Muriel Bradbrook on Shakespeare

M. C. BRADBROOK
Professor of English Emerita,
University of Cambridge and Fellow of
Girton College

THE HARVESTER PRESS · SUSSEX
BARNES & NOBLE BOOKS · NEW JERSEY

First published in Great Britain in 1984 by
THE HARVESTER PRESS LIMITED
Publisher: John Spiers
16 Ship Street, Brighton, Sussex
and in the USA by
BARNES & NOBLE BOOKS
81 Adams Drive, Totowa, New Jersey 07512

© M. C. Bradbrook, 1984

Editor: Sue Roe

British Library Cataloguing in Publication Data

Bradbrook, M. C.
  Muriel Bradbrook on Shakespeare.
  1. Shakespeare, William—Criticism and
  interpretation
  I. Title
  822.3'3   PR2976

ISBN 0-7108-0679-5
ISBN 0-7108-0687-6 pbk

Library of Congress Cataloging in Publication Data

Bradbrook, M. C. (Muriel Clara), 1909–
  Muriel Bradbrook on Shakespeare.

  Contents: Shakespeare's primitive art—Shakespeare
and the use of disguise in Elizabethan drama—Shakespeare's debt to Marlowe—[etc.]
  1. Shakespeare, William, 1564–1616—Criticism and
interpretation—Addresses, essays, lectures. I. Title.
PR2976.B568   1984   822.3'3   84-6273
ISBN 0-389-20487-0
ISBN 0-389-20488-9 (pbk.)

Photoset in 10 on 11 pt Linotron Sabon by
Rowland Phototypesetting Ltd
Bury St Edmunds, Suffolk

Printed in Great Britain by
The Thetford Press Ltd
Thetford, Norfolk

Contents

		page
Introduction		vii
1.	Shakespeare's Primitive Art	1
2.	Shakespeare and the Use of Disguise in Elizabethan Drama	20
3.	Shakespeare's Debt to Marlowe	28
4.	Beasts and Gods: the Social Purpose of *Venus and Adonis*	43
5.	Dramatic Role as Social Image: a Study of *The Taming of the Shrew*	57
6.	*King Henry IV*	72
7.	Shakespeare's Hybrid: *All's Well that Ends Well*	84
8.	What Shakespeare did to Chaucer's *Troilus and Criseyde*	99
9.	An Interpretation of *Hamlet*	110
10.	The Balance and the Sword in *Measure for Measure*	118
11.	*Othello*, Webster and the Tragedy of Violence	129
12.	The Origins of *Macbeth*	143
A Retrospective View		161
Acknowledgements		167

Introduction

The purpose of collecting here a dozen essays, written over the last thirty years, is to show the variety of approaches to Shakespeare. Enjoyment of his work is world-wide, and after a lifetime's study he remains for me a continuous source of refreshment and energy, giving new insights into my own time.

The order of presentation is the chronological order of Shakespeare's work. The first two general studies are concerned with the Elizabethan theatre, for Shakespeare's acting basically influenced his poetry. On his tombstone at Stratford, he is shewn holding a pen, but his lips are parted. He is declaiming.

He was also, in his young days, fired with literary ambitions that for a time led him into non-dramatic poetry; the essays on Marlowe and on *Venus and Adonis* place him among his fellow writers; some may prefer to skip these and move to his main theatrical development. *The Taming of the Shrew*, an early play, remains a success for the stage and the film; the even greater success of *King Henry IV* also depends on popular theatrical models, subtly transformed. Falstaff is the most famous of his creations before Hamlet. But Shakespeare, like his own characters, enjoyed a unique power of growth and development. The group termed the Problem Plays followed – *All's Well that Ends Well*, *Measure for Measure* and *Troilus and Cressida*. All three attained sudden popularity within the last half century, and are now frequently played; because they break or question accepted models, they appeal to contemporary moods. Accepted standards in love relationships and in the politics of power are put to the question – and these two problems of relationship are linked together.

Three great tragedies were presented to very different kinds of audience, so my essays may suggest something about the universality of the works. *Hamlet,* as an exploration of attachment and loss, of bereavement, was offered originally to the students of Hiroshima University, and to their Professor, Michio Masui, a survivor of the atomic bomb attack, who certainly knew what bereavement and mourning meant. The lecture on *Othello* and violence was given in 1981 in Washington D.C. That on *Macbeth*, presented to an audience of Shakespearean scholars from all over the world, gathered at Stratford upon Avon, shews that by 1606 Shakespeare was again redrawing his boundaries and reshaping his own earlier work.

To those interested in Shakespeare as an artist, the relations with Marlowe and with Chaucer, with Shakespeare's own earlier work may appeal more particularly; those concerned with social background may wish to turn first to the papers on *The Taming of the Shrew* and *Measure for Measure*; for those whose interest is in performance, the two opening papers and those on *All's Well that Ends Well* and *Macbeth* offer a start.

General and special topics, each involving a slightly different approach, may suggest how Shakespearean study enriches other topics; if one or two of these papers are rather technical, I have tried always to keep them readable. My own interests have developed in the two fields of social history, including the history of the theatre, and in actual performance, in the influence of Shakespeare on contemporary stages. These twin interests are examined in the Retrospect of the last fifty years in Shakespearean studies, with which this volume ends.

M. C. Bradbrook
Girton College, Cambridge

I

Shakespeare's primitive art*

Spectacle is that part of tragedy which has least connection with the art of poetry, as Aristotle believed: but, when the text of plays – even of Shakespeare's plays – provides only raw material for John Barton and other theatre directors, it might be thought 'So much the worse for poetry'.

Today Bali rather than Athens supplies dramatic models, and the cult of primitive theatre is so strong, that it may have been suspected I come to praise Shakespeare as a barbaric contemporary, after the fashion of Jan Kott – to enrol him in the theatre of cruelty. On the contrary, taking a conventionally historic view, I shall try to recover traces of the archaic spectacular tradition from which Shakespeare first started and to which, in the richly transmuted form of his final plays, he returned. I hope to identify the scenic proverb, the elements of that unspoken language which derives from the primal stage arts of gesture, costume, grouping, pantomime; to reveal the influence of those inexplicable dumb shows, which, although he rejected them, Shakespeare never forgot.

In doing this, it may be possible to uncover also something of his creative process. As his poetic imagination subdued itself to what it worked in, the visual and scenic basis of his art became absorbed into his poetry. An actor before he was playwright, Shakespeare carried always with him the memories of his repertory. It has been convincingly shown by Dr Edward Armstrong that Shakespeare's memories, as they sank below the level of consciousness, formed themselves into 'image clusters' or associative groups. Image clusters would have had visual and scenic counterparts, but since 'memory is an *imaginative* reconstruction',[1] what Shakespeare recalled from the stage, more especially when it need not have been conscious recall, was converted by that act 'into something rich and strange'.

*The annual Shakespeare lecture of the British Academy, 1965.

I would begin by distinguishing two traditions of spectacle in his inheritance, which might be termed the high road and the low road to drama proper. There are the lofty icons or tableaux of coronation, triumph, great marriages or funerals; and, at the other extreme, tumblers and jesters, comic quick-change artists, such as the poor tatterdemalion dwarf that William Dunbar introduced running through his parts at the Market Cross of Edinburgh (in 'The Manere of Crying of Ane Playe'). Both extremes met in the ring of Burbage's Theatre, London's 'game place' or 'playing place'; but Marlowe and Shakespeare began by taking the high road and rejecting 'such conceits as clownage keeps in play'. Marlowe's lofty first creation, Tamburlaine, is descended from the King of the Moors, who rode in many civic processions, followed by his train, and gorgeously attired in red satin and silver paper; the spectacle is transmuted into heroic poetry,[2] by which it has been preserved for posterity. The originals are long forgotten.

Marlowe's doctrine of power and glory was very largely a doctrine of sovereignty and he made use of another image by which it was forcibly brought home to the simple. Every parish church in the land contained a copy of Foxe's *Book of Martyrs* and the edition of 1580 has for frontispiece a crowned king mounting to his throne by trampling on a prostrate foe, whose triple crown is falling from him. The king is Henry VIII. The footstool is the Pope. Tamburlaine trampling on Bajazet repeats the image.

For many people the royal image assuaged a deep privation they felt in the loss of those older images that had been familiar for so long, whose simple wonder-working mechanisms the reformers had triumphantly torn out. Opponents of the stage were apt to charge the common players with what seems to us the very incongruous sin of idolatry, because they perceived a line of descent from the older icons to the new. One such sour cleric, writing in 1587 *A Mirror of Monsters*,[3] describes a marriage procession of Pride, Lord of the Theatre, and Lechery, Lady of Worldlings, which passed through the streets to the Chapel of Adultery at Hollow-well (that is, Burbage's Theatre in Holywell Street in the old grounds of a Benedictine nunnery). It was presided over by a magic winged image of a holy child, made of alabaster and painted in life-like colours. The Child Cupid carried emblems of torch and dart, and could nod the head in a magic fashion, which excited wonder as he was set up in a niche in the Parlour of Payne, where the North Wind assisted the miracle. The cleric adds to this infernal revelry a troop of monsters sent from Satan.

A grand wedding tableau also concludes *Tamburlaine*, Part I, where the royal virgin Zenocrate is crowned by a trinity of kings.

This, though doubtless without overt intent, recalls the sacred icon of a humbler Virgin crowned by a loftier Trinity; and the depth of conflict resolved in this play is suggested by its unconscious combination of Catholic and Reformed iconography.

In Marlovian style Shakespeare develops *Titus Andronicus* as a series of tableaux. The well-known contemporary illustration of the opening scene, by Henry Peacham, shows the Blackamoor flourishing a drawn sword over Tamora's doomed sons. In spite of the fact that he is himself a captive at this point, I think Aaron might have momentarily assumed the pose of a black-visaged headsman, to produce a tableau that must have been common enough in martyrology. The magician, the king, the blackamoor, the weeping queen, had long been familiar, so that imaginative roles of Shakespeare and of Marlowe are but half-emerged from a penumbra which surrounds and enlarges them beyond the dimensions of individual parts, to the sacred and archaic originals from which they derive.

The most powerful icon of *Titus Andronicus* is the silent figure of Lavinia mutilated. The first of her family to meet her unconsciously evokes the image of the green and the withered tree, one commonly used in festive procession to symbolize a flourishing and fading commonwealth; when she is next compared with a conduit running red wine, the shock of the conflicting festive image inflates the horror. She becomes herself, in metamorphosis, a stony silent image of violence and outrage:

> What stern ungentle hands
> Hath lopp'd, and hew'd, and made thy body bare
> Of her two branches – those sweet ornaments
> Whose circling shadows kings have sought to sleep in? . . .
> Alas, a crimson river of warm blood,
> Like to a bubbling fountain stirr'd with wind,
> Doth rise and fall between thy rosed lips . . .
> And notwithstanding all this loss of blood –
> As from a conduit with three issuing spouts –
> Yet do thy cheeks look red as Titan's face,
> Blushing to be encounter'd with a cloud.   (II. iv. 16–32)

The heraldic conventions of its images and the extreme violence of its plot[4] make *Titus Andronicus* unique among Shakespeare's works. In his English histories, I would like to think that he borrowed a tableau from that Coventry play given by the townsmen before Queen Elizabeth at Kenilworth in July 1575, when Shakespeare, a boy of 11, was living not far away. An old Hocktide contest between men and women had become associated with the memory of a battle between English and Danes, in which, after initial victories, the Danes were led captive by English women; this was combined with a drill display by the town's muster men. The image of this play may have been revived in *Henry VI* when Joan la Pucelle or Margaret of Anjou triumphed over English warriors; but since 'remembering is an imaginative reconstruction', the image has been reversed, and the foreign women triumph over Englishmen.

Londoners would not have recognized this image, since they did not know the original, but by the time he wrote the second part of *Henry IV*, Shakespeare felt sufficiently a Londoner to mock their local show. The London archery band was led by a small group of the élite, known as Prince Arthur's Knights, who marched annually in procession, each with his name from Arthurian story, and bearing his arms emblazoned. Justice Shallow, in recalling the exploits of his youth, claims to have played the part of the jester, Dagonet; but his memory prompts him rather to enact another part, that of a craftsmaster whom he had admired.

> I remember at Mile End Green, when I lay at Clement's Inn – I was then Sir Dagonet in Arthur's show – there was a little quiver fellow, and 'a would manage you his piece thus; and 'a would about and about, and come you in, and come you in. 'Rah, tah, tah!' would 'a say; 'Bounce!' would 'a say; and away again would 'a go, and again would 'a come. I shall ne'er see such a fellow. (*2 Henry IV*, III. ii. 271–8)

This is not very far from the open parody of Beaumont's *The Knight of the Burning Pestle*, when Ralph the bold Grocer-Errant reaches the culmination of his glory by playing the May Lord on a conduit head, and then leads out the musters to Mile End Green.

The high tradition of early tragedy had been established by Marlowe and mediated through the majestic presence of Edward Alleyn the tragedian. Alleyn was, however, a master of more than one style – of all the 'activities of youth, activities of age' that were found among strolling players, where he had learnt his trade. One of his star performances, the title role in Greene's *Orlando Furioso*, offers a display of virtuosity such as Dunbar's dwarf suggests. His own copy of the part, preserved at Dulwich, shows how gaily Alleyn could point it up. As he turned from lover to madman and back to warrior, Orlando must have raised both a shudder and guffaw. He tears a shepherd limb from limb (offstage) and enters bearing a leg on his shoulder; he fights a battle with spits and dripping pans (a familiar comic turn); his action and speech are constantly changing, and different rhetorical styles must have been put into play, as Alleyn, like a practised juggler whirling a set of clubs, spun up one after another his brightly coloured lines.

A single actor could hold an audience with such rapid transitions (the Admiral's Men later developed a group of plays for the quick-change artist) and the greatest actors prided themselves on 'Protean' mutability. 'Medley' plays rose from the mixed activities of the theatre. Burbage's playhouse could accommodate a monster, an antic, a grotesque dragon made of brown paper that 'would fright the ladies that they would shriek'. In medieval times such an irruption would have been termed a marvel; today, it would be a happening. The 'medley' evoked a mingled feeling of fright and triumph, gasps and laughter; but it was a professional show, as the older romantic adventures were not. There is much more professional distinction than at first appears between a shambling romance like *Sir Clyomon and Sir Clamydes*, which is older than the Theatre, and a medley like *The Cobbler's Prophecy*, written by Wilson in the late eighties. In his *Apology for Poetry* Sidney's description of a romance implies that the stage was set out with a group of symbolic objects, which, protected by the heavens, attracted the players into a variety of settings. The garden, the shipwreck, the cave with its fire-breathing monster, and the battlefield, must have made up a most elaborate play. Thanks to modern studies, we are now familiar with the visual aspects of the city gates, the tree, the cave, the ship, the arbour of the medieval and Tudor stages; these provided a gift for the artist's imagination to which only a Melanie Klein could hope to do justice.

Such symbolic objects were used also by Wilson and others in the medley plays, and in Shakespeare's early theatre. Studied coldly on the page, the medleys may appear to offer sheer nonsense, for their effect depends on what a modern French writer has termed 'the theatre's magic relation to reality and danger'. The magician with his wonderful shows (a type of the playwright) was a central figure, together with a pair of lovers, a clown, a speaker of riddles and prophecies, one or more of the classical gods and goddesses, and some fireworks. In Wilson's play one of the 'pavilions' was set on fire; in another, a juggler appeared to whisk away the serious title board 'Speculum' and to substitute 'Wily Beguiled'.

Medleys evolved their own set of sequences when they were the property of a famous troupe like the Queen's Men, and eventually must have delighted the audience only by an unpredictable mixture of predictable items, that belong together because they have been seen together before.[5]

In *The Old Wives' Tale* George Peele raised the romance to a similar professional level by setting it in the framework of a story about three actors who have lost their way in a wood. Antic, Frolic, Fantastic, the servants of a lord, whose names proclaim their quality, take refuge in a cottage, where the old wife's tale comes to life; but the audience are released from the confines of time and space and move freely between a magician's study, a well, a hillock with magic flames upon it, and crossroads in a wood. There is no need for a plot; the princess 'white as snow and red as blood', her two brothers, the wicked enchanter, the wandering knight, are as familiar as the set of emblematic objects among which they move. Gaps in the action are taken for granted. There are twenty-four parts (many silent) in this brief play, designed for a company of about ten.

Shakespeare began by turning his back upon medley and romance, to write classical plays like *Titus Andronicus* and *The Comedy of Errors*. The fecundity of the early staging was transferred to his vocabulary, where he poured out crowded images, mingled, as Dr Johnson was to observe, with endless variety of proportion and innumerable varieties of combination. The conflict of incompatible and paradoxical images which surges through his comedy derives indirectly from the physical crowding of the old stages, and therefore was readily acceptable to his audience. Ben Jonson thought that Shakespeare was carried away by his own facility – 'His wit was in his power; would the rule of it had been so too.' Charles Lamb noted that 'Before one idea has burst its shell, another has hatched and clamours for disclosure'. Primitive art, repudiated as spectacle, is transformed by Shakespeare into a characteristic mode of imaginative working, where the dumb language of shows combines with higher, more articulate, forms. Greene, railing on Shakespeare as an 'upstart Crow', was putting him in the shape of an Antic, the lowest and most scurrilous type of dumb player; but as author ('Johannes Factotum') Greene suggests he has turned the actor's versatility into writing, with the 'ease' and 'facility' that his friends were later to praise. He sees the connection between Shakespeare's two activities, the second an extension of the first.

Shakespeare has left at least three accounts of this process: Richard II's soliloquy in Pomfret Castle, Duke Theseus on the poet's eye, and the fifty-third Sonnet, all (as I would think) written somewhere about his thirtieth year, in 1594.

Alone in a prison cell, the uncrowned Richard peoples his little world with a teeming succession of diversified forms, which come nearer to the comic actors' multiple roles than to the playwright's art. [And Burbage, it should be remembered, was an even more Protean actor than Alleyn.]

> Thus play I in one person many people,
> And none contented. Sometimes am I King;
> Then treasons make me wish myself a beggar,
> And so I am. Then crushing penury
> Persuades me I was better when a king,

> Then am I king'd again; and by and by
> Think that I am unking'd by Bolingbroke,
> And straight am nothing. (V. v. 3 1–8)

Richard tries to hammer out his inner conflict to a set pattern; but a charm of music hushes his restless activity of mind and returns him to the hard immures of his prison. This suddenly begets an image or icon of the tragic mode.

> I wasted time, and now doth time waste me;
> For now hath time made me his numb'ring clock.
>
> (V. v. 49–50)

The prisoner develops the image of a clock at length, his finger becoming the hand, his face the dial (from which he is wiping the tears), and his groans the bell; while the gay motion of organic life is transferred in his imagination to the coronation of his supplanter. He sees himself as a wooden 'Jack o' the clock' such as provided a simple foolery for onlookers by its movement.[6]

Recalled again to his surroundings, he hears from a poor groom of the stable of the usurper's triumph, and 'in the quick forge and working house of thought' transforms himself in his degradation as Bottom was transformed, by the ass's head.

> I was not made a horse;
> And yet I bear a burden like an ass,
> Spurr'd, gall'd and tir'd by jauncing Bolingbroke.
>
> (V. v. 92–4)

A popular game with the Coventry men and others – mounted men on one another's shoulders for comic mock-tournaments.

The nature of our general perception of the world, and of our own body, is so primitive and deep-seated a foundation of our identity that we cannot imagine how these basic levels of perception may change from age to age. But from Shakespeare's work it may be gathered how the icon's immobility and the medley's ever-changing succession of 'streamy associations' became integrated in full poetic drama, the fusion of poetry and spectacle, of inner and outer worlds. This remains primitive art only in the sense that our perception of the world is itself analogous to a work of art – 'a complex ordering of attitude and belief achieved a stage earlier than discursive statement'.[8] It utilizes but is emphatically not the same as that mental process (conducted largely through visual symbols) which we meet in dreams – primitive thinking, as one psychologist terms it.[9] Plays are 'such stuff as dreams are made on' – they are not dreams.

The capacity for pre-conscious and intuitive ordering found in both Marlowe and Shakespeare is characteristic of drama, where preverbal and verbal languages combine in one total statement. As Duke Theseus observes, the 'seething brain' of the poet apprehends more than cool reason ever comprehends, giving to things unknown, to airy nothing a *shape* (which was the technical name for an actor's costume) a *habitation* (or 'locus' on the stage) and a *name* (which the early actors wore pinned to their chests on a scroll). *A Midsummer Night's Dream* is full of the magic of the early stage; Professor Coghill has recently pointed out some links with the play of magic and quick changes of identity, *John a Kent and John a Cumber*.

The Sonnets, which I take to have been written about the same time, open with a strong and familiar icon. A beautiful youth, embodiment of spring, is urged to marry and produce an heir. The choice of topic has caused some surprise, and C. S. Lewis went so far as to inquire: 'What man in the whole world, except a father in law or potential father in law cares whether any other man gets married?'[10]

But *was* the theme so very unusual? Was there not at least one great person, in whose excellence the red and white rose united, who for some thirty-five years had been constantly exhorted not to let beauty's flower fade unpropagated? Any poet approaching a new patron would find the royal model readily adaptable, since every noble household reproduced in miniature the patterns of royal service. Beginning to learn his courtier's alphabet, Shakespeare naturally fell to his copy book. That great icon of springtime beauty which Spenser had once delineated in his April Eclogue remained the fixed form for praises of the Queen, in her public capacity, though she was now sixty years old: Sir John Davies produced in 1596 *Astraea*, his enamelled acrostics, in which she magically controls the seasons, like Titania and Oberon.

> Earth now is green and heaven is blue,
> Lively spring, that makes all new,
> Jolly spring, doth enter;
> Sweet young sunbeams do subdue
> Angry, aged winter.
>
> Blasts are mild and seas are calm,
> Every meadows flows with balm,
> The earth wears all her riches.
> Harmonious birds sing such a charm,
> As ear and heart bewitches.
>
> Reserve, sweet spring, this nymph of ours,
> Eternal garlands of thy flowers,
> Green garlands never wasting;
> In her shall last our youth's fair spring,
> Now and for ever flourishing,
> As long as heaven is lasting.

In her private person Elizabeth might typify 'angry, aged Winter': but not as Astraea. Shakespeare's youth is more vulnerable than this changeless image; 'the world's fair ornament', he dwells where 'men as plants increase' and beauties must 'die as fast as they see others grow'. His beauty must therefore be transmitted to his heir (and this was also his duty as heir of a great family); yet the poet too, as father-creator, can dream that in his verse 'I engraft you new'. The play of fancy deepens, the royal icon gives way to a multitude of images, as the beloved is seen to sum up 'all those friends which I thought buried'. Now 'their images I loved, I view in thee', till ultimately the whole world becomes reflected in this one being and so integrated in the poet's mind. The beauty of the beloved, like that of God, is seen everywhere, and he sums up the loveliness of past and present, of both the sexes, of all the seasons, of history and poetry. In the fifty-third sonnet, Shakespeare's Adonis and Marlowe's Helen attend on the beloved, who combines the loftiness of a Platonic ideal with the Protean 'shadows' and 'shapes' of the actors' art.[11] Here is the swarming profusion of the medley – gods, shepherds, lovers, magicians with their attendant spirits – completely harmonized and introjected by a complex poetic image:

> What is your substance, whereof are you made,
> That millions of strange shadows on you tend?
> Since every one hath, every one, one shade,
> And you, but one, can every shadow lend.
> Describe Adonis, and the counterfeit
> Is poorly imitated after you;
> On Helen's cheek all art of beauty set,
> And you in Grecian tires are painted new.
> Speak of the spring and foison of the year:
> The one doth shadow of your beauty show,
> The other as your bounty doth appear,
> And you in every blessed shape we know.
> > In all external grace you have some part,
> > But you like none, none you, for constant heart.

Eventually, in Sonnet 104, Shakespeare denies that Time moves for his beloved, and in the last poem of all, the lovely boy, an emblem of eternal youth, stands charming the glass of old Father Time, stilling in its clockwise motion the onward sweep of Chronos' 'sickle hour'.

It is no part of my present argument to trace the development of Shakespeare's art after the stage of full integration represented by *Richard II*. From 1594 his career was bound up with the Lord Chamberlain's Men; stability and cohesion came to his theatre. It was true of the whole age, but especially of Shakespeare, that he united the cosmic with the human image, most powerfully in his great tragedies.

If I may quote a poet of our own day:

> Sorrow is deep and vast – we travel on
> As far as pain can penetrate, to the end
> Of power and possibility; to find
> The contours of the world, with heaven align'd
> Upon infinity; the shape of man!
>
> Kathleen Raine, 'Sorrow' (from *Living in Time*)

In *Hamlet* Shakespeare refashioned an old tragedy, where the original Hamlet may have offered the same kind of Protean jesting as Orlando Furioso, the comic madman. By transforming and incorporating such a role, Shakespeare regained imaginative access to a great fund of energy, and the character is his most complex creation. Yet there is a void at the centre of Hamlet the man – the unfocused, unplumbed grief, the 'pang without a name, void, dark and drear' which all his complex introspection leaves a mystery, an eloquent silence. And there is a ghost at the centre of *Hamlet* the play; the chthonic King is the only true ruler. Echoes of Marlowe cling to the part of the Ghost; for example, the story of his murder recalls a trick of the devilish Lightborn, murderer of Edward II:

> Whilst one is asleep to take a quill
> And blow a little powder in his ears,
> Or open his mouth and pour quicksilver down.
>
> (ll. 2366–8)

The great icon which unites the two Hamlets, father and son, is also Marlovian in style; it emerges with the arrival of the actors at Elsinore, in the First Player's speech of the death of Priam. The apparition of Pyrrhus, avenger of his father Achilles, upon Priam (with whom, as the murderer of Hector, Priam has pleaded for his son) is a figure of strange but arrested power. As he finishes the description of Pyrrhus, Hamlet hands over to the first Player, who recounts how the very wind of Pyrrhus' sword felled Priam, but at that moment the crash of the falling towers amid 'the nightmare of smoke and screams and ruin'[12] arrested his action. Pyrrhus stands in tableau, flourishing his sword, a mechanical figure of destruction in his black armour smeared with blood, a kind of iron man.

Like Tamburlaine, or like Aaron in *Titus Andronicus*, he remains larger than life:

> So, as a painted tyrant, Pyrrhus stood
> And like a neutral to his will and matter,
> Did nothing.
>
> (II. ii. 474–6)

and there was silence for a space, till the burning towers crashed thunderously again, and the blade fell.

After meeting this icon, Hamlet in a great burst of self-directed rage recognizes the embodiment of what he had before encountered in the Ghost, issuing its archaic but absolute command, Revenge! It is a compulsion, it is a *must*, laid upon a man by an archaic part of himself, a decayed part reactivated by his father's death. The compelling power of that part of ourself which we do not desire to meet can return only in such images. Yet the tempest of Hamlet's passion evokes in him the notion of the play-within-the-play, by which he catches the conscience of King Claudius, even as he himself has been caught. All this depends on the 'theatre's magic relation to reality and danger'; for Hamlet remembers how guilty creatures sitting at a play have been forced by what they saw to recount their crimes. After the play has indeed caught its victim, we see Hamlet stand with drawn sword flourishing over the kneeling figure of the praying Claudius, in exactly the same posture as that of Pyrrhus over Priam. The icon is re-enacted in the prayer scene; but Hamlet does not let his sword fall. He puts it up with the thought of yet more horrid and complete revenge, which shall damn Claudius both body and soul.

Shakespeare here appeals to the most primitive and terrifying aspects of theatrical participation; the sequel to this act is the second and final appearance of the Ghost.

When Shakespeare came to the writing of his final plays, popular art was dying in the countryside. Robin Hood and the hobby horse were everywhere put down; the court was evolving a new Italianate form of masque, and a new theatre. Shakespeare reactivated his own early memories and transformed into scenic terms for the new stage the medleys of twenty-five years before – 'tales, tempests and such drolleries' as Ben Jonson scornfully termed them. The utmost reaches of his imagination evoked the scenic emblems of Shakespeare's youth – the cave, the living statue, the ship – and some of the ancient roles – the may queen, the monster, and the magician – using them to explore an interior world where fine and delicate sensibilities alternated with 'imaginations foul as Vulcan's stithy'.

Pericles, first of these plays, is presented by the ancient poet Gower, who here performs the kind of Induction that old Madge, Frolic, and Fantastic had given in *The Old Wives' Tale*. But he is a Ghost.

> To sing a song that old was sung,
> From ashes ancient Gower is come . . .
> It hath been sung at festivals,
> On ember-eves and holy-ales;

> And lords and ladies in their lives
> Have read it for restoratives.   (Prologue, 1–8)

Much of the moral action is in dumb show, and much of the writing is absurd. Like the hero of the old romance, Sir Clamydes, the wandering knight Pericles is shipwrecked on a foreign coast and wins its princess for bride in spectacular tournament. His father-in-law plays fast and loose with the unknown prince and his own daughter in a style which burlesques the old quick changes:

> Will you, not having my consent,
> Bestow your love and your affections
> Upon a stranger, who, for aught I know
> May be, nor can I think the contrary,
> As great in blood as I myself?
> Therefore, hear you, mistress: either frame
> Your will to mine – and you, sir, hear you –
> Either be ruled by me, or I will make you . . .
> Man and wife.   (II. v. 75–83)

This clownish jocularity is exercised in a play which seems to exist only as matrix for the great tableau and icon, the discovery scene of the last act. When Marina's sacred charm of music has reanimated the frozen image of Grief that is Pericles, then a figure no longer of cosmic dimensions, but subject to cosmic influences, has been recalled from dereliction so extreme that it could have been embodied only in traditional forms, not originally carrying the personal stamp that Shakespeare here bestows upon them. In returning to these archaic forms Shakespeare breathed new life into them and recovered a 'radical innocence'.[13] The basis is so simple and the shaping spirit of imagination so concentrated that there is in *Pericles*, so to speak, more gap than play. This is no longer, as in the original old wives' tales, a gap in narrative, but a gap in realization. Shakespeare has gone so deep that he has momentarily lost his unifying power, so splendidly displayed in the Roman plays. The single icon emerges, surrounded by old-fashioned romance in debris, and by the macabre comedy of the brothel scenes. Shakespeare even needed to lean on the work of an inferior collaborator.

Cymbeline carries echoes of several medley plays, in particular of *Sir Clyamon and Sir Clamydes* and *The Rare Triumphs of Love and Fortune*.[14] From Jupiter to Cloten, the roles repeat earlier counterparts; Imogen's later adventures as Fidele have their counterpart in those of Fidelia and Neronis. In 1957, at Stratford, the stage was arranged in a simultaneous setting, Tudor-fashion, so that the emblems of castle, bedchamber, cave, and wood in surrealist fantasy appeared together, 'throwing over the whole production a sinister veil of faery, so that it resembled a Grimm fable transmuted by the Cocteau of *La Belle et la Bête*'.[15]

The costumes, disguises, tokens, tricks of this play, the medley of Roman, British, and medieval themes, turn all to dream and fairy tale; by this means the sensitive core of tenderness, anguish, and vital playfulness that Imogen embodies can come into being. Imogen is a heroine who would be at home in the high romance of Sidney's *Arcadia*, with Philoclea, her sister in affliction. She is one who makes an art of living, from cookery to leave-taking of her banished husband, devising 'pretty things to say' even for that moment of separation, after which, as she tells her father,

> I am senseless of your wrath; a touch more rare
> Subdues all pangs, all fears.   (I. i. 135–6)

When she reads Posthumus' accusation, Pisanio comments:

> What shall I need to draw my sword? The paper
> Hath cut her throat already.   (III. iv. 30–1)

These are wedded lovers, and the poisoned imagination of Posthumus sinks far below Sidney's world of romance, to the level of Iago and of the brothel scenes in *Pericles*. Yet in spite of his words, Posthumus' actions suggest that he believed in Imogen's innocence all the time; the letter which summons her to Milford on the dangerous journey from her home would have had no effect on one who had really forgotten him completely, and given away 'the manacle of love', the bracelet which was his last token. When he himself appears in real gyves, Posthumus has spontaneously repented; and a vision of his dead father and two brothers mysteriously links with the next scene, in which Imogen also meets again her father and her two long-lost brothers. Thus the union of the wedded lovers is shown to exist at a level beyond that of overt statement.

The fairy tale gives underlying support to the impossibilities of this play. To reach the totally unfamiliar, it is necessary to cling to the familiar; from moment to moment this new kind of medley convinces, although the princess so wounded by the accusation of Posthumus could not have assumed the role of Fidele, and lived to be struck down once again. It is a kind of posthumous life for *her*, she is playing a part; the grotesque symbolism of Cloten's dead figure in her husband's garments is impossible and hideous, but perhaps also a kind of black comedy of actors' 'shapes'. The magic drinks, changes of identity, and visionary spectacles of the last part of the play no longer carry any relation to reality and danger; they are the means by which Shakespeare can leave gaps in his work. They also seem to function by some associative process in the release of energy from below; the primitive art assists or accompanies or is a necessary concomitant of new, difficult poetry for which the play reaches out.

The original of the next play, *A Winter's Tale*, belongs to the same period as the medleys and was a narrative of Shakespeare's old enemy and detractor, Robert Greene. The old tale ended tragically and was named *Pandosto or the Triumph of Time*. Construction through gaps in the story is emphasized by the appearance of Time as Chorus, who separates the two halves of Shakespeare's play: but the action is clearer, and firmer, the poet has regained his mastery of plot. In the first half, Leontes is overwhelmed by that poisoned level of the imagination which Posthumus had shown, and which had been displayed in the brothel scenes of *Pericles*. Leontes' jealousy invades him suddenly and spontaneously at the moment when he *sees* his wife and his friend in playful familiar talk together. The image speaks to him of what might be. All this is imaginatively realized, but then the marvels begin. They are the work of Apollo, a much more effective deity than Diana in *Pericles* or Jupiter in *Cymbeline*. First comes an oracular message, then the death of Mamilius, and finally the icon of Hermione as she appears in Antigonus' dream. The significance of this dream was pointed out by Anne Righter in a paper read last year at the International Conference at Stratford. As the instrument of Leontes' vengeance, Antigonus is accursed, and the vision of the Queen comes to warn him of this fate. Although she appears 'in pure white robes, Like very sanctity', her eyes 'become two spouts'; she is portentously like Lavinia. Antigonus falsely accepts this as an omen that the babe is indeed a bastard; no sooner has he laid it on the earth than thunder is heard, and the sounds of a hunt. It is the god Apollo, descending in storm, Apollo the Hunter, who chases the guilty man as Prospero and Ariel hunt the guilty with dogs in *The Tempest*. Antigonus himself becomes the quarry, and the 'Marvel' of the bear, at once grotesque and horrifying, would raise the old mixture of fright and laughter in the audience – especially if a real bear were let loose among them.

By contrast, in the last scene, the high magic of the holy statue that comes to life is Christian in its forms. The icon of Hermione is kept in a chapel 'holy, apart' as Paulina tells the penitent king. Perdita kneels before it with the pretty proviso:

> Give me leave,
> And do not say 'tis superstition that
> I kneel, and then implore her blessing. Lady,
> Dear Queen, that ended when I but began,
> Give me that hand of yours to kiss.   (V. iii. 42–6)

The coldness of the stone has chid his own coldness in Leontes, but Paulina tells him

> It is requir'd
> You do awake your faith. (V. iii. 94–5)

The magic is powerful, the charm is musical; the figure is transubstantiated back to flesh and blood, and Leontes puts all in three words: 'Oh, she's warm.'

Although a statue which comes to life is not unknown to earlier plays, or to later ones for that matter,[16] this single scene offers the deepest integration of spectacle and poetry in the last plays; and for the audience, who have been given no more than hints and guesses that Hermione may be living, the final descent is a most powerful *coup de théâtre*, made eloquent by silence and music wedded to poetry.

In this, it is a wonderful advance on the descent of Jupiter, spectacularly the highlight of the whole play *Cymbeline* but poetically a gap and a void. Hermione has replaced the gods in this scene; the triumph is that of a divine humanity. Was there here some unconscious recall of a Catholic image of the mother, mingled with the semi-divine Elizabeth, Virgin Queen but nursing mother of her people (as she termed herself to Parliament), wedded to her kingdom, whose reign was already assuming legendary greatness as the weakness of her successor appeared?

In its spontaneous-seeming, yet perfectly disciplined, form, *The Tempest* represents the final triumph of art, an art based on imagination perfectly attuned to the stage. Spectacular but not naïve, classical in form, poetic but no longer with the poetry of the gaps, it presents a close, delicate wholeness:

> A condition of complete simplicity
> Costing not less than everything.

The Tempest is a play of high magic throughout, although its ruling intelligence is human and fallible. Prospero's magic is Pythagorean, based on that 'monstrous imagination' that Bacon was to reject:

> that the world was one entire perfect living creature; insomuch as Apollonius of Tyana, a Pythagorean prophet, affirmed that the ebbing and flowing of the sea was the respiration of the world, drawing in water as breath and putting it forth again . . . They went on, and inferred that if the world was a living creature, it had a soul, and spirit, calling it spiritus mundi. (*Sylva Sylvarum*, century x)

White magic, by 'giving a fit touch to the spirit of the world', can make it respond. Prospero is at first subject to the stars and courts an auspicious influence; whereas the monstrous Sycorax had worked black magic by the manipulation of physical charms on the sublunary level. She was able to exert physical compulsion on the higher spheres, even those beyond the moon – for so I read the crux

> That could control the moon, . . .
> And deal in her command without her power.
>
> (V. i. 270–1)

To the guilty Alonzo the whole world speaks with one voice:

> O, 'tis monstrous, monstrous!
> Methought the billows spoke and told me of it;
> The winds did sing it to me; and the thunder,
> That deep and dreadful organ pipe, pronounced
> The name of Prosper.
>
> (III. iii. 95–9)

It is from the spirit Ariel that Prospero himself learns to feel sympathy with Alonzo, returning from his stony remoteness to that quick freshness of feeling with which his own child responds.

> Oh, the cry did knock
> Against my very heart.
>
> (I. ii. 8–9)

Ariel's strange shapes, which include that very old-fashioned one of a coat of invisibility, sometimes reflect the inner states of those he works on. Dozens of strange shadows attend on him, and not every one of them is a blessed shape; for the men of sin he plays the Harpy, for the lovers a bounteous Ceres; when he comes to the clowns 'like the picture of Nobody', he plays old tricks from the repertory of earlier spirits,[17] and piping a merry catch, leads them into a horse-pond. His imprisonment, told by Prospero, recalls a potent device of the early stage; in *The Fairy Pastoral*, William Percy described exactly how the Hollow Tree was constructed. The clowns are clowns of the old type, and to them Caliban is but a fairground monster, to be shown to gaping crowds. He is confined by Prospero in a rock, another familiar scenic device. The old emblems of the ship and the cave are used, and a special 'quaint device' for the banquet that vanishes, leaving a bare table, which is carried out by spirits. Pure shows, like the dance of harvesters, unite the Jacobean masque with the revels of *The Old Wives' Tale*, where there is also a harvesters' dance.

Prospero's physical needs are served by Sycorax's son till, by way of ordeal, Prince Ferdinand takes his place as logman. Caliban accuses Prospero of usurping his island, and Prospero later accuses Ferdinand of this design, thus visiting the sin of the father upon his child. The murderous conspiracy of the false princes and the grosser rebellion of the clowns are alike frustrated by Prospero (whose art of government had certainly improved in exile) and the theme of usurpation dissolves in a lovers' jest, in the final tableau where

Miranda and Ferdinand are revealed playing with ivory kings and queens at chess.

> *Miranda.* Sweet lord, you play me false.
> *Ferdinand.* No, my dearest love,
>   I would not for the world.
> *Miranda.* Yes, for a score of kingdoms you should wrangle,
>   And I would call't fair play.   (V. i. 171–5)

Alonzo greets this restoration of the son he had lost as 'a most high miracle', but the disclosure has not the startling quality of that in *The Winter's Tale*, and Gonzalo's quiet comment points the distinction:

> I have *inly* wept.   (V. i. 200)

Finally, the whole dramatic action is dissolved by a series of transformations. For what is the magician but, as always in the old plays, a stage manager of shows, with his wand and his magic inscribed 'book' – what is this but a sublimated Master of the Revels? What the fellowship of the bottle with their stolen frippery and their game of kings and subjects, but a reductive mockery of the poorest players in the service? Pointing to the royal badge of Naples on the sleeves of Trinculo the fool and 'King Stephano', Prospero asks,

> Mark but the badges of these men, my lords,
> Then say if they be true.   (V. i. 267–8)

A man wearing King James's badge spoke the lines.

Finally, with no more dignity than a fashionable hat and rapier will confer, yet as one who dares more than Dr Faustus did – to make every third thought his grave – the old man appeals in his epilogue to the theatre's magic relation of reality and danger in a prayer of primal simplicity:

> As you from crimes would pardon'd be,
> Let your indulgence set me free.   (Epilogue 19–20)

The final plays represent an interior conflict, resolved in association with revived memories of a more primitive stage, and asserted with ever clarifying force.[19] It would be dangerous to speculate further than this. We may note the prevalent themes of death and rebirth, petrification and release; the common element of false accusation, banishment, and usurpation; the relations of fathers and children; the combination of extreme purity and scurrility. Do these suggest some possible conflicts of an ageing man? Prospero's farewell to Art, though not actually Shakespeare's last word (things do not work out quite so tidily as that) may represent an inner acceptance, that only at great price could be put into speech, and after many attempts; but here, as always, the Actor-Poet found, for his familiar ritual, the fitting words.

Notes

1 E. A. Armstrong, *Shakespeare's Imagination* (London, Lindsay Drummond, 1946), p. 122, quoting Sir Frederick Bartlett.
2 See J. P. Brockbank, *Dr Faustus* (London, Edward Arnold, 1962), pp. 23–4. The following paragraphs develop from chapter 3 of my book *English Dramatic Form* (London, Chatto & Windus, 1965).
3 William Rankins, *A Mirrour of Monsters*, 1587, sigs. C.1–C.2. The image of Cupid and the presence of Venus seem to point to the infernal Venus of Robert Wilson's play, *The Cobbler's Prophecy*, and her adultery with 'Contempt', which is celebrated by a masque of animal forms led by Folly.
4 See Eugene Waith, 'The Metamorphosis of Violence in *Titus Andronicus*', *Shakespeare Survey*, 10 (1957), 39–49.
5 Among such plays are *The Cobbler's Prophecy, The Rare Triumphs of Love and Fortune, John a Kent and John a Cumber*; perhaps *Friar Bacon and Friar Bungay* and *The Woman in the Moon* might be considered variants on this form.
6 The famous figures of the pageant in the clock of St Mark's, Venice, are the best-known examples; but a crowd will gather today to watch the figures in what was Fortnum and Mason's clock in Piccadilly. It is interesting to compare Marvell's satire on kings:

> 'Image like, an useless time they tell
> And with vain sceptre, strike the hourly bell.'
>
> (The First Anniversary', ll. 41–2)

7 The term is Edward Armstrong's; *Shakespeare's Imagination*, ch. 13.
8 D. W. Harding, *Experience into Words* (London, Chatto & Windus, 1963), p. 182.
9 J. A. Hadfield, *Dreams and Nightmares* (London, Penguin Books, 1954), ch. 6.
10 C. S. Lewis, *English Literature in the Sixteenth Century* (Oxford, Clarendon Press, 1954), p. 503.
11 According to Stephen Gosson, a 'shadow' is a minor actor; compare Macbeth's 'Life's but a walking shadow', and Puck's 'If we shadows have offended'.
12 The phrase is Harry Levin's.
13 'All hatred driven hence,/The soul recovers radical innocence/And learns at last that it is self-delighting,/Self-appeasing, self-affrighting.' Yeats, 'A Prayer for my Daughter' from *Michael Robartes and the Dancer*.
14 See *Cymbeline*, ed. J. C. Maxwell, New Cambridge Shakespeare (Cambridge, Cambridge University Press, 1960), pp. xxii–xxvii.

15 *Ibid.* p. xl (quoting Kenneth Tynan).
16 A statue on a grave comes to life in *The Trial of Chivalry*; and pictures in Massinger's *The City Madam*. There is a portentous set of statues in Middleton's *A Game of Chess*, but these are idols of the Black, i.e. Spanish party.
17 For instance, Shrimp of *John a Kent* and Robin Goodfellow of *Wily Beguiled*.
18 A. M. Nagler, *Shakespeare's Stage* (New Haven, Yale University Press, 1958), p. 100, discusses this trick; in medieval terms a 'secret'.
19 That there was perhaps a general movement in this direction does not modify the nature of Shakespeare's achievement, for he was the only actor-playwright with personal knowledge of the earlier stage. For a useful summary of the common stage practice, see Dieter Mehl, *The Elizabethan Dumb Show* (London, Methuen, 1965), ch. 2.

II

Shakespeare and the Use of Disguise in Elizabethan Drama

Today disguise is a living part of the drama. Sir Francis Crewe of *The Dog beneath The Skin*, the mysterious stranger at *The Cocktail Party*, the intrusive little girls of Giraudoux's *Electra* do not bear the limited significance which naturalism and the set characters of the nineteenth century imposed. Disguise was then reduced to a subterfuge, restricted to the Scarlet Pimpernel, the hero of *The Only Way* or the heroine of *East Lynne* ('Dead! and he never called me mother!'). Ibsen and Chekhov transformed it. Those implications of self-deception and fantasy which are the stuff of *A Doll's House* and *The Cherry Orchard* lurk in a masquerade dress, or a few conjuring tricks at a ball. Yet even in its revival, disguise has not attained the manifold significance which it enjoyed in the Elizabethan theatre and which Shakespeare alone fully revealed.

A study of the subject was provided by V. O. Freeburg as long ago as 1915 and has not been superseded (*Disguise Plots in Elizabethan Drama*, Columbia University Press, New York). Dr Freeburg's conception of disguise belongs, however, to the nineteenth century: 'Dramatic disguise ... means a change of personal appearance which leads to mistaken identity. There is a double test, change and confusion.' He eliminates the mere confusion of *The Comedy of Errors* and the substitution of Mariana for Isabella in *Measure for Measure*, where, as in the similar situation of *All's Well*, Shakespeare himself actually uses the word:

> So disguise shall, by the disguised,
> Pay with falsehood false exacting,
> And perform an old contracting.
>
> Only in this disguise I think't no sin
> To cosen him that would unjustly win.

I should prefer to define disguise as the substitution, overlaying or metamorphosis of dramatic identity, whereby one character sustains two roles. This may involve deliberate or involuntary masquerade, mistaken or concealed identity, madness or possession. Disguise ranges from the simple fun of the quick-change artist (*The Blind Beggar of Alexandria*) to the antic disposition of Edgar or Hamlet: it may need a cloak and false beard, or it may be better translated for the modern age by such terms as 'alternating personality'.

Dr Freeburg distinguishes five main types of disguise, all of which Shakespeare employs. These are the girl-page (Julia, Rosalind, Viola, Imogen), the boy-bride (*Taming of the Shrew* and *The Merry Wives*), the rogue in a variety of disguises (Autolycus) the spy in disguise (Vincentio) and the lover in disguise (Lucentio in *The Taming of the Shrew*). All go back to classical comedy, and except for the girl-pages they do not represent important aspects for Shakespeare. The boy-bride and the rogue are bound to lead to farce, and are handled better by Jonson in *Epicoene*, *Every Man In His Humour* and *The Alchemist*.

For the Elizabethans, 'disguise' still retained its primary sense of strange apparel, and 'disguising' was still the name for amateur plays. In Jonson's *Masque of Augurs* one player uses 'disguised' in the slang sense (to be drunk, as in *Antony and Cleopatra*, II vii 131) and is told 'Disguise was the old English word for a masque'. But it also carried the senses of 'concealment', and of 'deformity' ('Here in this bush disguised will I stand'; 'Her cheeks with chaps and wrinkles were disguised') from which the transition was easy to 'dissembling' ('disguise not with me in words'). The word thus retained a strong literal meaning yet also carried moral implications.

> Disguise, I see thou art an wickedness
> Wherein the pregnant enemy does much

says Viola, in the accents of Malvolio. New Guise and Nowadays, the tempters of *Mankind*, had been named from a dislike both of innovations and of that elaboration of dress which was so feelingly denounced by moralists from Chaucer to Tourneur.

The two archetypes were the disguise of the serpent and the disguise of the Incarnation. The devil's power of deceit furnished plots for many moralities. In Medwall's *Nature*, in *Republica* and in Skelton's *Magnifycence*, the vices take the virtues' names: in the last, Counterfeit Countenance becomes Good Demeanance, Crafty Conveyance becomes Sure Surveyance, Courtly Abusion becomes Lusty Pleasure and Cloaked Collusion becomes Sober Sadness. The two fools, Fancy and Folly, become Largesse and Conceit. The very names of such vices as Ambidexter and Hardy-dardy signify their power to juggle with appearance as they juggle with words. Slippery speech belongs with disguise:

> Thus like the formal Vice, Iniquity,
> I moralize two meanings in one word.

Both are combined in the great figure of the Marlovian Mephistopheles, disguised as a Franciscan friar. It is this tradition which lends such strength to Shakespeare's concept of the false appearance or *seeming*. There is no direct disguise in Angelo, Claudius, Iago, Iachimo or Wolsey, but an assumed personality. Miss Spurgeon has shown the force of the image of borrowed robes in *Macbeth*. The witches' invocation, recalling an important passage from Spenser on the fall of man, first states the theme: 'Fair is foul and foul is fair.' Lady Macbeth counsels her husband to look like the innocent flower but be the serpent under it. Macbeth himself speaks of 'making our faces vizards to our hearts, / Disguising what they are.' The clearest dramatic presentation of the theme occurs when the porter of Hell gate assumes a role which is no more than the mere truth. Here direct and planned concealment stirs pity and terror less than the disguise which is rooted in poetry and action, and perhaps not outwardly signified at all.

The diabolical villains, Richard III, Iago and the rest were, of course, not derived from any single original. Conscienceless Machievels such as Barabas, and Lorenzo of *The Spanish Tragedy* were behind them, as well as the Father of Lies; yet Donne's *Ignatius his Conclave* may serve as evidence that the old diabolism and new Machievellianism were linked in the popular mind.

Opposing infernal deceit was the heavenly humility of the Incarnation. The ruler of the world, concealed in humble garb, ministering to the needy, and secretly controlling every event is reflected in the disguised rulers (God's vicegerants), who wander among their subjects, living with them, and in the end distributing rewards and punishments in a judgement scene. Heavenly disguise enables Vincentio to test the virtue of his subjects, Henry to learn the secrets of his soldiers' feelings before Agincourt. Each of these roles has a long stage ancestry, but Shakespeare has strengthened the force of the disguise, which is in each case his own addition to the play. *Measure for Measure* contains a number of pronouncements upon disguising, and a wide variety of instances. The bride and the condemned prisoner have each their substitutes, 'Death's a great disguiser', as the supposed Franciscan says to the Provost. Lucio, a direct descendant of the old Vice is 'uncased' in his own act of 'uncasing' the Duke. This is Shakespeare's fulle: t study of disguise.

Disguises generally mean a drop in social status (except in farce) and in comical histories came a whole series of rulers who wooed milkmaids, learnt home-truths from honest countrymen, stood a buffet with their subjects and finally revealed themselves with all graciousness. The exploits of King Edward in *George-a-Greene*, King Edward IV in Heywood's play, and King Henry VIII in *When You See Me You Know Me* foreshadow Henry V's jest with Williams. These jovial revellers seem related to the stories of Robin Hood and the King: Robin himself appears in some of the plays. Noble wooers in disguise often played a rustic part (as in *Friar Bacon, Mucidorus, The Shoemakers' Holiday* and *Fair Em*), and in his wooing, King Henry V again slips back into a rustic role, which, though it is not a disguise, is certainly an assumed part, and recalls such popular songs as:

> To marry I would have thy consent,
> But faith I never could compliment;
> I can say nought but 'Hoy, gee ho!'
> Words that belong to the cart and the plough.
> Oh, say, my Joan, will not that do?
> I cannot come every day to woo.

In the old chronicle play of *King Leir*, France wooed Cordella in such disguise. In his adaptation of this story, Shakespeare used another old tradition, that of the disguised protector. The tenderness and devotion of Kent to Lear, and Edgar to Gloucester are however but faintly suggested by Flowerdale of *The London Prodigal* or Friscobaldo of *The Honest Whore*, who in the guise of servants tend their erring children. In these plays, the disguise is comic as well as pathetic; yet the father who pities his children, like the husband who pities and succours his erring wife, must have had a biblical origin, and Shakespeare recalled this old tradition to its first significance.

Different aspects of the same disguise could be played upon (even Kent has his moments of comedy) because there was an 'open' or unresolved view of individuality behind Elizabethan character-drawing, which corresponded to the open use of words in Elizabethan poetry. Fixed denotation, which is encouraged by a standardised spelling and pronunciation, a dictionary definition, and controlling prose usage was still unknown. The great key-words had a radiant nimbus of association; they were charged with life, so that a writer could allow their significance to reverberate through a whole play. The meaning of poetry is not to be extracted but to be explored;

and the creative uses of the pun, as illustrated in recent articles in this journal, are analogous to the use of multiple personality or disguise. Characters are fluid, and the role may vary from a specific or strictly individual one to something nearer the function of the Greek chorus. The antic disposition of Hamlet, or Edgar as Poor Tom, create an extra dimension for these plays as well as giving depth and fullness to the parts. Hamlet's coarseness and Edgar's wildness are parts of themselves, but they are more than merely that. Madness is a protective ruse, deriving in part at least from the disguise of Hieronimo, and of Antonio's disguise as a fool in Marston's *Antonio's Revenge*. Through this mask Hamlet penetrates the disguises of Polonius, Rosencrantz and Guildenstern, and Claudius. Edgar as madman has something of the insight of

> the eternal eye
> That sees through flesh and all.

The revengers, Hamlet and Vindice, have x-ray eyesight; their double roles of revenger and commentator correspond to the antinomy of their characters. Here again there is an easy gradation from the choric to the individual. The Revenger was also both good *and* evil; for revenge was deadly sin, yet also the inevitable result of the greater sins which the hero so pitilessly anatomised. Such double roles had not only a verbal correspondence in the pun but a structural parallel in the 'shadowing' of mainplot by subplot, most fully developed in *King Lear*. As Poor Tom, Edgar describes as his own the sins of Oswald and Edmund: his sinister disguise helps finally to turn the wits of the old king: he talks of the devils that inhabit him, till at Dover Cliff they are exorcised; finally he appears vizarded, the unknown challenger who executes a just vengeance, and forgives his dying enemy.

The Elizabethan theatre included a wide range of representation. Ghosts, spirits and visions appeared, or could even be used as disguise (as in *The Atheist's Tragedy*, where the hero dresses as a ghost). The appearance of Caesar's or Banquo's ghost also adds an extra dimension to the dramatist's world. Unearthly and almost unbearably poignant is Paulina's revival of the ghostly Hermione from dead marble to flesh and blood:

> I'll fill your grave up: stir, nay come away,
> To death bequeath your numbness, for from him
> Dear life redeems you.

Leontes has but three words 'Oh, she's warm', and Hermione, save to Perdita, has none. It is the dream of all bereaved, handled with a sureness and delicacy that could come only from long mastery. In his last plays, Shakespeare makes disguise an essentially poetic conception, and varies the level of it more subtly than ever before. It is necessary only to think of Imogen, her brothers and Belarius, Posthumus as the poor soldier, Cloten in Posthumus' garments, the false seeming of the Queen and the vision of the ghosts and the gods; or of Perdita's contrast with Florizel, both of them with the more conventional muffling of his father and Camillo, and the many disguises of Autolycus. Perdita is seemingly a shepherdess, pranked up as a goddess for the May sports: Florizel is obscured as a swain. As they dance together, the disguised Camillo says:

> He tells her something
> That makes her blood look out: good sooth, she is
> The queen of curds and cream.

Truly it is royal blood that rises, even as Florizel's youth shows 'the true blood which fairly peeps through it.' Here the threefold meaning of 'blood' – passion, descent, blushing – corresponds with the complex function of the disguises. Like those of Imogen and her brothers, they isolate the innocence and truth of the young, they are vestures of humility which disclose true worth; and yet they give the action a masque- or pageant-like quality which sets it apart from the rest of the play. In *The Tempest*, the varying of shapes belongs principally to Ariel, to Prospero, who can go invisible, and to the spirits of the masques. Yet Ferdinand and Miranda are in some sense obscured, and the anti-masque of Trinculo and Stephano with their frippery adds at least a further visual pattern.

The physical basis of disguise remained indeed of great importance. When the actors were so well known to the audience, it must have been easy for the spectators, like the playwright, to translate 'Enter Dogberry and Verges' into 'Enter Kempe and Cowley'. Costumes had to produce the stage atmosphere now given by scenery, lighting and make-up, and changes of costume must therefore have been valuable. Apparel was not thought of as concealing but as revealing the personality of the wearer. 'The apparel oft proclaims the man', and some of the most bitter and prolonged religious quarrelling of the age centred in the Vestarian controversy. Sumptuous clothing was a subject for satirists both off and on the stage; the Puritans attacked the theatre with the plea, based on the Mosaic injunction that for a man to put on the garments of a woman was an abomination. Hence there could be no such thing as a mere physical transformation. As the body revealed the soul, so appearance should reveal the truth of identity. A character could be really changed by the assumption of a disguise. The modern woman who restores her self-confidence with an expensive hat, the soldier who salutes the Queen's Commission and not the drunkard who happens to be wearing its insignia act in a manner familiar to Elizabethans. Hence Prospero's discarding of his magic robe symbolised most adequately his transformation from Magician back to Duke of Milan.

Such deepened power of guise and disguise did not prevent Shakespeare from using it in a practical and even thoroughly stagey fashion upon other occasions. His earliest plays are full of disguisings of a superficial kind: the complexities emerge in *The Merchant of Venice*, where he builds up a scale of contrast between Jessica's purely formal disguise, Nerissa's imitative one, and the significant robing of Portia. Viola's disguise, complicated by her likeness to her twin, is also contrasted with the literal dis-guise of Malvolio in yellow stockings and cross garters, and with the clown's assumption of Sir Thopas's part. Shakespeare on occasion used all the conventional tricks, as in *The Taming of the Shrew*, *The Merry Wives*, or Margaret's disguise as Hero, which leads to Claudio's pretended unmasking of the false semblant in the church scene, and to the final comedy of the masks.

The girl-pages, who would perhaps occur most readily to the mind as Shakespeare's favourite line in disguise, were already familiar from earlier narrative and drama. In comedy, there is less open characterisation than in tragedy: instead, the roles become stereotyped, based on sets of 'characteristics'. When the heroine is disguised as a boy, her two roles may be sharply contrasted, giving an effect as of shot silk, as the boyish wit or the feminine sensibility predominates. Shakespeare allows some very stagey jests, such as the broad farce of Viola's duel with Sir Andrew: yet such parts as hers, with their obvious advantages for the boy-actors, also allowed Shakespeare to depict the relationship of men and women with a new ease and frankness. Rosalind enjoys her disguise and frankly exploits its possibilities, but even the most demure of the heroines is given a chance by indirection to find directions out. In spite of the clear contrast between appearance and reality, the disguised heroines owe the peculiar delicacy and felicity of their depiction largely to masquerade.

This particular convention remained popular, long after Shakespeare's day; Fletcher, in Bellario and Aspatia, drew a new and sophisticated version. Bellario's true sex is not revealed till the end, though by this time any theatrical page might be assumed to be a woman in disguise. In the later seventeenth and eighteenth centuries, 'breeches parts' were as popular with the actresses as they had been with the boys, and from the stage they re-entered the Romantic poem. Sir Walter Scott has two such characters, one the heroine of *The Lord of the Isles*, the other in *Harold the Dauntless*, where an utterly incredible Viking is attended for years by a devoted page, whose sex is finally revealed to the imperceptive warrior by no less a personage than Odin himself.

The deeper implications of disguise, however, did not long survive Shakespeare's day. Writers of today have rediscovered its possibilities for tragedy as well as comedy, and are no longer limited to the presuppositions governing *Charley's Aunt*, *Vice Versa*, or even *The Happy Hypocrite*. Yet the triple flexibility of language, characters and plotting which give the Elizabethans so strong and delicate a weapon belongs to them alone. Only occasionally in lyric verse, as in Yeats's sequence of *The Three Bushes* – where the old trick of *Measure for Measure*, the false bride, is put to new uses – disguise provides a statement of philosophic themes. The antithesis of Body and Soul, even of the One and the Many is symbolised in this folk story, written in ballad style and set to a popular tune. (Yeats's source, however, is actually a Provençal *tenzon*, which he may have learnt of from Ezra Pound; hence the mixture of courtly love convention with reminiscences of *Fair Margaret and Sweet William*.)

It may be that Shakespeare too drew some of his inspiration from popular literature, especially from ballads, where disguises of all kinds are of primary importance, both for comedy and for tragedy. Whilst disguise has been used in the drama, the pathos and depth of feeling in the ballads, dramatic in form as many of them are, far exceeds that of the pre-Shakespearean stage in general. Tom a Bedlam, Hind Horn, Fair Annie may have been the seed-plots for Edgar, Hamlet and Imogen, as the Robin Hood ballads were for the comical history plays. Shakespeare turned to the popular ballad in moments of deepest pathos for Ophelia and Desdemona, he turned to old wives' tales and riddles for the visionary horror of *Macbeth* and the visionary beauty of *The Winter's Tale*, as many times he drew his purest poetry from the diction of common life.

III

Shakespeare's Debt to Marlowe

'Who chooseth me shall gain what many men desire.'
Why, that's the lady! All the world desires her;
From the four corners of the earth they come
To kiss this shrine, this mortal-breathing saint.
The Hyrcanian deserts and the vasty wilds
Of wide Arabia are as throughfares now
For princes to come view fair Portia.
The watery Kingdom, whose ambitious head
Spits in the face of heaven, is no bar
To stop the foreign spirits, but they come
As o'er a brook to see fair Portia.
                    (*The Merchant of Venice*, II vii 37–47)

At the moment of high ritual when the first of Portia's suitors, the
Prince of Morocco, is to make his choice, a heightening of the verse
attests his ardour. The dancing rhythm, with its onward flow, its
panoramic view, and its refrain, is modelled on Tamburlaine's
speech at the death of Zenocrate. Her apotheosis is celebrated with
images of the cosmic grandeur that have marked Tamburlaine
throughout, tinged here it would seem with some echoes of the Book
of Revelations; Morocco uses the ritual of pilgrimage to express his
reverence, although presumably his holy place is Mecca.

Morocco like Tamburlaine is a solar figure, clad in 'the shadowed
livery of the burnished sun' (II i 2), and like Tamburlaine's the
conclusion of his quest is a death's head. Tamburlaine's grief at the
death of Zenocrate is his first acknowledgement of mortality; he
enshrines his dead Queen 'not lapped in lead, but in a sheet of gold'
(*2 Tamburlaine*, II iv 131), the gold casket of Morocco's choice.

Now walk the angels on the walls of heaven,
As sentinels to warn th'immortal souls

To entertain divine Zenocrate.
Apollo, Cynthia, and the ceaseless lamps
That gently looked upon this loathsome earth,
Shine downwards now no more, but deck the heavens
To entertain divine Zenocrate.
The crystal springs, whose taste illuminates
Refinèd eyes with an eternal sight
Like trièd silver runs through Paradise
To entertain divine Zenocrate.
The cherubins and holy seraphins,
That sing and play before the King of Kings,
Use all their voices and their instruments
To entertain divine Zenocrate.
And in this sweet and curious harmony,
The god that tunes this music to our souls
Holds out his hand in highest majesty
To entertain divine Zenocrate.

(2 *Tamburlaine*, II iv 15–33)

The music is kept back for Bassanio, and for the last scene of all, but the dark quality behind the choice, the hint of regality tempered with grief, has been established. This dramatic recollection is designed to evoke audience memories, and to give a heightened audience-response in the theatre; it is more than a literary evocation.

Marlowe is found both at Belmont and Venice; the main Marlovian connections, though more diffused, lie in Shylock's role.

In making use of *The Jew of Malta*, Shakespeare may have drawn on his own memories as an actor – for the play, unlike *Tamburlaine*, was not in print, but it had been put on by Lord Strange's Men in 1592, and was subsequently given by the Admiral's Men. If Alleyn played Barabas, Burbage as Shylock acquired a subtler version of the stage Jew. Shakespeare took over certain situations, particularly from the role of Abigail the Jew's daughter, but Barabas's joy at the stratagem by which his daughter recovers his gold from its hiding place –

O my girl,
My gold, my fortune, my felicity!
. . .
O girl! O gold! O beauty! O my bliss! –
(*The Jew of Malta*, II i 46–53)

becomes Shylock's grief at the flight of Jessica as mocked by Solanio:

I never heard a passion so confused,
So strange, outrageous and so variable,

As the dog Jew did utter in the streets.
'My daughter! O my ducats! O my daughter!'
(II vii 12–15)

The subtle use of one Christian to entrap another was a practice of
Barabas which Shylock greatly expands when he pleads that the law
of Venice, and international confidence in its stability, demand the
fulfilment of his bond. That Antonio stands surety for Bassanio is no
of Shylock's contrivance, as the mutual destruction of Mathias and
Lodowick is of Barabas's.

Shakespeare can assume certain conventions about his stage
figure, and upon them work his own tranformation. Barabas's
justification for his treacheries, that 'Christians do the like', is
sufficiently demonstrated; zest in planning these as a 'savage farce' he
whetted the ironic plots in earlier plays, particularly *Titus Androni-*
cus and *Richard III*, where malignant delight in evil extrudes itself
in lively action. The most direct borrowing from *The Jew of Malta*.
Aaron's death speech in *Titus Andronicus*, is closely modelled on
Barabas's counsel to Ithamore (*The Jew of Malta*, II iii 165–99),

First be thou void of these affections:
Compassion, love, vain hope, and heartless fear;
(165–6)

but becomes active:

Even now I curse the day – and yet, I think,
Few come within the compass of my curse –
Wherein I did not some notorious ill.
(*Titus Andronicus*, v i 125–7)

The list of crimes that make up Barabas's life story include unprovoked murders (though of a secret kind) and more elaborate
stratagems; beginning

As for myself, I walk abroad a-nights,
And kill sick people groaning under walls;
Sometimes I go about and poison wells;
(*The Jew of Malta*, II iii 172–4)

and ending with the macabre image of a man hanging himself for
grief, with pinned upon his breast a long great scroll 'how I with
interest tormented him'. Aaron's crimes are more openly violent, but
the list ends with an equally macabre image of death; he digs up dead
men and sets them at

> their dear friends' door
> Even when their sorrows almost was forgot,
> And on their skins, as on the bark of trees,
> Have with my knife carvèd in Roman letters,
> 'Let not your sorrow die, though I am dead.'
> (*Titus Andronicus*, v i 136–40)

The scrolls transform these two Death figures into emblems of Judgement, which lies beyond death.

As Aaron's last dying confession, an occasion when a man was expected to give an exemplary speech, and ensure his future life by dying well, his diabolic manifesto has more force than the counsel imparted to a slave by reason of the position which it occupies. Unquenched evil holds its addict fast. Barabas's own death speech is comparatively short, and entails a triumphant acknowledgement of what he has brought about, with a final curse on Christians and Turks alike. The theological implications of his end have been studied in detail by G. K. Hunter. Aaron's choice of the devil's part is explicit, and more purposefully aimed:

> If there be devils, would I were a devil,
> To live and burn in everlasting fire,
> So I might have your company in hell
> But to torment you with my bitter tongue!
> (v i 147–50)

A just doom is to set him breast deep in earth, and famish him – 'There let him stand and rave and cry for food.' This is the end meted out to the negro bond-slave in the second part of *The Pleasant History of Tom a Lincoln*: it seems symbolic of the end of Base Desire. Aaron, who would 'have his soul black like his face', is one of a line of villainous Moors, Turks and Jews who supplied the material for atrocity plays like *Selimus* and *Lust's Dominion*; but his role in the retinue of the Empress allows for a mixture of ferocious comedy in Marlowe's manner, as he kills the nurse who has delivered the black infant born to him by the Empress, or as he instructs her sons in his own diabolic arts. This diabolic, jesting vitality has a Marlovian ring, though Shakespeare's sense of natural detail is as always much nearer the soil:

> Come on, you thick-lipped slave, I'll bear you hence;
> For it is you that puts us to our shifts.
> I'll make you feed on berries and on roots,
> And feed on curds and whey, and suck the goat,
> And cabin in a cave, and bring you up

> To be a warrior and command a camp.
>
> (*Titus Andronicus*, IV ii 176–81)

Aaron initiates most of the action in the play; when at the end Tamora and her sons disguised as Revenge, Rapine and Murder, they are, as it were, entering a figurative level which Aaron has already presented. In a play as deeply indebted to Kyd's Revenge dramas as *Titus Andronicus*, the Marlovian ingredient has brought something more characteristic of Shakespeare the poet into the remarkably well-constructed tragedy; and into its sombre and heraldic symmetries something of the countryside. Even Aaron's final catalogue of crimes includes some that sound like country witchcraft; to

> Make poor men's cattle break their necks;
> Set fire on barns and hay-stacks in the night,
>
> (V i 132–3)

are crimes not really worthy of the imperial court.

Shakespeare's imitations of Marlowe, even at their closest, invite consideration of the differences between the two. Marlowe's was incomparably the most powerful dramatic voice which he encountered at the beginning of his career, and Tamburlaine's were the accents which first had liberated the drama. Blended with the voice of the Jew in Aaron is the voice of Tamburlaine, especially in his opening soliloquy:

> Now climbeth Tamora Olympus' top,
> Safe out of fortune's shot, and sits aloft,
> Secure of thunder's crack or lightning flash,
> Advanced above pale Envy's threatening reach.
> . . .
> Away with slavish weeds and servile thoughts!
> I will be bright and shine in pearl and gold.
>
> (II i 1–4, 18–19)

The superb assurance of these lines, the triumph over Fortune, is Marlovian, in so grand a style that the fact that Aaron sacrifices his pride to secure the life of his bastard comes with a startling reversal. It is as if recalling Marlowe pushed Shakespeare into a further degree of inventiveness. This was the thesis maintained by Nicholas Brooke in the most cogent study of their relationship, *Marlowe as Provocative Agent in Shakespeare's Early Plays*.[2] As the sequence of history plays by Shakespeare and Marlowe ricochet one from another, each is seen borrowing in turn from the other. Henry VI's weakness shows the distintegrative force of a culpable innocence that lacks all will to power, and is in strongest contrast to Tamburlaine's power drive. Greene's parody from that play in his warning, addressed to Marlowe, against Shakespeare, 'O tiger's heart wrapped in a woman's hide',[3] is indeed the key to the catatonic movement by which Margaret becomes a spirit of Nemesis. Finally, as the embodiment of evil, Richard Crookback betters the Marlovian villain-heroes, for while they were pupils of Machiavelli he could 'set the murderous Machiavel to school'. His opening speech also betters theirs, for he is his own prologue, whilst they are preceded by various kinds of chorus.

Edward II, Marlowe's riposte, is clearly indebted to *Richard III*, since Mortimer's role as protector derives in some details from Richard's (see Harold Brooks, 'Marlowe and the Early Shakespeare'),[4] but, as the study of an obsession, the play lacks that wider sense of the country's plight, the desolation of England's trampled garden, so prominent in Shakespeare's counter-play, *Richard II*. Here the plot of the deposed and libertine king has many parallels with Marlowe's, but whilst for instance the ritual of the deposition scene is greatly expanded, the homosexual element is so played down that Bushy, Bagot and Green seem almost irrelevant. Some of the Marlovian magniloquence heard in the opening scenes does not come from *Edward II*, but the earlier plays.

> I would allow him odds
> And meet him, were I tied to run afoot,
> Even to the frozen ridges of the Alps.
> (*Richard II*, 1 i 62–4)

> O, who can hold a fire in his hand
> By thinking on the frosty Caucasus?
> (1 iii 294–5)

The two dramatists, contending with and reacting from each other, select their material to make contrasting effects. Richard's fall is more richly developed; 'Down, down I come like glistering Phaeton' is mirrored in the actual descent from the uppper to the lower stage; in the deposition scene itself, 'Fiend, thou torments me ere I come to hell' stands in apposition to the many comparisons with Christ and evokes Dr Faustus, whose last speech is echoed in the cry

> O that I were a mockery king of snow
> Standing before the sun of Bolingbroke,
> To melt myself away in water drops!
> (IV i 260–2)

But here there is the double image of the King's present tears, and of his former heraldic badge, the sunburst, which was applied to him in the earlier scene. The effects of *Dr Faustus* are felt most powerfully where they are most indirect, in the final moments of self-knowledge at Pomfret, though here the depth of tragic knowledge is more analytic than Marlowe's.

The question remains that this rivalry in the theatre may have accompanied rivalry outside the theatre. What is the relation of *Venus and Adonis* to *Hero and Leander*? And is Marlowe the rival poet of Sonnets 85 and 86?

The order in which the two Ovidian romances were composed is not easy to decide. *Hero and Leander* was entered to John Wolf in the Stationers' Register on 28 September 1593, only a few months after Marlowe's death on 30 May; but it did not appear till Edward Blount published it in 1598. *Venus and Adonis* was entered on 18 April 1593 to Richard Field, and was certainly in print by June. A second edition appeared in 1594 and it was frequently reprinted. G. P. V. Akrigg, in his *Shakespeare and the Earl of Southampton*,[5] called attention to the Latin poem 'Narcissus' by John Clapham, secretary to Lord Burghley, which was printed by Thomas Scarlet in 1591 with a dedication to the Earl of Southampton. It was the first dedication the young Earl had received, but it may not have been particularly welcome.[6]

For this 'short and moral description of Youthful Love and especially Self-Love' was intended as a warning fable to the young ward who was refusing to accept the plans of his guardian, Burghley, that he should marry Burghley's granddaughter, Lady Elizabeth Vere, a marriage which had been in the Lord Treasurer's mind since the previous year.

The scene is England. Narcissus visits the Temple of Love – which, like the temple in *Hero and Leander*, is painted with stories of famous victims – where he is received by Venus, and instructed in Ovid and Petrarch; but Love prophesies that Narcissus will perish of self-love. Having drunk of Lethe, and thereby forfeited self-knowledge, Narcissus is borne on an untameable horse named 'Lust' to the Fountain of Self-Love, where, according to legend, he is drowned – in despair that night has removed the image of himself from the waters.

Here, then, is the warning which was extended to the recalcitrant youth, and here much of the material which Shakespeare was to catch up and present in a far less offensive guise. The prime model for *Venus and Adonis* is not Marlowe, but Clapham, who supplies the moral, as well as reason for the inset of the horse and jennet, and the version of the story, reduced to a mere illustration in the persuasion of Venus, that Narcissus drowned himself (and was not, as in Ovid, pulled into the water by amorous nymphs).

> Is thine own heart to thine own face affected?
> Can thy right hand seize love upon thy left?
> Then woo thyself, be of thyself rejected;
> Steal thine own freedom and complain on theft.
>> Narcissus so himself himself forsook,
>> And died to kiss his shadow in the brook.
>>> (157–62)

Clapham has

> Deficiunt vires, et vox et spiritus ipse
> Deficit, et pronus de ripa decidit et sic
> Ipse suae periit deceptus imaginis umbra.
>> (sig. B3v)

Marlowe dismisses the story of Narcissus as a mere adjunct or mark to show Leander's surpassing beauty:

>> let it suffice
> That my slack muse sings of Leander's eyes,
> Those orient cheeks and lips, exceeding his
> That leapt into the water for a kiss
> Of his own shadow, and despising many,
> Died ere he could enjoy the love of any,
>> (*Hero and Leander*, i 71–6)

as the story of Venus and Adonis is merely a tale embroidered on the hem of Hero's sleeve:

> Her wide sleeves green, and bordered with a grove,
> Where Venus in her naked glory strove
> To please the careless and disdainful eyes
> Of proud Adonis that before her lies,
>> (i 11–14)

and the 'hot proud horse' an image of Leander's imperviousness to the counsel of his father (ii 141–5). The temple of Venus, where Marlowe's poem opens, may recall more precisely the same Temple in Clapham's poem: although commonplace, it fits in the catena of images linking all three poems.

Venus and Adonis shows a far closer relation with the first group of the Sonnets (1–19); the two Ovidian poems seem rather to be running parallel to each other, both deriving from Clapham. If

Marlowe's poem were complete as it stands (and there are precedents for such selective treatment) it would provide a persuasion to love quite devoid of warnings. Blount of course refers to it as an 'unfinished tragedy' in his dedicatory letter to Sir Thomas Walsingham, with whom Marlowe had been residing at the time of his death. But the full story would defeat the special purpose.

In Shakespeare's poem, the natural beauty of the landscape and of the animals is totally unlike the jewelled exotic world of Marlowe's poem; Shakespeare had already brought more of the natural scene into his Marlovian portrait of Aaron, and much into *Richard II*. It is one of the distinguishing marks between the imagination of the one and the other poet.

The comedy is equally contrasted; Shakespeare's is muted, incidental:

> Her song was tedious, and outwore the night,
> For lovers' hours are long, though seeming short;
> . . .
> Their copious stories, often times begun,
> End without audience and are never done,
>
> (841–2, 845–6)

whilst Marlowe's, enclosed in the taut couplet form, is more pervasive, an exultant triumph at the expense of mortals and gods, who are alike befooled, self-deceiving, and subjected to deflating comment:

> Albeit Leander, rude in love and raw,
> Long dallying with Hero, nothing saw
> That might delight him more, yet he suspected
> Some amorous rites or other were neglected.
>
> (ii 61–4)

Both are addressing an audience whose appetite for the pure honey of Ovidian eroticism is tempered by a taste for witty 'arguments of love'. This is one of the games people play when they have to lead a good deal of their private life in public, as courtiers did. Though it is so near in theme to the Sonnets, *Venus and Adonis* is a more public affair; indeed, it was licensed for printing by the Archbishop of Canterbury himself – did he actually read it, or was it one of his chaplains?

Kenneth Muir and Sean O'Loughlin noted the almost satiric outlook of *Venus and Adonis* in parts, and its ironic use of hyperbole.[7] This becomes appropriate in a context that asks for a 'correction' of John Clapham's sententiousness. This unwilling

Adonis (not a traditional role for him) must be offered a more artful persuasion to love.

As I have indicated elsewhere,[8] I think *Venus and Adonis* was also Shakespeare's response to charges of ignorance made by Robert Greene, which were couched in the form of a warning to Marlowe, the 'famous gracer of tragedians'. It was designed to obliterate the impression he had tried to make by its implicit claim to Art, set out in its motto

> Vilia miretur vulgus; mihi flavus Apollo
> Pocula Castalia plena ministret aqua . . .

Ovidian lines which Marlowe had translated

> Let base-conceited wits admire vile things,
> Fair Phoebus lead me to the Muses' springs.
> (*Elegy* xv 35–6)

If *Venus and Adonis* is an answer to Clapham's Latin, its claim as 'Art' increases.

During the winter of 1592–3, when the theatres in London were closed by the plague, poets scattered to country retreats – the kind of retreat that Boccaccio depicted in *The Decameron*, if they were fortunate, or the kind that is suggested in *Love's Labour's Lost*. It was during this period of retreat that Shakespeare wrote *Venus and Adonis* – T. W. Baldwin dates it just a few months or weeks before publication.[9] In the seventeenth century it would have been a country-house poem – as, in some respects, it is.

The danger from plague, which did not spare the young or the beautiful, lies behind its note of urgency. The plea for 'breed' was intensified by such circumstances. Here the two poets re-echo each other. 'Beauty alone is lost, too warily kept' parallels 'Beauty within itself should not wasted', and the familiar argument of usury re-occurs, Shakespeare here being the more succinct. Venus has been describing all the maladies that 'in one minute's fight bring beauty under', comparing the body to 'a swallowing grave' if it buries its own posterity – an act worse than suicide or parricide.

> Foul cank'ring rust the hidden treasure frets,
> But gold that's put to use more gold begets.
> (767–8)

Leander's sophistry lacks this pressure but his eye certainly glances from earth to heaven. Ships were made to sail the sea, strings to play upon, brass pots to shine with use, robes to be worn, palaces to live in:

> What difference betwixt the richest mine
> And basest mould but use? For both, not used,
> Are of like worth. Then treasure is abused
> When misers keep it; being put to loan,
> In time it will return us two for one.
>
> (i 232–6)

The familiar innuendo spices this trade catalogue, but Hero's reply, which is very brief, seems not amiss: 'Who taught thee rhetoric to deceive a maid?' (i 338) Marlowe is not involved; and this spirited series of conflicts – between gods, between the lovers, within Hero herself – taught Shakespeare more about how to write plays, and fit conflict within conflict.

Sonnets 85 and 86, as I believe, describe a poetry contest between Shakespeare and the Rival Poet. These contests of recitation – one thinks of the *Mastersingers* of Wagner – had been held in London since Chaucer's time at the festival of the Pui (the guild of foreign merchants); at a lower level there were scolding matches or 'flytings'.[10]

> Was it the proud full sail of his great verse,
> Bound for the prize of all-too-precious you,
> That did my ripe thoughts in my brain inhearse,
> Making their tomb the womb wherein they grew?
> Was it his spirit, by spirits taught to write
> Above a mortal pitch, that struck me dead?
> No.
> . . .
> But when your countenance filled up his line
> Then lacked I matter; that enfeebled mine.
>
> (Sonnet 86)

Marlowe was so often credited with 'inspiration' by his fellow poets, with the 'brave translunary things' that made his spirits 'all air and fire' that the fifth line does not derogate from the recognisable fitness of the opening lines to Marlowe and to him alone. (Chapman, chief alternative, had at this time written nothing, was only newly out of the Low Countries, and found composition extremely difficult and agonising by his own accounts.)

If Marlowe were the rival poet (and he seems to me the most likely candidate), this would explain why his verse re-occurred to Shakespeare in *The Merchant of Venice* within the high ritual atmosphere of a prize contest. In Sonnet 85 the winning poem was to 'reserve [its] character with golden quill', which was what happened to the prize poem at the festival of the Pui, where the winner was given a 'crown' for the song he had made in praise of the newly elected 'Prince' of that fraternity. It was then hung up under the 'Prince's' arms. (A mock challenge at wooing is set up in Jonson's *Cynthia's Revels*.) In *The Merchant of Venice* the contest is for a much nobler reward; Morocco, the first contestant, departs with the mournful echo of what he had read on the scroll, 'Your suit is cold':

> Cold indeed and labour lost!
> Then farewell, heat, and welcome, frost,
> (II vii 74–5)

whilst, after the interlude of Aragon (whom Nicholas Brooke compares with Marlowe's figure of the Guise in his contempt for things common), Bassanio approaches with that note of love and springtime which is heard in the plays as well as the poems:

> A day in April never came so sweet
> To show how costly summer was at hand
> As this fore-spurrer comes before his lord.
> (II ix 93–5)

The after-effects of *Hero and Leander* can be sensed in *Romeo and Juliet*. The resemblance is general and is a matter of the high assurance of Juliet's 'Gallop apace, you fiery-footed steeds', or Mercutio's bawdy wit (perhaps also the tragic suddenness of his death in a futile brawl may be taken to reflect Marlowe's own). The sustained note of lyric joy, the physical obstacles that separate the lovers, the blindness of destiny that opposes them do not add up to a challenge to Marlowe; they are in Shakespeare's own mode.

From time to time he looked back on Marlowe. Among Pistol's playscraps the 'hollow pamper'd jades of Asia' appear along with Callipolis and Hiren the Fair Greek. Then, in 1598, *Hero and Leander* appeared in print, and Shakespeare, for the only time in his life, identified and quoted a contemporary

> Dead shepherd, now I find thy saw of might:
> 'Who ever loved that loved not at first sight?'
> (*As You Like It*, III v 80–1)

Two scenes earlier there had been a reference to Marlowe's death:

Touchstone: I am here with thee and thy goats, as the most capricious poet, honest Ovid, was among the Goths.

Jaques:	O knowledge ill-inhabited, worse than Jove in a thatched house!
Touchstone:	When a man's verses cannot be understood, nor a man's good wit seconded with the forward child understanding, it strikes a man more dead than a great reckoning in a little room. (III iii 4–13)

It is generally conceded that the 'great reckoning in a little room' recalls Marlowe's death in a quarrel over the reckoning in a tavern. The jest about 'honest Ovid' might have brought him to mind; but the catastrophe that when a man's verses cannot be understood it strikes him dead also recalls Sonnet 86:

> Was it his spirit, by spirits taught to write
> Above a mortal pitch, that struck me dead?

Not literally, of course; he had 'dried' – the actor's worst fear, a fear already described in Sonnet 23. The image here is a double one, of the reciter 'struck dead' and that later death after 'a great reckoning in a little room'. Tenderest of all is Rosalind's denial that any in 6000 years had met Leander's fate (untold in Marlowe's poem).

> Leander, he would have lived many a fair year, though Hero had turned nun, if it had not been for a hot midsummer-night; for, good youth, he went but forth to wash him in the Hellespont, and, being taken with the cramp, was drowned; and the foolish chroniclers of that age found it was – Hero of Sestos. But these are all lies: men have died from time to time, and worms have eaten them, but not for love. (*As You Like It*, IV i 83ff.)

The playfulness covering so much hesitant and withheld feeling, which is Rosalind's charm, chimes with the memory of a contest for love and favour, ended so abruptly. A later memory of Marlowe is also associated with death. Hamlet's favourite piece of verse has a distinctly Marlovian ring, though he cannot remember it exactly ('"The rugged Pyrrhus, like th' Hyrcanean beast" – Tis not so; it begins with Pyrrhus' (*Hamlet*, II ii 444–5)).

This enormous icon, much bigger than life, with 'sable arms / Black as his purpose', foreshadows, with his arrested action as he stands over Priam, his sword held aloft, an image we are to see, of Hamlet himself standing over the kneeling Claudius. It is something that has risen from the depth of the mind, and that is to return; in its primitive violence and rhetorical emphasis quite unShakespearian, though of course very well suited to stand out from the text of this play. This, in itself, it would appear, was the reworking of a tragedy that had belonged to Marlowe's day.

Shakespeare's relation to Kyd, and to Lyly, is often of a more detailed kind than his relation to Marlowe, for what they offered were theatrical models of rhetorical speech and dramatic patterning. What Shakespeare learnt from Marlowe, the only figure whose poetic powers approached his own, was shown rather in reaction. The greatest of Marlowe's creations, *Dr Faustus*, makes the least identifiable contribution; yet as Macbeth stands waiting for the sound of the bell, there is but one scene with which it may be compared.

Psychologists affirm that the slighter the indication of an adjustment, the deeper its roots may well lie. Shakespeare reacted to Marlowe in a selective way, and as a person; that is to say, there is an emotional train of association in his borrowings. Marlowe, it is clear from *Edward II*, also reacted to Shakespeare; and Greene's warning to Marlowe may have gained in point and malice if the two were already known in some sense to be in contest for the poetic 'crown'. Such a contest, in the plague years, would have been part of the courting of favour that had survived in Spenser's day, but was by the mid-1590s not without its alternatives. To these Shakespeare returned, throwing in his lot with the common players.

Notes

1 'The Theology of Marlowe's *The Jew of Malta*', *Journal of the Warburg and Courtauld Institutes*, XXVII (1964), pp. 211–40. Reprinted in G. K. Hunter, *Dramatic Identities and Cultural Tradition* (1978).

2 *Shakespeare Survey* 14 (Cambridge, 1961), pp. 34–44.

3 Greene's well-known passage in his *Groatsworth of Witte* (1592): 'There is an upstart crow, beautified with our feathers, that with his *Tiger's heart wrapped in a player's hide*, supposes he is as well able to bombast out a blank verse as the best of you, and being an absolute *Johannes fac totum*, is in his own conceit the only Shake-scene in a country.' This is the first reference to Shakespeare in the literature of his time. The line is *3 Henry VI*, I iv 137.

4 In *Christopher Marlowe*, ed. Brian Morris (London, 1968).

5 London, 1968.

6 The dedication ran: 'Clarissimo et Nobilissimo Domino Henrico Comiti Southamptoniae; Johannes Clapham virtutis, atque honoris incrementum multosque annos exoptat.' For John Clapham, see Joel Hurstfield, *The Queen's Wards* (London, 1958), especially p. 263 where Clapham is quoted as saying Burghley 'oft-times gratified his friends and servants that depended and waited on him.' It was presumably for Burghley's gratification, not the dedicatee's, that the poem was written.

It is unfortunately not given in Bullough's *Narrative and Dramatic Sources of Shakespeare. STC* lists only the London copy (*STC*, 5349).

7 See *The Voyage to Illyria* (London, 1937), pp. 44–5, where it is also said Shakespeare owed most to Marlowe in this poem.

8 See my article 'Beasts and Gods; Greene's *Groatsworth of Witte* and the social purpose of *Venus and Adonis*', *Shakespeare Survey* 15 (Cambridge, 1962), pp. 62–80. *Collected Papers* vol. 1.

9 T. W. Baldwin, *On the Literary Genetics of Shakespeare's Poems and Sonnets* (Urbana, Illinois, 1950), p. 45: 'It would seem ... *Venus and Adonis* was written no long time before its entry for publication.'

10 For the festival of the Pui, see my *Shakespeare the Craftsman* (London, 1969), pp. 31–2.

Beasts and Gods: the social purpose of *Venus and Adonis*

The player's challenge

Precisely because it is of a different kind, there has been very little attempt to see *Venus and Adonis* as the work of one whose nature was already subdued, like the dyer's hand, to the popular stage-writings of his day. In this Shakespeare has succeeded in what was surely his initial intention, to make a second reputation for himself. To appear in print was to make a dignified bid for Fame; the author at once achieved recognition and respectful notice, even among those who despised, or affected to despise, the work of the common stages. In a few years the students of St John's College, Cambridge, in the person of Judicio would commend William Shakespeare the poet – 'Who loues not *Adons* loue or *Lucrece* rape?' – while they gave a pulverizing defence of William Shakespeare the playwright to Kempe:

> Few of the university pen plaies well, they smell too much of that writer *Ouid*, and that writer *Metamorphoses*, and talke too much of *Proserpina & Iuppiter*. Why heres our fellow *Shakespeare* put them all downe, I and Ben Ionson too.[1]

This elegant poem, redolent of Ovid, joins Marlowe and Shakespeare; for like *Hero and Leander*, it is witty and challenges abstinence on behalf of the flesh. Both poets had also been joined for rebuke, though each for very different reasons, in a work which appeared a few months before *Venus and Adonis*. Shakespeare's first venture into print, while not a direct reply to Greene's *Groats-worth of Witte*, may be regarded as a response provoked by this piece of vilification. Because I would see Greene's attack as more sustained and even more insulting than it is usually thought, I would suggest it produced a degree of irritation that writing alone could cure.

Shakespeare's intention is signified by the dedication to the Earl of

Southampton, and by the motto. He was dissociating himself from baseness:

> Vilia miratur vulgus . . .

is more characteristic of Ben Jonson (who translated it 'Kneel hinds to trash') than of the tolerant Shakespeare; it betrays the spirit in which the work was published. *Venus and Adonis* furnishes a literary equivalent of the application to Herald's College for a coat of arms:

> mihi flavus Apollo
> Pocula Castalia plena ministret acqua.

The gulf that lay between popular playwriting and courtly poetry may be measured in that scene of *Histriomastix*, where the artisan players presented Troilus boasting to Cressid:

> Thy knight his valiant elboe weares,
> That When he shakes his furious Speare,
> The foe in shivering fearefull sort,
> May lay him downe in death to snort. (ii. i)

They were dismissed in disgrace and an Italian lord observed:

> I blush in your behalfes at this base trash;
> In honour of our Italy we sport,
> As if a Synod of the holly Gods,
> Came to tryumph within our Theaters. (ii. i)

If both Shakespeare's poem and Greene's pamphlet are read, not in terms of their classical background but as pictorial imagery, they seem to me to provide a coherent pattern – a disparagement, or rhetorical invective, against the common player; and a counter-challenge of nobility, by a common player. Greene in scorn affixes the beast's mask upon his enemy: Shakespeare counters this by evoking a goddess, and celebrating the triumphs of the senses and the flesh in divine, human and animal forms.

The antics and the upstart crow

It may be well here to recall a few dates:

> 3 September 1592: Death of Robert Greene.
> 20 September 1592: Registration of Greene's *Groats-worth of Witte*.
> 8 December 1592: Registration of Henry Chettle's *Kind-Harts Dreame*, containing an apology for printing the *Groats-worth of Witte*.
> 18 April 1593: Registration of Shakespeare's *Venus and Adonis*.

To which might be added the conclusion of T. W. Baldwin, based on an examination of the literary sources, that *Venus and Adonis* was written 'most likely just a few weeks or at most months before' registration, and the fact that it was announced in the letter of dedication as Shakespeare's first work in print.[2]

In a passage which ever since the eighteenth century has caused much throwing about of brains, Greene had addressed three gentlemen-playwrights (Marlowe, Nashe, Peele):

> Base minded men all three of you, if by my miserie you be not warnd: for vnto none of you (like mee) sought those burres to cleaue: those Puppets (I meane) that spake from our mouths, those Anticks garnisht in our colours. Is it not strange, that I, to whom they all haue beene beholding: is it not like that you, to whome they all haue beene beholding, shall (were yee in that case as I am now) bee both at once of them forsaken? Yes trust them not: for there is an vpstart Crow, beautified with our feathers, that with his *Tygers hart wrapt in a Players hyde*, supposes he is as well able to bombast out a blanke verse as the best of you: and beeing an absolute *Iohannes fac totum*, is in his owne conceit the onely Shake-scene in a countrey.[3]

Greene puts Shakespeare among the lowest and most scurrilous type of actor, the antic or mome; these grotesque characters with animal heads and bombast figures came into court revels with mops and mows, for dumb shows of detraction and scorn. In the first unbridled Christmas festivities of Elizabeth's reign, cardinals, bishops and abbots appeared at court in the likeness of crows, asses, and wolves; in 1564 Cambridge students pursued the Queen to Hinchingbrooke with a dumb show presenting the imprisoned Catholic prelates – Bonner eating a lamb, and a dog with the Host in his mouth – a dumb show from which the Queen rose and swept out, taking the torchbearers and leaving the players in darkness and disgrace.[4] Such antics were no longer in favour at court; but they were seen in country merriments and in the afterpieces of the common stages. The players had brought their enemy Gosson on the stage in some such monstrous form. 'We will have, if this fadge not, an antique' (*Love's Labour's Lost*, v. i. 154–5) suggests that even village players rated the form below a show.

In 1570 first appeared *A Marvellous History entitled, Beware the Cat*, a 'Christmas Tale' attributed to William Baldwin. He describes how he had been at Court with Edward Ferrars, King Edward VI's Lord of Misrule, and some others; they lay abed together discussing the play of *Æsop's Crow* which the King's players had been learning, and which Baldwin discommended, saying:

> it was not Commicall to make either speechlesse things to speake: or brutish things to commen resonably. And although in a tale it be sufferable . . . yet it was vncomely (said I) and without example of any authour

to bring them in liuely personages to speake, doo, reason, and allege authorities out of authours (ed. 1584, A4⁴⁻ᵛ).

This introduction to a queer, ribald collection of witch stories about Irish cats – by turns horrific and bawdy, and like the shows at court, with a strong anti-papal bias – implies that a play of *Æsop's Crow* first gave speaking parts to antics. It might have been remembered, and thus might have given point to Greene's earlier rebuke to the actors:

> why *Roscius*, art thou proud with *Esops* Crow, being pranct with the glorie of others feathers? of thy selfe thou canst say nothing, and if the Cobler hath taught thee to say, *Aue Caesar*, disdain not thy tutor, because thou pratest in a Kings chamber: what sentence thou vtterest on the stage, flowes from the censure of our wittes.⁵

Whether Greene's upstart crow be, in the literary sense, Æsop's crow, or as Dover Wilson would have it, Horace's crow,⁶ he is primarily neither, but an antic taught to speak by poets and unnaturally spurning his teachers. Garnished in the 'colours' of Greene's rhetoric, as in the colours of brilliant playing suits, if his plumes were pulled, he would appear a mere crow of the old kind. Yet there is one of these crows who has not only learnt to speak verses but to write them; with him, the beast form is an inward one, for like all players, he is treacherous and cruel; by concealing his predatory nature within, he is transformed from crow to tiger. As an antic took to speech so a player has now taken to writing; Shakespeare, like the original crow, violates decorum.

The kind of player Greene suggests is one who had begun as a tattered, gaudily dressed stroller, with the slipperiness, the capacity for betrayal, of all wandering tribes – gipsies, fiddlers, minstrels, tinkers. The disparagement laid on him is akin to that of the mock-blazon devised for the Duttons when they claimed the academic title of Comedians:

> Three nettles resplendent, three owles, three swallowes,
> Three mynstrellmen pendent on three payre of gallowes,
> Further sufficiently placed in them
> A knaves head, for a difference from alle honest men.
> The wreathe is a chayne of chaungeable red,
> To shew they ar vayne and fickle of head;
> The creste is a lastrylle whose feathers ar blew,
> In signe that these fydlers will never be trew . . .⁷

Greene's bespattering is of this kind, with bestial comparison, and social denigration. Its theatrical, not its literary echo, is cruellest. Three years before the appearance of Greene's *Groats-worth of Witte*, Martin Marprelate had been brought on the common stages to be lanced and wormed in the form of an ape; and when the shows were banned, Lyly lamented:

> He shall not bee brought in as whilom he was, and yet verie well, with a cocks combe, an apes face, a wolfs bellie, cats clawes, &c.[8]

Several years after, at the end of *Poetaster*, Jonson showed Tucca gagged and vizarded, Fannius fitted with fool's coxcomb and cap, and in the epilogue proclaimed:

> Blush, folly, blush: here's none that feares
> The wagging of an asses eares,
> Although a wooluish case he weares.
> Detraction is but basenesse varlet;
> And apes are apes, though cloth'd in scarlet.　　(v. iii. 626–30)

There were plenty of hybrids as extraordinary as the crow with a tiger's heart. Greene was not writing for scholars; the context evoked a direct visual memory for his readers. Stage pieces would naturally spring to mind, though a Latin phrase might follow for the few.

The structure of Greene's *Groats-worth of Witte*

This passage on Shakespeare, the highest point of Greene's invective, is not detachable from the rest of the pamphlet, in which the poet tells his life-story as the tale of the prodigal Roberto, born in a rich mercantile city [Norwich], disinherited by his father, cheating his brother, and cheated later by a drab. As Roberto sits lamenting under a hedge, he is accosted with smooth and consoling words:

> But if you vouchsafe such simple comforte as my abilitie may yeeld, assure your selfe, that I wil indeuour to doe the best, that either may procure you profite, or bring you pleasure: the rather, for that I suppose you are a scholler, and pittie it is men of learning should liue in lacke.　　(p. 33)

The stranger, so civil in his demeanour, turns out to be a player:

> A player, quoth *Roberto*, I tooke you rather for a Gentleman of great liuing, for if by outward habit men should be censured, I tell you, you would bee taken for a substantiall man. So am I where I dwell (quoth the player) reputed able at my proper cost to build a Windmill. What though the world once went hard with me, when I was faine to carry my playing Fardle a footebacke; *Tempora mutantur*, I know you know the meaning of it better than I, but I thus conster it, its otherwise now; for my very share in playing apparell will not be sold for two hundred pounds. Truly (said *Roberto*) tis straunge, that you should so prosper in that vayne practise, for that it seemes to mee your voice is nothing gratious.　　(pp. 33–4)

This player with the ungracious voice goes on to say he is famous for acting Delphrigus and the King of the Fairies, that he has thundered in the Twelve Labours of Hercules, and played three scenes of the Devil in *The Highway to Heaven*. Moreover, he is author as well as player – a 'countrey Author' 'passing at a Morrall' who wrote *The Dialogue of Dives*; finally, for seven years he was absolute interpreter of the puppets. His repertoire was on the level of the Antic, though more respectable.

> But now my Almanacke is out of date:
>> *The people make no estimation,*
>> *Of Morrals teaching education.*
> Was not this prettie for a plaine rime extempore? if ye will ye shall haue
>> more.   (p. 34)

This caricature of an untrained player-poet, who is none the less wealthy, and can speak ingratiatingly, must not be taken for an individual likeness. For apart from anything else, some of it is stock stuff, borrowed from Nashe's preface to Greene's own *Menaphon*:

> Sundry other sweete gentlemen I know, that haue vaunted their pennes in priuate deuices, and tricked vp a company of taffata fooles with their feathers, whose beauty if our Poets had not peecte with the supply of their periwigs, they might haue antickt it vntill this time vp and downe the Countrey with the King of *Fairies*, and dined euery day at the pease porredge ordinary with *Delphrigus*. But *Tolossa* hath forgot that it was sometime sacked, and beggars that euer they carried their fardels on footback . . .'

Nevertheless, there was one especially noted player-poet when Greene was writing; one who according to a later tradition had been a schoolmaster in the country, and therefore might well have been supposed to begin with morals teaching education; this is the player-poet alluded to by name later as a so-called Comedian who is fit only to antic it up and down the country. The player with the ungracious voice might have been recognizable to contemporaries; for it is worth noting that Chettle begins his apology with a tribute to Shakespeare's acting ability ('excellent in the quality he professes'). The kind of play in which this player began is the kind which in Shakespeare's 'lost years', before the arrival of the University Wits, must have provided the repertory of all common players.

Greene used the popular method of detraction, taking a pre-existing formula, and working in an ascription or two which would fit a particular person – a method of denigration by suggestion, still practised, for example, in the speeches of learned counsel or of politicians who know their art. Seaside photographers of the past invited sitters to pose with their heads stuck through a cardboard

cutout, so that they appear to be taking part in a comic donkey race
or rowing on a choppy sea. So, in this kind of caricature, the personal
touch and the public property are conjoined; the individual is dressed
in an ass's head or a calf's skin and the joke depends on contrast
between the human and the dummy parts. Clowns who sought
voluntary ridicule at an Elizabethan fair would compete at the sport
of grinning through a horse-collar; here ready-made detraction was
clapped on a selected victim.[10]

In the *Groats-worth of Witte* Greene makes two contrasting uses
of beast-fables, literary equivalent of the antic show of scorn. The
cheating courtesan gives Roberto a 'caveat by the way, which shall be
figured in a fable' of the Fox and the Badger, directed against the
red-haired fox who was also the red-haired Greene. The whole work
ends with a 'conceited fable of that old Comedian Æsop' told by
Greene; in this farcical afterpiece to his tragic story, the improvident
Poet appears as the Grasshopper, while the provident Ant represents
the Player, who refuses succour in time of need:

> Packe hence (quoth he) thou idle lazie worme,
> My house doth harbor no vnthriftie mates:
> Thou scorndst to toile, & now thou feelst the storme,
> And starust for food while I am fed with cates.
> Vse no intreats, I will relentlesse rest,
> For toyling labour hates an idle guest.   (pp. 48–9)

Here is the 'forsaking' and cruelty of which Greene has already
complained – and in his letter to his wife, he reveals he was like to
have died in the streets.

It is when, in the course of the narrative, Roberto's time for
repentance comes that the narration turns into confession, and
Greene speakes for the first time in his own person:

> Heere (Gentlemen) breake I off *Robertoes* speach; whose life in most parts
> agreeing with mine, found one selfe punishment as I haue doone. Heer-
> after suppose me the saide *Roberto*, and I will goe on with that hee
> promised . . .   (p. 39)

Having thrown off the vizard, Greene gives his precepts, and appeals
to the gentlemen playwrights; in exactly parallel manner, having
presented the unnamed player-poet in the narrative, he then attacks a
similar figure, but directly and by name, in the confession. Some link
may be supposed between the two. The construction of this pamphlet is not as haphazard as it at first appears.

Chettle's reply to Greene

In the epistle to the 'Gentlemen readers' prefixed to *Kind-Harts Dreame*, Chettle makes handsome apology to Shakespeare as player, as citizen and as poet:

> my selfe haue seene his demeanor no lesse ciuill than he exelent in the qualitie he professes: Besides, diuers of worship haue reported, his vprightnes of dealing, which argues his honesty, and his facetious grace in writing, that approoues his Art.[11]

Shakespeare is cleared from the imputation of being an antic, or a dishonest skipjack player, and though he has not published, he is allowed by report facetious grace in Art. But against this must be set a tribute to Greene in the body of the work, where his ghost appears to protest against the cruel imputations that are being put about after his death:

> the fifth, a man of indifferent yeares, of face amible, of body well proportioned, his attire after the habite of a schollerlike Gentleman, onely his haire was somewhat long, whome I supposed to be Robert Greene, maister of Artes; of whome (howe euer some suppose themselves iniured) I haue learned to speake, considering he is dead, *nil nisi necessarium*. He was of singuler pleasaunce the verye supporter, and to no mans disgrace bee this intended, *the only Comedian of a vulgar writer in this country* [my italics].   (p. 13)

Kind-Harts Dreame is a reply to the general case against players, a humble plea for the liberty of honest, if lowly, wanderers. The pamphlet consists of five newsletters from five apparitions (including Greene, and Richard Tarlton the clown, who defends harmless pastime) seeking to deliver a 'bill invective against abuses now reigning' to be borne by Piers Penniless' Post to the infernal regions. The fiddler, the juggler, the simple-hearted narrator come from London fairgrounds. There is little chance that William Cuckow or Kind-Hart the toothdrawer could be taken for anyone but themselves; that is perhaps the purpose of the very full description they are given.[12]

That Greene's name is often attached to scurrilous pamphlets and that he appears so often coupled with Tarlton,[13] whose jests were exceptionally bawdy, may appear surprising to anyone who remembers the inoffensiveness of his romance and the delicacy of much of his work: though it should be recalled that Chettle said he had expunged from the *Groats-worth of Witte* a certain accusation against Marlowe, which to publish 'was intollerable'.

The whole chain of scurrilous invective and lachrymose repentance put out under Greene's name shows his sales-value for printers;

in the *Groats-worth of Witte*, from the first appearance of the player with falsely 'civil demeanour' to the afterpiece of the Ant and the Grasshopper, Shakespeare might not unjustly consider himself to be bearing the brunt of a widely-read invective. That the attack cut deep may be easily supposed. Years later, even Polonius remembered that 'beautified' was a vile word. After extracting an apology from Chettle, Shakespeare went on to safeguard his reputation with a work whose elegance and modishness was recognized within the walls of Greene's own college and university. His 'facetious grace in writing' was publicly shown by a work of learning (Art). Its un-abashed celebration of the delights of the flesh gave an answer more convincing than a directly aimed reply to the terror-stricken repent-ance of the poor wretch who, by his own confession, had been guilty of all the faithlessness and promise-breaking with which he charged the players.

Venus and Adonis

Venus and Adonis, sumptuous and splendidly assured, was designed not to answer Greene, but to obliterate the impression he had tried to make. In this it seems to have succeeded. Yet, because Shakespeare was a player, there remain a few traces in the poem of the very different Venus he had known upon the common stages – the Venus of the first actor-playwright, Robert Wilson, a contemporary of Tarlton. It is a vindication of the goddess, no less than of the player.

Love appears as a character in each of Wilson's three plays, as well as in some others which Shakespeare may have known.[14] On the stage she is more often condemned than praised, especially by Wilson, who marries her to Dissimulation, and sets her to woo Contempt. The language of scorn employed by Adonis is mild compared with that of Contempt, who first seduces Venus from Mars and then leaves her to lament:

> So flies the murderer from the mangled lims,
> Left limles on the ground by his fell hand.
> So runnes the Tyger from the bloodles pray,
> Which when his fell stomacke is of hunger stancht,
> Thou murdrer, Tyger, glutted with my faire,
> Leaust me forsaken, map of griefe and care.[15]

There may be a faint echo in the final prophecy of Shakespeare's mourning Venus; a more curious similarity is that Contempt, like Adonis, is described as being most incongruously smaller than Venus; if Shakespeare's Venus can tuck Adonis under her arm,

Wilson's Contempt is described as a sort of false Eros, a 'little Goosecap God', a 'little little seeing God'. Greene himself had written a lyric in which Adonis seems almost confused with Eros:

> In *Cypres* sat fayre *Venus* by a Fount,
> Wanton *Adonis* toying on her knee,
> She kist the wag, her darling of accompt,
> The Boie gan blush, which when his louer see,
> > She smild and told him loue might challenge debt,
> > And he was yoong and might be wanton yet.[16]

The climax of Wilson's *The Cobler's Prophecy* is the denunciation of Venus by other gods and her degradation from heavenly rank, since she is known to be but 'Venus alias Lust'; and so is given only 'the detested name of Lust or Strumpet Venus'.

Shakespeare's goddess is admonished by Adonis:

> 'Call it not love, for Love to heaven is fled,
> Since sweating Lust on earth usurp'd his name . . .
> Love comforteth like sunshine after rain,
> But Lust's effect is tempest after sun:
> Love's gentle spring doth always fresh remain,
> Lust's winter comes ere summer half be done;
> > Love surfeits not, Lust like a glutton dies;
> > Love is all truth, Lust full of forged lies.   (793–804)

The same attitude prevailed on the private stage, for in Court plays Venus was in conflict with Diana's nymph, Elizabeth. The comedies of Lyly gave Shakespeare a model, especially for the one which was shortly to follow *Venus and Adonis*, in the winter of 1593–4, *Love's Labour's Lost*.[17] This was eventually published 'as it was presented before her Highness this last Christmas', the first of Shakespeare's plays to achieve this honour. In his poem Shakespeare also addressed himself to the courtly group, Lyly's select audience. Socially Greene and Lyly were poles apart, and to turn from the one to the other was to step from tavern to presence chamber.

Many of Lyly's plays, especially *Midas* and *Campaspe*, are like Ovidian romance in dramatic form, yet they lack its vivid sensuous expansiveness. Lyly's was an artificial world; his 'natural' objects were a collection of rarities brought together by simile. The Venus of Lyly may, like Shakespeare's, fall in love with a fair boy *(Sapho and Phao)*, but she remains a voice only, a speaking part undefined by sympathy, in a series of rhetorical statements:

O Cupid, thy flames with Psyches were but sparks, and my desires with Adonis but dreames, in respecte of these vnacquainted tormentes . . . (iv. ii. 14–16)

In *Gallathea* Venus loses Cupid to Diana, and in *Sapho and Phao* to Sapho; in *The Woman in the Moon*, she is shown at her worst, inspiring the heroine with nymphomaniac fury. Venus in Lyly always represents lust; the cool impersonality of his style, no less than the need to consider his royal patroness, would not admit the true goddess. Cupid is a more important figure than Venus for Lyly; desire not passion presides. The fragile elegance of his dialogue combined with an underlying stratum of conventional morality, in spite of its airy mockery and sophistication. Elizabeth, in the person of Sapho, triumphed over Venus:

> Venus, be not chollerick, Cupid is mine, he hath giuen me his Arrowes, and I will giue him a new bowe to shoote in. You are not worthy to be the Ladye of loue, that yeelde so often to the impressions of loue. Immodest Venus, that to satisfie the vnbrideled thoughtes of thy hearte, transgressest so far from the staye of thine honour! . . . Shall I not rule the fansies of men, and leade Venus in chaines like a captiue?   (v. ii. 57–67)

Except by Adonis, Shakespeare's goddess is never condemned in the moralizing manner of Wilson or Lyly. The poem is finely balanced between accepted animalism and a strange pathos. Although at the end she flies away to Patmos, in the poem itself Venus displays all the helpless weakness as well as the beauty of the flesh. She sweats, pants, weeps, swoons – or pretends to swoon[18] – runs like a country lass with no power to save her lover from the boar, though by an instinct of prophecy she foretells his death and the inevitable woes of all who love. She frantically compares herself with the boar; her wooing is paralleled with the hunt. The little hunted hare, the snail who 'shrinks backward in his shelly cave with pain' and the wounded hounds embody more poignant forms of pain and fear than Venus herself. Proud horse and raging boar provide splendid cartoons of lustihood and fury. As he transformed the squalid Venus of the stage, so Shakespeare transformed the grotesque animal forms of his detractor into genuine instinctive creatures, conceived in full naturalistic detail. *Venus and Adonis* is a great work of release, an assertion of natural energies. The artificial beasts of the mime, like the artificial world of Lyly, have been exorcized and left behind; instead, the true animal world – including the human animal – appears, so palpable and so warmly evoked that Shakespeare's contemporaries were quite swept away. Many a Gull besides Gullio was beautified with Shakespeare's feathers:

> Marry I thinke I shall entertaine those verses which run like these:
> Euen as the sunn with purple-coloured face
> Had tane his laste leaue on the weeping morne, etc
> O sweet Mr Shakespeare, Ile haue his picture in my study at courte.[19]

Venus and Adonis is at once a claim to social dignity for its author, a justification of the natural and instinctive beauty of the animal world against sour moralists and scurrilous invective, a raising of the animal mask to sentient level, the emancipation of the flesh. Since, however, he did not continue this kind of poetry after the *Rape of Lucrece*, it may be that without the stimulus of Greene's attack Shakespeare would not have been moved to write Ovidian romance, or, if he wrote, to insist at once upon the dignity of print, with all that this implied of a bid for Fame.

Of Shakespeare it might be said,

> Cet animal est très mechant,
> Quand on l'attaque, il se défend

— not with the common style of disclaimer but with positive demonstration of new and dazzling capacities. In *Venus and Adonis*, a lofty form and classic authority is invoked to display the continuity of animal, human and divine passion; the 'vulgar' are rejected only in their narrow prejudice, for the natural at all levels is celebrated.

The player has shown his capacity to move in a world of gorgeous paganism, to write upon a noble model, and to deal with love in aristocratic boldness and freedom. The dedication to Southampton, with its modest apology for 'these unpolished lines' is at once disarming and 'gentle', the tone courtly but unaffected. This could not be calculated; it is the natural consequence of that civility of demeanour which Chettle had so admired.[20]

Notes

1 *Second Part of the Return from Parnassus*, ed. J. B. Leishman (London, Nicholson & Watson, 1949), I, ii, 301–3 and IV, iii, 1766–70.
2 T. W. Baldwin, *On the Literary Genetics of Shakespeare's Poems and Sonnets* (Urbana, University of Illinois Press, 1950), pp. 45–8.
3 *Greene's Groats-worth of Witte*, ed. G. B. Harrison, Bodley Head Quartos (London, 1923), pp. 45–6.
4 E. K. Chambers, *The Elizabethan Stage* (4 vols., Oxford, Clarendon Press, 1923) I, 128 describes the Hinchingbrooke affair; p. 155, the mumming in Coronation year, which happened on Twelfth Night. For late examples of similar shows, see Sheila Williams, 'The Pope-Burning Processions of 1679, 1680, and 1681', *Journal of the Warburg and Courtauld Institutes*, XXI (1958), 104–18.
5 *Francesco's Fortunes* (1590), B4ᵛ-C1ʳ. See Chambers, *op. cit.* IV, 236. *Francesco's Fortunes*, a version of Greene's life-story preceding his *Groats-worth of Witte*, contains further abuse of the players. Ferrars actually presented masks of cats and bagpipes before Edward VI in 1553

(A. Feuillerat, *Documents Relating to the Revels*, Bang's Materialien, no. 44 (Louvain, 1914), p. 145).

6 J. Dover Wilson, 'Malone and the Upstart Crow', *Shakespeare Survey*, 4 (1951), 56–68 returns to Malone's view that Greene accused Shakespeare of plagiarism. I would still incline to that set out in Peter Alexander's *Shakespeare's Henry VI and Richard III* (Cambridge, Cambridge University Press, 1929), for reasons which the present article will indicate.

7 Chambers, *op. cit.* II, 98–9. The Duttons were nicknamed 'Chameleons' because they changed their livery and allegiance so often. Cf. *The Defence of Coneycatching* where Greene is accused of saying 'as they were comedians to act, so the actions of their lives were chameleon-like: that they were uncertain time-pleasers, men that measured honesty by profit, and that regarded these authors not by desert but by necessity of time' (Chambers, *op. cit.* III, 325. This refers to actors in general).

8 *Pappe with an Hatchet*. See Chambers, *op. cit.* IV, 229–33 for this and other examples of the stage attack on Martin Marprelate.

9 Chambers, *op. cit.* IV, 236. Such borrowing is constant; for example, in his *Farewell to Folly*, Greene borrows the description of a morris dancer, in burlesque style, from Laneham's Letter on the Princely Pleasures of Kenilworth.

10 C. R. Baskervill, in *The Elizabethan Jig* (Chicago, University of Chicago Press, 1929), p. 67, quotes a 'box' rhyme into which any names could be fitted that the reciter desired:

> 'If I had as fair a face
> As John Williams his daughter Elizabeth has
> Then would I wear a tawdry lace,
> As Goodman Bolt's daughter Mart does:
> And if I had as much money in my purse
> As Cadman's daughter Margaret has,
> Then would I have a bastard less
> Than Butler's maid Helen has.'

Ready-made rhymes may have been used by Clowns in their 'extempore' afterpieces. This one was heard in Oxfordshire in 1584.

11 Ed. G. B. Harrison, Bodley Head Quartos (London, 1923), p. 6.

12 Such care was not misplaced. Nashe in writing to his printers to deny his authorship of 'a scald trivial, lying pamphlet, cald *Greens Groats-worth of Wit*' says of the very knight of the Post whom Chettle uses in *Kind-Harts Dreame*: 'In one place of my Booke, *Pierce Penilesse* saith but to the Knight of the Post, *I pray how might I call you*, & they saye I meant one *Howe*, a Knave of that trade, that I never heard of before' (*Works of Thomas Nashe*, ed. R. B. McKerrow (5 vols., London, A. H. Bullen, 1904–10), I, 154).

13 *Tarlton's News out of Purgatory*, supposedly published by Robin Goodfellow, and *The Cobbler of Canterbury*, with an invective against *Tarlton's News*, both collections of fabliaux, appeared in 1590. *Greene's Vision* (1592) denounces *The Cobbler*, which had been attributed to Greene. *Greene's Newes from Heaven and Hell* (1593) presents

both Tarlton and Greene, who ends as 'the maddest goblin that euer walked in the moonshine' (was Robin Goodfellow a nickname for him perhaps?).

14 *Three Ladies of London* (1582?), *The Pleasant and Stately Moral of Three Lords and Three Ladies of London* (1590), and *The Cobbler's Prophecy* (before 1594). Wilson was a member of Leicester's Men and afterwards of the Queen's Men, *The Rare Triumphs of Love and Fortune* was played before the Queen by Derby's Men at Windsor, 30 December 1582; published 1589. Love appears also, with Death and Fortune, in the Induction to *Solyman and Perseda* (anonymous, company unknown, published 1592).

15 *The Cobbler's Prophecy*, eds. A. C. Wood and W. W. Greg, Malone Society Reprint (Oxford, 1914), 1540–5. Armado compares his own wooing to the roaring of the Nemean lion! (*Love's Labour's Lost*, IV, i, 81–6).

16 From *Perimides the Blacke-Smith* (1588). See T. W. Baldwin, *op. cit.* p. 88.

17 I do not know whether it has been noted how completely Trachinus' speech in praise of the court against academics (*Sapho and Phao*, I, ii, 6–25) agrees with the arguments of Berowne in *Love's Labour's Lost*. In an article in *Shakespeare's Styles*, eds. P. Edwards, I.-S. Ewbank and G. K. Hunter (Cambridge, Cambridge University Press, 1980) I have argued for its indebtedness to John Clapham's *Narcissus* (1591), a warning fable addressed to Southampton.

18 Wilson's Venus also pretends to swoon when rebuked by Mars, in order to win her lover to penitence.

19 *First Part of the Return from Parnassus*, ed. J. B. Leishman (London, Nicholson & Watson, 1949), III, i, 1028–33.

20 Cf. Herbert Howarth, 'Shakespeare's Gentleness', *Shakespeare Survey*, 14 (1961), 90–7; the view of the social purpose of *Venus and Adonis* is similar to that expressed here.

V

Dramatic role as social image: a study of *The Taming of the Shrew*

I

Since the approach to Shakespeare's plays through poetic imagery rather than character was first propounded, about thirty years ago, the unwary have seen it as an alternative method to the approach through character and story. The antithesis is, of course mistaken, since dramatic characters are only another, though the most complex, form of image, projections of the poet's inner vision, interpreted by the actors and re-formed within the minds of spectators, in accordance with those inward images which shape and dominate the deeper levels of thought and feeling in every one.[1]

This 'internal society' is made up of images first imprinted in early childhood, which though differently charged with love or hate, and differently arranged, are basically the same in all men. The more truly representative an artist's work the more completely can it offer to the artist and the spectator an opportunity to harmonize the conflicts of their 'inner society' by projection upon the persons imaged. Art thus becomes a species of abreaction, with a directly therapeutic function. No one need resort to those fanciful clinical reductions with which certain psychiatrists have attempted to explain the tragic characters of Shakespeare,[2] since this is a process which applies equally to the 'normal' and healthy; indeed the production and appreciation of art may be taken in itself as a sign of health.

It has always proved difficult to extract from the comedies any structure of images other than images of man; and some of these are well-known stage types, which might seem at first sight to be too stiff and rigid to supply the delicate and complicated adjustment required for individuals, each differing from the other. In real life, to see persons as merely fulfilling one or two roles, as merely a lawyer, a priest, a mother, a Jew, even as merely a man or a woman is to see them as something less than images of God; for practical purposes this may be necessary. The distinction between acquaintances and friends may be measured by the greater variety and flexibility of roles in which we meet our friends. Assigning and taking of roles is in fact the basis of social as distinct from inward life; in comedy, characters tend to be presented socially, in terms of roles, which, as in the case of classical comedy or the *commedia dell'arte*, are fairly stereotyped. Recipes for depicting clowns, young lovers, pantaloons, boastful cowards are necessary as the social basis for drama; the images must be current coin, negotiable in the common market, but the artist will always select, recombine, and break up the ingredients of the familiar roles.[3] He may in addition, by means of those subsidiary images through which one character in a play describes another (imagery that is, of the kind usually opposed to character-drawing) suggest attitudes and approaches for the audience which may run contrary to or modify the main presentation of the role; such images indeed constitute minor alternative roles for the character in question. Other images may not be verbalized but presented only in mime. Thus the constant grouping and regrouping of roles for any dramatic figure may be varied by different spectators or actors (who will notice those which suit themselves and ignore those which do not). So many men, so many Shylocks, Falstaffs, Rosalinds, Katharines.

To accept liberty of interpretation yet accept also community of experience is perhaps an act of faith, yet of rational faith. In looking at the role as image, it is necessary to remember always the nature of Shakespeare's theatre and audience, as providing not the last word in interpretation, but the first. He was addressing a crowd socially heterogeneous, mostly masculine, who required a delicate adjust-ment of native popular traditional art with the socially more esteemed classical and foreign models.

In his earlier plays these different needs are met by different groups, serious lovers, comic clowns; as his art developed, he succeeded in blending the roles more subtly and freshly.

II

The Taming of The Shrew repays examination from this point of view. It is an early comedy (before 1594),[4] with a main plot based on the popular dramatic role of the Shrew, but highly original in treatment, and a subplot drawn from an Italian model, Ariosto, as adapted in Gascoigne's *Supposes*; both deftly worked together and strengthened by an Induction organically related to the main theme. In *The Taming of A Shrew* mediocrity shows what could be done to

…estroy the inner fabric of the vision while preserving the outlines of the story.

The wooing of Katherine takes up rather less than half the play, and her part is quite surprisingly short; although she is on the stage a good deal, she spends most of the time listening to Petruchio. The play is his; this is its novelty. Traditionally the shrew triumphed; hers was the oldest and indeed the only native comic role for women. If overcome, she submitted either to high theological argument or to a taste of the stick. Here, by the wooing in Act II, the wedding in Act III and the 'taming school' in Act IV, each of which has its own style, Petruchio overpowers his shrew with her own weapons – imperiousness, wildness, inconsistency and the withholding of the necessities of life – combined with strong demonstrations of his natural authority. Petruchio does not use the stick, and Katherine in her final speech does not console herself with theology. To understand Shakespeare's skill in adaptation, the traditional image of the shrew, as she had developed from Chaucer's time, must be recalled.

Shrews might be expected to be especially common in England, that 'Hell of horses, purgatory of servants and paradise of women', but stories of shrews belong to the general medieval tradition of bourgeois satire, as well as to folk tales. Jean de Meung's portrait of 'La Veille', Eustace Deschamps' *Miroir de Mariage*, *Les Quinze Joyes de Mariage* and the *Sottie* have their English equivalents in Chaucer, the Miracles and the interlude. The Wyf of Bath is the great example of the shrew triumphant; in the Miracle plays Noah's wife evolves from simple boozing and brawling to a notable housewife, from a formula to a simple dramatic role. The gossips' league which appears in the plays is given a courtly setting in Dunbar's poem, 'Twa Mariit Wemen and the Wedo'.

Two short plays on shrews from the early Tudor stage are *Johan Johan* (1533/4) and *Tom Tyler and his Wife* (c. 1561). In both these plays, the pusillanimous husband is the centre of the picture. Tib, wife of Johan Johan, deceives her husband with the parish priest; his tremendous opening speech, in which he proclaims his intention of beating her, and beating her horribly, directs the audience's attention firmly to his abject but boastful state. Only at the end does a three-cornered fight develop. The remarkable miracles with which Sir Jhan the priest edifies the supper party, his smooth graciousness give him an odious mastery over poor Johan Johan who, deprived of his eagerly expected pie (like Katherine of the beef) and sent away from table is so poor-spirited a wretch that his sudden onslaught most unexpectedly relieves all the pent-up hatred of priestly hypocrisy which is the serious, though covert, intention of Heywood's farce.

Tom Tyler is another such meek-hearted husband; misled by
Desire, the Vice, he has married with Strife. She, with her gossips
Sturdy and Tipple, forms a drinking party, but chases Tom back to
his work when he ventures to seek a pot of beer. His valiant friend
Tom Taylor puts on the Tyler's coat, and undertakes the correction
of Strife; but after he has beaten her into submission, Tom Tyler
foolishly confesses the trick and gets a worse drubbing than ever.
Two sage parsons, Destiny and Patience, introduce and wind up the
gay little frolic, in which the rival conspiracy of men to combat the
gossips' league, though at first unsuccessful, is able with the church's
help finally to tame a shrew. Flat morality is in sharp contrast to
lively fun; the two artisans alone are characterized as people, and this
helps to concentrate the sympathy on them. They are wage earners
whose wives do not share their work as country wives must do, but
are free to gad about with no supervision and to spend their
husband's earnings. The valiant Taylor is contrasted with the hulk-
ing inoffensiveness of the Tyler, and both with Strife, who is much
less of a morality figure than the rest, being one of those 'sklendre
wyves' 'egre as a tygre yond in Inde' whom Chaucer had celebrated, a
true daughter of the Vice. She exploits her husband as drudge and
provider:

> What a husband have I, as light as a flye?
> I leap and I skip, I carry the whip,
> And I bear the bell; If he please me not well,
> I will take him by the pole, by cocks precious soul.
> I will make him to toil, while I laugh and smile,
> I will fare of the best, I will sit and take rest . . .
> I will teach him to know the way to Dunmoe.
> At board and at bed I will crack the knave's head,
> If he look but awry, or cast a sheep's eye;
> So shall I be sure to keep him in ure,
> To serve like a knave and live like a slave.[5]

All the moralizing is subject to parody, including that of Patience,
who leads the final song and dance, and, after the fighting, justifies
submission all round, with a perhaps unintended hit at a very exalted
personage:

> Which God preserve our noble queen.
> From perilous chance that has been seen,
> And send her subjects grace, say I,
> To serve her highness patiently.

Tom Tyler is close in spirit to the ballad and the jig; in 'The Wife
Wrapt in a Wether's Skin' (Child, 277) a timid husband finds a surer
method of punishment by proxy; his wife is too highborn to spin,

wash, or work, so Robin wraps her in a wether's skin, and since he may not beat her because of her great kindred, he beats the wether's skin till he has tamed his wife. In a longer, more savage version, the wife is beaten till she swoons and then wrapped in the salted hide of Morell, an old horse. This seems to be a magic charm: she is to stay in the salt hide for ever if she does not submit. The jest ends with a party at which the wife shows her obedience, and the conclusion reads

> Finis quoth Mayster Charm her
> He that can charme a shrewde wyfe,
>   Better than this
> Let him come to me and fetch ten pound
>   And a golden purse.
>
> (Hazlitt, *Early Popular Poetry*, iv, 179)

Tom Taylor and Tom Tyler, at the height of their triumph, likewise rejoice in a song which puts a wife among the higher domestic animals:

> Blame not Thomas if Tom be sick,
> His mare doth prance, his mare doth kick,
> She snorts and holds her head so high,
> Go tie the Mare, Tomboy, tie the Mare, tie.

The two plays differ in their appeal, though they are alike in theme. *Johan Johan* has shown anticlerical colouring; *Tom Tyler* in spite of its moral framework is the more frivolous. They are alike in stressing the husband's part, and in the similarity of name that links him with the tamer, who seems therefore like another self. Johan Johan has been server to Sir Jhan the priest and Tipple observes of Tom Tyler 'Belike he hath learned in a new school'.

III

The theme of the School for Henpecked Husbands was one of those taken up by Shakespeare. Although he used many features of the older tradition, his play has the advantages both of novelty and familiarity. It is unnecessary to postulate a lost source play unless Shakespeare is held to be constitutionally incapable of inventing a plot; for there is no sound external evidence for it.

Petruchio, keeper of the taming school in which the 'tutors' Hortensio and Lucentio are his immediate pupils (IV. ii. 54–8) and Christopher Sly a more remote one, owes his victory to his eloquence and his natural vigour. He enters full of enthusiasm to see the world and enjoy his inheritance, blown by

> Such wind as scatters young men through the world
> To seek their fortunes farther than at home,
> Where small experience grows.   (I. ii. 48–50)

and the first two dozen lines show his readiness to let his fists walk about a man's ears. Shrews commonly marry old men, or their social inferiors; Petruchio undertakes his 'labour of Hercules' in the spirit of an explorer, and the challenge of his America, his Newfoundland, exhilarates him. When she breaks his friend's head, he asserts with a significant oath:

> Now, by the world, it is a lusty wench,
> I love her ten times more than e'er I did.
> O, how I long to have some chat with her!   (II.i.159–61)

His demonstrations of physical exuberance, wit and bawdry are provocative courting plumage, of Mercutio's style in wooing rather than Romeo's. The wedding night has as climax his sudden bout of unclerkly asceticism. 'Come, I will bring thee to thy bridal chamber' he exclaims, and the servants, stealing back, observe:

> He kills her in her own humour.
> Where is he?
> In her chamber. Making a sermon of continency to her,
>   And rails, and swears, and rates, that she, poor soul,
>   Knows not which way to stand, to look, to speak.   (IV. i. 164–9)

For contrast, there are no less than four old men. Katherine is the first shrew to be given a father, the first to be shewn as maid and bride; she is not seen merely in relation to a husband. The savage and hysterical attack on her sister is counterbalanced by the comic description of her bash at her tutor. She is unteachable; the point is explosively made.

At the beginning both characters are shewn at their least attractive. Kate's first speech is vulgar, thick-sown with proverbs; she threatens to 'comb' her suitors' 'noddles' with a three-legged stool and they in turn defie her roundly:

> From all such devils, Good Lord deliver us.   (I. i. 66)

'This fiend of hell', 'the devil's dam', 'Is any man so very a fool as to be married to hell?' The image persists through the first scene, with the charitable alternatives that she is 'stark mad' or that she should be 'carted' like a whore. It is all very violent and in a 'low' style. Petruchio is introduced in a low comedy turn with his servant, and with a great flourish proclaims his intention to marry for money – a wife as hideous and old as the hag of the Wife of Bath's Tale if need be (I. ii. 69). Money is always to the fore in tales about shrews, and Katherine's father, by offering his younger daughter to the highest bidder, effectively shews that he prizes it; Petruchio after all takes little trouble to secure the best offer, but takes the first good one that comes. When at the end, he bets on Katherine's duty – a very safe bet, and a large one –

> I'll venture so much of my hawk or hound,
> But twenty times so much upon my wife.   (V. ii. 71–2)

Baptista backs Bianca, but at the end sportingly comes forward with a second dowry for Katherine 'for she is changed as she had never been'. The 'old Italian fox' lives like a lord; but money helps to set the shrew where she belongs, within the merchant class. When Henry V woos another Kate, he thinks in terms of fair French towns, though he too finds that the role of a bumpkin has its value in a whirlwind courtship.

Petruchio gets a plain description of Katherine's accepted role; she is 'renowned in Padua for her scolding tongue'; but his tongue is equally renowned among his own servants (I. ii. 106–15). Natural exuberance is matched in him by variety and colour of speech; he has every rhetorical weapon at command, from the high-flown terms of his address to Vincentio to the fluent cursing which he bestows upon servants and tradespeople. The basis is bluntness, 'russet yeas and honest kersey noes', and when he uses the high style it is a spirit of mockery, in contrast with the learned eloquence, in the opening scene, of Lucentio, the student.

The short scene between his resolution to woo, and the wooing scene itself shows Katherine beating Bianca and Bianca subtly retaliating under the guise of sweet compliance:

> If you affect him, sister, here I swear
> I'll plead for you myself, but you shall have him.   (II. i. 14–15)

Katherine frankly wants a husband, and abuses her father for preferring Bianca.

She is met by her wooer with a teasing shower of contradictory epithets: 'plain . . . bonny . . . sometimes curst . . . prettiest Kate in Christendom . . .' that ends according to a plan already confided to the audience by Petruchio:

> Hearing thy mildness praised in every town . . .
> Myself am mov'd to woo thee for my wife.   (II. i. 190,193)

Kate's wits are waked, and a quick crossfire of repartee leads to the traditional slap. If however the audience expect a fight they do not get it; Petruchio, in his role of Hercules, simply holds his Protean enemy fast, and indulges his humour of finding everything agreeable, provoking her with oratorical flourishes to another wit combat and then issuing his absolute fiat.

> For by this light, whereby I see thy beauty,
> Thy beauty that doth make me like thee well,
> Thou must be married to no man but me;
> For I am he am born to tame you, Kate.　　　(II. i. 265–8)

Katherine furiously tells her father that he has offered to wed her to a lunatic. She repeats it, as later she stands waiting for her bridegroom; he is a 'frantic fool' maliciously jesting with 'poor Katherine' as she tearfully calls herself, so that she may be mocked by the world:

> 'Lo there is mad Petruchio's wife,
> If it would please him come and marry her'.　　(III. ii. 19–20)

It is in fact as a madman that Petruchio appears in the end. He has assumed the part she assigned him, the traditional fate of a shrew's husband, as the Abbess had lengthily explained to Adriana in the *Comedy of Errors* (V. i. 68–86). The most important passages about the wedding are given in description; the broken-down horse, who is anatomized at much greater length than his rider, with Petruchio's wild attire, prepare the listener for the church scene in which the bridegroom swears, hits out and plays the part of a madman who is also possessed. The likeness of the pair only brings out Petruchio's pre-eminence.

> He's a devil, a devil, a very fiend
> —Why, she's a devil, a devil, the devil's dam.
> —Tut, she's a lamb, a dove, a fool to him . . .
> Such a mad marriage never was before. (III. ii. 151–3, 178)

Though at one point it is suggested that 'he hath some meaning in his mad attire', no one seems to disagree when Bianca sums up at the exit of the pair, 'Being mad herself, she's madly mated'. The central point, the knot of the play, is here.

Petruchio has already invited the audience to stand with him; he confides his plan just before the wooing starts (II. i. 167–79). He will ignore Kate's forward behaviour and describe it instead as if it were what it ideally should be. He will assume a virtue for her if she has it not; maintain before her the image of perfection which he is trying to create; or (if the audience are prepared to be so subtle) will pierce below the surface of Kate's angry, thwarted, provocative abuse to the desire to be mastered and cherished which her conduct unconsciously betrays.

This mastery he asserts immediately after the wedding, with an unequivocal statement of his legal rights, and a mimic marriage by capture.

> I will be master of what is mine own—
> She is my goods, my chattels, she is my house,
> My household stuff, my field, my barn,
> My horse, my ox, my ass, my anything . . .   (III. ii. 225–8)

In the next scene, after the full horrors of the journey – again given to one of the clowns for embellished description – Kate does not fail to address him respectfully as 'husband'.

Having drawn his ideal in wooing, he now holds up a mirror to her worser self, and gives her a travesty-performance of her own behaviour. She had beaten Hortensio; he beats his men. She had tied up Bianca; he hurries her breathlessly about. All is done, as he explains to the audience in the central soliloquy which is the grand exposition of his strategy, to 'curb her mad and headstrong humour'.

He is not preparing the audience for what is to happen, but directing them how to take it. The image he uses is that of manning a falcon.[6]

> My falcon now is sharp and passing empty,
> And till she stoop, she must not be full-gorg'd,
> For then she never looks upon her lure.
> Another way I have to man my haggard,
> To make her come, and know her keeper's call:
> That is, to watch her, as we watch these kites,
> That bate and beat, and will not be obedient . . .
>
> (IV. i. 174–80)

Kate is not to be wrapt in a wether's skin; a more subtle form of the animal tamer's art is called for, but it is animal taming none the less. Only it allows Petruchio to maintain a pretence which may be taken as rather more than a subterfuge:

> Ay, and amid this hurly I intend
> That all is done in reverend care of her . . .
> This is the way to kill a wife with kindness. (IV. i. 183–4,192)

He concludes with a triumphant and direct appeal to the audience (both Sly and the Globe spectators) to identify themselves with him:

> He that knows better how to tame a shrew,
> Now let him speak; 'tis charity to shew.   (IV. i. 194–5)

The full torrent of his eloquence is finally loosed in the tailor's scene, not without some occasional plain hints to Kate ('When you are gentle, you shall have one too', if she wants a gentlewoman's cap). All the usual desires of the shrew, clothes, feasts, company, lovemaking, are dangled before her only to be snatched away. She is shewn what it means to be Petruchio's household stuff; finally she capitulates and enters his private universe, in which 'it shall be what o'clock I say it is', in which Petruchio decides whether the sun or the moon is shining in the sky.

But this universe turns into the public one without warning; at the end of the act it is Kate whom he accuses of madness, when, obediently following his eloquent lead, she greets Vincentio in high style as

> Young budding virgin, fair and fresh and sweet.   (IV. v. 36)

She meekly apologizes for 'my mad mistaking'.

Petruchio's last demand is a mere flouting of decorum; he wants a kiss in the public street. He gets it, with one un-called-for endearment that shows how far Hortensio's

> Petruchio, go thy ways, the field is won   (IV. v. 23)

falls short of the fullness of victory. The shrew's role is transformed, and the charming young woman whom Petruchio imagined, he has now, like Pygmalion, obtained in the flesh.

Katherine has never been in league with society, like older shrews, but always at odds with it. Henceforth her relations to others, as she shows in Act V, are to be through Petruchio. Very early in the play he had based his confidence of taming her on his knowledge of a man's world:

> Think you a little din can daunt mine ears?
> Have I not in my time heard lions roar?
> Have I not heard the sea, puff'd up with winds?   (I. ii. 196–8)

Have I not above all, he concludes, been in battle!

On the same ground Katherine bases her final plea for obedience. Her grand oration does not invoke the rather muddled theology which winds up *The Taming of A Shrew*, but recalls man's social claims as breadwinner, protector and temporal lord (those claims which Tom Tyler's wife so shamelessly ignored). A man

> commits his body
> To painful labour, both by sea and land,
> To watch the night in storms, the day in cold,
> While thou liest warm at home, secure and safe.(V. ii. 148–51)

Women are incapable of man's work; their minds should be as soft as their bodies. Kate's plea is in the high style, directly opposed to the 'low' style of her first speeches; but it has little more weight than the sermon of Patience in *Tom Tyler*. It is the lovers' battle that the audience is really invited to enjoy – the raillery which conceals attraction, the 'war' of wits which allows love and hate open play, in the fashion of Berowne and Rosalind, Benedick and Beatrice. Kate, though overmatched, remains the lusty wench Petruchio had sought;

even at the end, she demonstrates her powers by haling the other recalcitrant wives before their husbands. She is not simply transformed into the image of Bianca, who at the opening had displayed such readiness to strip off her finery at Kate's bidding, as Kate now does at Petruchio's. Bianca takes Kate's likeness more completely; for with her violent retort to the bridegroom's plaint, 'The more fool you, for laying on my duty', the younger sister clearly assumes the scold. The third bride, being a widow already, has a tone of easy practised insolence; it is she who flings back the old taunt of shrewishness, Kate's original role, of which in the last couplet she is divested for ever.

> —Now go thy ways; thou hast tam'd a curst shrew.
> —Tis a wonder, by your leave she will be tam'd so. (V. ii. 188–9)

IV

Three later examples of the shrew in Elizabethan drama may be considered to show how the part developed. Dekker and Middleton's *The Honest Whore* (1604) and Fletcher's *The Woman's Prize or the Tamer Tamed* (?1604/1610) both depict a shrew who voluntarily relinquishes her role and submits to her husband. In *The Honest Whore* the subplot shows Candido the patient man, a linen draper, subjected to a series of very rough tests by his wife, who has a woman's longing to provoke him. He refuses to be provoked, and when finally, having committed him to Bedlam, she repents and gets him out again, he turns the tables by assuring her that she was the madder of the two, that he has cured her humour by submitting to it; concluding with a set speech in praise of patience. In Part II, he is shewn married to a second wife; here he is instigated by a courtier to be severe with her and even threaten her with the yard measure, whereupon she instantly capitulates and delivers an oration against the sovereignty of women. The tricks which the patient man endures, very like those described in the Elizabethan translation of *Les Quinze Joyes de Mariage*, add up to a series of merry jests. Simple fun turning to simple didacticism is well within the popular sympathies of a city audience: toughness is represented by the prentices who attempt to defend Candido against his wife and her accomplices.

In *The Woman's Prize*, a sequel to Shakespeare's play, Fletcher shews Petruchio in his old age. He has come to London and for second wife taken an Englishwoman, who, under the leadership of 'Colonel Bianca', barricadoes herself on her wedding night and starts a campaign against husbands. The mock-battle is exactly calculated for a courtly audience's humour; but in the last three acts, wiles succeed defiance. By a series of tricks which include pretending that her husband has caught the plague and so shutting him up and depriving him of all his goods, pretending to run mad herself, and finally, when he shams dead, preaching a sermon to the 'corpse' on his unmanliness, Maria sufficiently shows the mettle of her pasture. As Petruchio finally observes:

> Well, little England, when I see a husband
> Of any nation stern or jealous,
> I'll wish him but a woman of thy breeding.

Both plays depend on gulling the husband by a series of fantastic tricks; yet Maria, no less than Candido's wife, having conquered, suddenly submits and vows herself her husband's servant. The chief mood being that of farce, a milder age seemed to require this happy ending.

Maria at one point recalls Petruchio's main speech from the older play and praises the wild bird, the haggard.

> Hang these tame hearted eyasses, that no sooner
> See the lure out, and hear their husband's hollow,
> But cry like kites upon 'em; the free haggard
> (Which is that woman that hath wing and knows it,
> Spirit and plume) will make an hundred checks,
> To show her freedom, sail in ev'ry air,
> And look out ev'ry pleasure, not regarding
> Lure nor quarry till her pitch command
> What she desires; making her founder'd keeper
> Be glad to fling out trains, and golden ones,
> To take her down again.

The tanner's wife who leads the regiment of country women, invokes a still older play, when she swears that Maria shall march off with terms of victory.

> She shall, Tom Tiler's,
> And brave ones too. My hood shall make a hearse cloth.
> And I'll lie under it like Joan O'Gaunt,
> Ere I go less; my distaff stuck up by me,
> For the eternal trophy of my conquests,
> And loud Fame at my head, with two main bottles
> Shall fill to all the world, the glorious fall
> Of old Don Gillian.

The gossips' league is here revived; but Petruchio still insists that his first wife was 'a fury to this filly'. There is a feeling of the audience being asked to play old parts and strike the old attitudes; the romp is somehow a little too self-conscious; there is too much burlesque in the farce.

Jonson, the most masculine of Elizabethan comic dramatists, does not give weight to any woman's part. He himself was married to 'a shrew, but honest'. His sketches of female violence culminate in *The Silent Woman* (1609) which dissolves and distributes the role of the shrew among a number of characters, and places it in a wider general context of social satire. Low comedy is provided by Mistress Otter, the rich shopkeeping termagant who has married a broken-down captain: she gives her husband a beating in the good old-fashioned style, to the accompaniment of drums and trumpets and she draws up articles of obedience for him before she marries him. The Ladies Collegiate are a foundation of courtly dames, resembling the cabals of Restoration comedy or even the *School for Scandal*:

> that live from their husbands; and give entertainment to all the wits and braveries of the time, as they call them; cry down, or cry up, what they like or dislike in a brain or a fashion, with most masculine or rather hermaphroditical authority.

Epicoene, the Silent Woman, whose marriage to Morose transforms her, as it transformed Bianca, from modesty to a scold, is discovered at the end, to be no more a woman than was Sly's lady-wife, and so Morose is freed; all the other shrews remain triumphant. In the course of the play, Truewit, the connoisseur of women, delivers a tremendous Character of an Ill Wife to Morose, and an equally lengthy oration on how to court a woman to his nephew: Morose also catechizes his future wife on her longing for chattering, courtship and fine clothes. The social follies of a whole troupe of gulls and fops counterbalance those of the Collegiate Ladies, and all join in brutal torment of Morose. Poor Captain Otter, who among his boon companions pretends to despise and rule his tyrant 'princess', has a humour of drinking toasts from the three cups he calls his bear, his bull and his horse; Morose's humour of silence shows itself not only in his choice of a wife but in the fantastic arrangement of his household, which in its way, is as odd as Petruchio's; every character is an eccentric, an original variant upon a familiar stage type. In Jonson's play the theme of the shrew has become only one role in a society where the tension lies in the whole action, not in parts: in which roles are fixed, sharply defined, Theophrastian. Unity of action and of tone, control of a consistently ironic point of view hold them together. There are two standards of what constitutes right social behaviour: that of the fops and the Ladies Collegiate and that of the wits, Dauphine and his friends; but there is no free play of sympathy. Satire offers the audience a direct and assured moral judgment, the pleasure of siding with authority: it offers also the covert satisfaction of surveying the baseness which is to be judged.

Jonson stands to Shakespeare in this respect as Dunbar stands to Chaucer. The audience are invited throughout to identify themselves with the point of view of the wits, which is detached, amused, ironic and merciless. The whole plot turns on Dauphine's stratagem of 'marrying' his uncle to a boy; but life and vivacity is stronger in the parts of the chief victim and of the fools and gulls than in that of the cool young cavalier who plays with his victim, velvety as the Lord with Christopher Sly, but does not confide either to the spectators or to his friends what he is about. The loudest horseplay and the nearest approach to the old comic tradition is Captain Otter's drinking scene, where he boasts in the manner of Johan Johan:

> Wife! buz! titivilitium! there's no such thing in nature. I confess, gentlemen, I have a cook, a laundress, a house drudge that serves my necessary turns and goes under that title; but he's an ass that will be so uxurious to tie his affections to one circle.

Immediately Mistress Otter enters and falls upon him; but even this is by the malicious contrivance of Truewit. Similar grand roles are assumed by the two gulls who claim to have enjoyed Epicoene's favours; by the Ladies Collegiate who claim freedom for a life of gallantry, but are tricked by Dauphine into competing for his attentions and betraying each other to him treacherously; and of course by Epicoene, whose disguise is maintained to the end. Disguise turns Otter and the Barber into a lawyer and a divine, to the ridicule of both professions. Money is, as usual, the basis of the intrigue; Dauphine extracts a settlement from Morose.

Jonson's 'humours' were said to be drawn from the life, and in the Prologue he gives a warning against 'particular sleights of application'; this suggests not only that the social images he created were based upon eccentric individuals (as the character of Morose is said to be) but that the audience's impulse to reject these roles and fasten them on to somebody else is very strongly aroused. Morose, the hero victim, is the dark antithesis to his nephew; a wit himself, in spite of his defeat he possesses a power, a massiveness of character, that the young men do not show. The main conflict lies between two men, representatives of Crabbed Age and Youth; although all the conscious identification is with Youth, yet it is in his saturnine foe that the deeper, more Shakespearean complexity of character is to be found. All the characters are static, inflexible, all equally interconnected in a web of purely external relationships: in Morose alone some reflexion of an 'inner society', troubled and rejected, may be discerned.

Notes

1 For a brief and lucid discussion, see John Rickman, *Selected Contributions to Psychoanalysis* (London, Hogarth Press, 1957), p. 159.
2 See Kenneth Muir, 'Some Freudian Interpretations of Shakespeare', *Proceedings of the Leeds Philosophical Society*, VII, part 1 (July 1952), 43–52.
3 See Bernard Hart, *The Psychology of Insanity*, 5th ed. (Cambridge, Cambridge University Press, 1957), pp. 115–16.
4 The date of publication of *The Taming of A Shrew*, which I take to be derivative from Shakespeare.
5 This does not prevent her complaining of his unmanliness in striking a woman.
6 Taming a falcon by keeping it without food or sleep brings about a strong sense of conflict described by the modern falconer T. H. White.

VI

'King Henry IV'*

There was once a summer school at the other Stratford where, in two successive hours, a first speaker said that anyone who doubted the unity of the great continuous ten-act play was disqualified to understand Shakespeare; while a second said that anyone who thought 2 *Henry IV* more than a feeble 'encore' must be illiterate. The link that I would see is that of adaptability, the imaginative ability to create a part and to play it. In Part 1, this playful, heroic, or sometimes merely crafty capacity distinguishes each of the main characters. In Part 2, the role-taking (to use familiar jargon) is subtle, Machiavellian and by no means subjected to plain ethical judgments of right and wrong. In dismissing Falstaff, Henry V appears both kingly *and* treacherous – because his two roles can no longer be played by the same man; the King cannot be true to the reveller of Eastcheap. In the play as a whole, the width of reference and ambiguity of response shows Shakespeare's full maturity. 'The solution to the problem of life is seen in the vanishing of this problem', said the philosopher Wittgenstein; and Machiavelli's contribution to political thought consisted in dropping theories of political government and observing the facts of behaviour, in all their awkward complexity. 'We are much beholden to Machiavel', said Bacon, 'who openly and unfeignedly declares . . . what men do, and not what they ought to do'. A famous book on princely education, Elyot's *Book of the Governor*, had aimed in the early sixteenth century at producing a traditionally good, well-equipped and high-principled ruler. Machiavelli perceived the emergence of secular sovereignty; and the rest of the world was horrified at what he saw. It had already arrived when Warwick the Kingmaker, in Henry VI's reign, putting pressure on the Vatican to back his policy, manoeuvred in a way any modern student of

*A lecture given at the summer school at Stratford, Ontario, 1966.

politics would readily define; but the next century still had no words for it. Behaviour was ahead of statement; for it is the artist that first catches the implications of behaviour. 2 *Henry IV* came out shortly after the first edition of Bacon's essays; these men, however different their minds, were observing the same phenomenon. Shakespeare gave it imaginative form, Bacon gave it definition.

As an actor, Shakespeare was gifted with a special insight into the quick-change aspects of political life; Protean variety, which was the outstanding quality of Elizabethan acting, elicits exactly what the new politics demanded of the ruler. Many have noted that Richard III is a natural actor in his wooing of Anne, his scenes with Clarence, with Edward. However, he is drawn as conventionally wicked; for 'men should be what they seem'. In *Henry IV* Shakespeare is questioning the popular frame of assumptions more radically; yet he had to avoid shocking his audience.

The uncertainties, the troubles, the doubtful roles, the lack of any suitable heir – these issues were calculated to touch powerfully the feelings and engage the interest of any audience in the late 1590s. And the glorious resolution of all doubts in the triumphant corona-tion of Henry V was exactly what the country was momentarily to feel when James I peaceably succeeded in 1603. Alas! James was no Plantagenet – but instead of leading his people to war against France, he at least united them with Scotland.

Shakespeare was not writing a political treatise or constructing an allegory, but he was playing variations on a live political issue; in these plays the whole of society enters into the conflict. The colour-less citizens of *Richard III*, the symbolic gardeners, Welsh tribesmen, the groom of the stable who appear in *Richard II* play minor roles. But here the life of London, and Gloucestershire, and the north is fully drawn into the play; while Shakespeare presents, in ever varying forms, a generous and yet sceptical questioning of that traditional principle which his earlier plays assume. This is political drama in a far profounder way than its dynastic interests would suggest, for the psychology of political life is here developed; the most successful man is he who can adapt himself most flexibly while retaining a clear sense of direction and purpose. This was exactly what the apparently changeable but really determined Elizabeth had done. Unlike her successor, she did not theorize; but she was a superb practitioner.

The Queen *was* the government; so throughout her reign the question of what would happen if she died untimely had troubled her subjects. A disputed succession meant the possibility of civil war – the ultimate worst thing for the sixteenth century (as perhaps it still is). This was a topic which no writer would dare directly to treat on the stage, for the consequences would have been extremely serious;

but in the mirror of history it had been reflected ever since the young lawyers in 1561 put on *Gorboduc* – a play written by one of the Queen's gravest counsellors. This play enjoyed a great and continuing success; it is about the wickedness of dividing a kingdom – as Hotspur and the conspirators propose to do. Other plays dealt with similar subjects – *Horestes, Locrine, The Misfortunes of Arthur.* These are now little more than names in a textbook; but then they were the means by which the warnings and counsels of her subjects might be tendered to the Queen herself. They were played before her; when later still in 1601 Essex and his friends wanted to raise the city of London, they put on the old play of *Richard II.*[1] We see this use of history today in such plays as Brecht's *Galileo*, Eliot's *Murder in the Cathedral*, Sartre's *Lucifer and the Lord.*

Within *Henry IV*, each character plays several roles, and the leading characters often substitute for each other. Falstaff is the father of Hal's wit, the King father of his chivalry; Harry Monmouth is the son of Henry's loins, but Harry Hotspur the son of his wishes.[2]

Falstaff plays any and every part. His imagination devises ever-fresh fancies for himself and his followers, which are taken up and discarded as fast as they are conceived. He describes Hal and himself as thieves, in gorgeously poetic terms; he next promotes himself to judge – but is ready to turn hangman; he then becomes melancholy and repents. In the heat of exploit Falstaff is a 'young man' that 'must live', and the victim of Hal's love charm; in the next scene he is 'poor old Jack'. Having justified himself for robbery on the grounds of a vocation for it, he raises a tempest of rage when his pocket is picked, and takes the opportunity to repudiate all his debts. Playing the knight of chivalry, he asks Hal to bestride him if he is down, and boasts that his deeds surpass Turk Gregory's. He rises in fact from his mummer's sham death to claim the spoils of victory.

Against Falstaff's instinctive mobility, Hal's role-taking looks deliberate. He early casts himself for the role of Percy, playing it in a mixture of admiration and irony; in his revels, he plays the part of Prodigal Prince, with Falstaff as his father; and then, assuming the King, deposes and banishes Falstaff as later he will do in earnest. But he can play the potboy in a leather apron, equally well. The fantasy life of Eastcheap (even the robbery is a jest), playing at capital crime, at exhortation, at soldiering, is sharply dismissed by the Prince, even while he enjoys it. It is Idleness – according to Puritan opponents, the capital sin of all players. Idleness and Vanity are keywords in Part 1; both were favourite terms of abuse for the players, but Shakespeare draws their sting. It is in the comedy of Gadshill, sweeping along through the first two acts, that the grand genial theme of Robbery is stated. Thief . . . hangman . . . gallows . . .: the sinister possibilities are suggested only to be brushed aside, for the thieves are in company with 'nobility and tranquility, burgomasters and great oneyers'. In the older plays, it is the King's own money which is taken. Later the note is graver; the rebels carve up the commonwealth and use her as their booty; the King himself is confessedly one who stole the diadem and put it in his pocket; the tussle with Hotspur over the prisoners is an attempt at Gadshill measures. According to Holinshed, Hotspur said of Mortimer, 'Behold the heir of the realm is robbed of his right, and yet the robber with his own will not redeem him.'

Falstaff of Gadshill is succeeded by Captain Falstaff, robbing under royal warrant by his misuse of the King's press. At Shrewsbury the Prince robs Hotspur of all his honours, and finally, most shameless of all, Falstaff robs the Prince of the glory of killing Percy, and staggers off, a porter of the 'luggage' that once was the fiery Hotspur. The Prince, with an indifference more telling than contempt, offers to 'gild' what he at the same time labels as a 'lie'.

Falstaff's chief weapon is neither his sword nor his bottle of sack, but his jests; his power to defend the indefensible springs partly from nimble wits and partly from that innocent and unstudied shamelessness which breeds lies gross, open and palpable as the fantasies of childhood. Somewhere in Falstaff lurks the small boy who boasts that he has just killed a lion. Only by degrees does he penetrate from his Castle of Misrule, the Boar's Head Tavern, to the world of heroic action in which Percy moves; only in Part 2 to the world of judgment, organization, political theory which surrounds the King. He is an Actor, not in the calculating fashion of Richard III, but with the instinctive, ductile mobility of a jester who takes up any position you throw him, and holds it.

Henry IV, as in the play of *Richard II*, stands for the life of judgment against that of the fantasy and imagination; it is his superior skill in deploying his forces that defeats the dash and fire of Hotspur.

Percy's scornful mimicry of the popinjay lord reveals that he, like Hal and Falstaff, lives in the life of the imagination. To think of a plot is enough for him; he can feed on his motto *Esperance*; mappery and closet-war are quite alien to him. Yet when he meets the more primitive imagination of Glendower with its cressets and fiery shapes, its prophecies out of the common lore, Hotspur baits Glendower mercilessly. Glendower is Hotspur's Falstaff.

Before Shakespeare wrote, Hotspur was already a potent name in such common lore. Every member of the audience would have known that old ballad of Douglas and Percy by which Sir Philip Sidney had confessed himself stirred more than with the sound of the trumpet. Hotspur's contempt for balladmongers is ill-deserved; for they were to keep his fame alive. In *The Battle of Otterburn* a single combat, such as the Prince offers at Shrewsbury, is offered by Douglas to Percy, and the conqueror salutes his gallant foe, as the Prince, laying his royal favours on the mangled face, salutes the dead Hotspur. In the ballad, it is Percy himself who

> leaned on his brand
> And saw the Douglas dee:
> He took the dead man by the hand,
> Saying, Woe is me for thee;
>
> To have saved thy life, I would have parted with
> My lands for years three;
> For a better man, of heart, nor of hand
> Was not in all the north country.

The resurrection of Douglas to join the conspirators in this play adds greatly to their potency. Hotspur could so easily have won at Shrewsbury; the battle against odds is a true foretaste of Agincourt – the little troop with its Welsh and Scots contingent, led by one man's courage. Harry learns his role at Agincourt from Hotspur's at Shrewsbury.

Harry Monmouth, the changeling prince, born in the enchanted west, publicly takes up the role of chivalrous knight in Vernon's splendid description of his mounting his horse; and Hotspur cries:

> Come, let me taste my horse,
> Who is to bear me like a thunderbolt
> Against the bosom of the Prince of Wales.   (IV. i. 119–21)

The essence of chivalry is the mounted charge: knights must have horses – and rivals to encounter. The images are cosmic, grand. As Harry says 'Two stars keep not their motion in one sphere'. The image of the rising sun dispelling clouds, which the Prince uses in his opening soliloquy, is inevitably parodied by Falstaff: 'Shall the blessed sun of heaven prove a micher and eat blackberries? a question not to be ask'd. Shall the son of England prove a thief and take purses? a question to be ask'd' (II. iv. 394–7).

Harry of Monmouth and Hal of Eastcheap are different roles for the same young man, who had learnt manysidedness among the pots of ale, where Hotspur contemptuously places him. The opening soliloquy shows the Prince as a passionless manipulator of events, whereas Hotspur is carried away by rage, ardour or mockery. In his presence, calculation fails; his uncle Worcester, the supreme Machiavel, gives up schooling him and at the last dupes him. (In his source, Shakespeare could have found that Worcester had in fact

een tutor to Hal; a suitable appointment, had he cared to develop
.)

Hal's many parts, however, do not cohere as naturally as do
alstaff's. In Falstaff the contradictions spring from a great natural
itality; they are the fruit of abundance; in his presence, jests alone
re plotted. The Prince is nimbly versatile, witty in a biting style and
oble in a restrained one; irony and control are his modes, as
istiness and shamelessness are Falstaff's. In wit they are evenly
latched; but Hal dispenses patronage, and a follower can never be
uite a friend. The mixture of apparent intimacy and real insecurity
·hich Falstaff develops at the Boar's Head is like that attained by
layers with such noble patrons as Southampton or Pembroke; and
le real Boar's Head Tavern was one of the players' winter houses.
alstaff harps constantly on Hal's position as heir apparent, and
lough he may dare to call him 'cuckoo' and ask, 'Help me to my
orse, good king's son', there is behind the Prince's retort, 'What,
lall I be your ostler?' something of the sting that appears in 'I know
ou all', with its later, more dramatic sequel, 'I know thee not, old
lan'.

Falstaff's gross body, his constant and clamorous needs, for sack,
ir wenches, for a hand to his horse (the Prince can vault into the
iddle), makes him helpless at times with the helplessness of the flesh
nd of old age, which raises its voice in the shrill reproaches of the
ing-suffering Mistress Quickly. Falstaff needs his wits to live; Hal
eeds his only to jest, and is an extraordinarily ascetic Rioter. In the
ld plays of the Prodigal Son, an addiction to harlots always
haracterized the Rioter. In Part 1 Falstaff represents misrule and
ood cheer rather than riotous life. Dover Wilson noted the many
nages of food which are applied to him – the most frequent is
utter'; he 'lards the earth' and is 'as vigilant as a cat to take cream'.
hough gross, these images are rich, nourishing, festive.

It is because he inhabits such a mountain of flesh that his wit
trikes fiery off'. He uses his bulk as a shield to turn reproaches into a
·st, and in his extraordinary union of the child, the animal and the
riminal, never pursues any single aim, so that all his disabilities serve
nly to illustrate his freedom. The dexterity with which he extricates
imself from danger is a quick and natural response; when he hacks
is sword or attempts to cozen, he is always exposed. His confidence
i himself is deep, animal, instinctive; in this, he resembles Hotspur.
hey represent the nobility of instinct, a feckless, unthrifty splendour
i living which is unknown to the prudent court. Coarseness and
iolence, the stench of the battlefield and the smell of the stable, cling
) Hotspur, who would have his Kate swear like a mosstrooper, and
ave modest oaths to citizens' wives. The praise of instinct which

Falstaff bestows on himself has some truth in it. He swears commonly and most properly by himself, for out of himself a whole world of
living roles is created for himself and others to play.

Henry IV has only one role to play – that of the King. He ha
shown courage, and a disregard for conventional restraint and for al
the sacred taboos in assuming the crown; as L. C. Knights ha
observed, he remains the embodiment of the guilt that is inseparable
from getting and keeping power. His vision of a united England sets
him above his enemies; but against his deep repentance, and that of
the Prince in face of his father's 'dear and deep rebuke', is set the
mock repentance of Falstaff, couched in the canting whine of the
sectaries. Falstaff thus protects himself against the uncou' guid by
stealing their thunder.

Interplay of character, exchange of roles, melting of mood into
mood, and free range combine to give Part 1 its 'divine fluidity'. All is
lucent, untrammelled in the consequence. The consequences are
presented in Part 2.

II

Here the characters are sharper, clearer, more definite; they do not
blend but contrast. Instead of lambent interplay, division or fusion of
roles is provided, with clear separation of man and office. There i
more oration and less action; the action belongs to the common
people, while the King utters his great soliloquies and Falstaff talks
directly to the audience on the virtues of sherris sack.

The embodiment of some of the leading themes appears in the
Prologue Rumour, and I was sorry that this Prologue was cut in your
production. Morally, Rumour embodies the Lie; socially, she represents 'rotten Opinion' or Seeming; politically, the unstable and
troublesome times. The rebels are first shown a false image of
victory, then a false peace which is prelude to a new conspiracy, and
finally a false show of war, when the true grief lies in the King's death
She addresses the audience as her 'household'; it is a slightly malicious opening jest.

The last abortive rebellion of Henry IV's reign is led by the two
symbolic figures of Mowbray and York; Mowbray, the son of
Bolingbroke's first public challenger, and York, the prince of the
church who echoes Rumour on the 'still discordant wavering multitude':

> The commonwealth is sick of their own choice; . . .
> An habitation giddy and unsure
> Hath he that buildeth on the vulgar heart.   (I. iii. 87,89–90

A religious rising in the north was the only rebellion of Elizabeth's reign: as a boy of five, Shakespeare might have seen the levies marching up against the Catholic earls, the Nevilles and Percies. Perhaps some of his London audience had marched too.

To his King's anxious calculations of his enemies' strength, Warwick, who is Shakespeare's countryman and speaks always with the voice of Truth, replies:

> Rumour doth double, like the voice and echo,
> The numbers of the feared.   (III. i. 97–8)

Like voice and echo, opposed rulers of church and state recall the deposition and death of Richard II, the Archbishop dwelling on the treachery of the multitude who then denounced and would now worship him, Henry dwelling on the treachery of Northumberland, once Richard's friend, then his, and now his sworn foe.

The connection between ecclesiastical and temporal rule is debated when the armies meet. Lancaster says the Archbishop is misusing his position as God's deputy to take up arms against God's temporal substitute, the anointed King.

> You have ta'en up,
> Under the counterfeited zeal of God,
> The subjects of his substitute, my father,
> And both against the peace of heaven and him
> Have here up-swarm'd them.   (IV. ii. 26–30)

But the treachery of John of Lancaster's ruse is hardly excused by his neat explanation that wrongs will be redressed, while traitors will suffer; and a final blasphemy is not lacking:

> Strike up our drums, pursue the scatter'd stray:
> God, and not we, hath safely fought today.   (IV. ii. 120–1)

Comment is provided in the last scene of this act by Henry himself:

> God knows, my son,
> By what by-paths, and indirect crook'd ways
> I met this crown.   (IV. iv. 184–5)

No one, least of all Bolingbroke, denies the guilt of usurpation or the conflicts it brings. Treachery in the political sphere replaces the mock robberies of Part 1; the presiding Genius is not Valour, but Wit, not Chivalry but Statecraft. God send us His peace, but not the Duke of Lancaster's, the commons might exclaim.

The lament of Hotspur's widow is immediately followed by the appearance of Falstaff's whore; it is one of the telling silent strokes. Doll hangs on Falstaff's neck and tells him whether she sees him again there is nobody cares. The life of the play resides in these

common parts, the roles of his followers who do not think of Hal as
their future governor. He himself plays the prentice's part: this was a
shrewd touch to endear him to all the prentices in Shakespeare's
original audience – an important playgoing group. The action of
Falstaff's own followers is largely parody. Pistol presents a great
parody of the imaginative life; he outgoes even Falstaff's soaring
inventions, a wild impossible creature who talks in scraps of play-
speech, and feeds on his own mad imagination. If the ghost of
Hotspur walks in Part 2, he is named Pistol. It has been said that we
always fundamentally talk about ourselves, or aspects of ourselves;
so, if Falstaff represents something of Shakespeare's own assessment
of himself, may not Pistol be a player's nightmare? A parody of Ned
Alleyn's rant, perhaps, but also an embodiment of Shakespeare's
deepest fear – a wild tatterdemalion spouter of crazy verses,
hopelessly mistaken in all he says and does, thrown off even by
Falstaff. Pistol embodies the life of dream, of playmaking at its most
distorted and absurd. It is fitting that he brings the deceptive good
news of Hal's succession to Falstaff. When the King wakens from his
dream of Eastcheap mirth, both Falstaff and Pistol are jailed. Pistol
roaring his defiant Spanish tag as he is carried off, in cruel parody of
Hotspur's motto, *Esperance*: 'Si fortuna me tormenta, spero me
contenta.'

The great mythological popular scene of the stolen crown is
haunted not by an explicit recollection of Richard II, but an echo of
his fate, the sad ceremony by which Bolingbroke unkings himself.
Giving shape to his imaginary fears, Henry mockingly hails his son
by the new title which for all the audience evoked the 'star of
England', victor of Agincourt.

> Harry the Fifth is crown'd! Up, vanity:
> Down, royal state! . . .
> O my poor kingdom, sick with civil blows.
>
> (IV. iv. 120–1, 134)

Behind the dying king, the anxious father peers out, as death bores
through his castle wall. The man fenced in by office, the body fretted
by care, bequeath themselves to dust. Bolingbroke admits that even
his expiatory crusade had not been without its prudential aspect; he
had known only a 'supposed Peace', but he prays for 'true peace' at
home in his own son's time. And pat to the catastrophe comes the old
prophecy's fulfilment – he is to die in Jerusalem, if not quite the
Jerusalem his rather stumbling piety expected.

The transmission of office, the demise of the crown as distinct from
the death of Henry Bolingbroke, involves Prince Henry in the last
death-pangs of his old self. In his brief appearance before the King's

last sickness, the Prince is shown with Poins, who, unlike Falstaff, is
bluntly honest. The Prince must mock his own greatness, gird at
Poins, but half confide in him. Hal of Eastcheap has no right to weep
for a father's sickness, and is well aware of it. He takes up the
prentice's part and surveys from this vantage Falstaff's descent 'from
a god to a bull'. The encounter is momentary: there is a revival
momentarily of the old manner ('Why, thou globe of sinful conti-
nents') a recollection of Gadshill; and a carefully casual goodbye,
whose finality was beautifully suggested in the playing: 'Falstaff,
good night'. This is the Prince at his most sensitive, subtle and
inconsistent. When he finally takes up the poisoned gold of the crown
and receives absolution from his natural father, he becomes warmly
and simply a tearful son in the closet; but in public, wearing the 'new
and gorgeous garment, majesty', he stands as father to his brothers,
son to the Lord Chief Justice, and to Falstaff an image of the Last
Judgment itself (the Exhortation of the York Judgment Play might
serve as parallel to the rejection speech).

In his fears Henry Bolingbroke had given a 'character' of his son, in
which sharp changes of mood and irreversible decisions are the
leading traits. A strong personality, when its deeps are broken up by
an internal earthquake, shows a new and unrecognizable landscape.
The 'noble change' so coolly predicted in Part 1 is painfully accom-
plished in Part 2. The Lord Chief Justice, like the Archbishop a
symbol of office, represents the better side of the last reign, all that
was true in its 'supposed Peace'. This is how he justified the jailing of
the unreformed Prince:

> I then did use the person of your father
> The image of his power lay then in me.   (V. ii. 73–4)

He suggests that Henry should imagine a future son of his own
spurning his own image; and the King allows the argument as 'bold,
just and impartial'. He is no longer an individual, but a power whose
image may by delegation reside in other bodies than his own, such as
those of Judge or Prelate. The shadows of past and future kings melt
away as the Sun of England mounts with measured confidence an
uncontested throne.

Yet he sets himself under the law: 'You shall be as a father to my
youth'. Henry, who had played so many parts, now accepts only one.
Complete identification of man and office closes the visor of his
golden armour upon him, and he becomes the centre of the group of
brothers, an impersonal Lancastrian King. Henceforth he has an
uncontrollable tendency to speak like a royal proclamation. However, in one jest dexterously combining religious reproof and a
recollection of old times, Falstaff is symbolically buried:

> Leave gormandizing; know the grave doth gape
> For thee thrice wider than for other men.   (V. v. 54–5)

In a metaphor derived perhaps from the parable of the tares, the Archbishop of York had seen the fourth Henry's friends and foes growing so inextricably together that he might not pluck up the one without destroying the other. This is not Henry V's problem in weeding his garden now. Falstaff, and that old father antic the law, Justice Shallow, are swept off to prison by Henry's new father and his colder self, John of Lancaster, who, fresh from the beheading of an Archbishop, can hardly see Falstaff's banishment as anything but a 'fair proceeding'.[3] It is a highly conventional scene, the traditional judgment scene for a bitter or moralist comedy, so that even Doll and Mistress Quickly are swept into the net. Rumour is confounded, Seeming is cast off, and Order restored.

At the height of his second military triumph, the capture of Colville, Falstaff boasts, 'I have a whole school of tongues in this belly of mine, and not a tongue of them all speaks any word but my name'. This elaborate way of saying that 'Everyone that sees me, knows me', by its metaphor suddenly clothes Falstaff in the robe which Rumour had worn in the prologue. Within the play, he is her chief representative; as indeed he admits by implication in a self revealing comment on Shallow: 'Lord, lord, how subject we old men are to this vice of lying'.

The delights of the Boar's Head and of Gloucestershire, with their undertones of death and old age sounding through the revelry, like the coming of winter in a harvest play, depict the wide commonwealth, the unthinking multitude of common folk about whom Bolingbroke and the Archbishop have been so loftily eloquent. Among the least of the rout, a little tailor with the 'only man-sized voice in Gloucestershire', suddenly echoes one of Prince Harry's proverbs from Shrewsbury: 'We owe God a death'. Feeble, who outbuys a whole army of Pistols, serves to link the multitude and the throne, as in earlier comical histories such local heroes as George-a-Greene had done.

The audience feels no compulsion to take the side of law and order; indeed the tragic themes predominate in reading, but on the stage this is Falstaff's play. The imaginative life of the action lies less in the sick fancies, the recollections and foreshadowing of Bolingbroke than in the daydreams and old wives' tales of Mistress Quickly and Justice Shallow. Neither Hal nor Falstaff daff the world aside with quite the carelessness they had shown before. More wit and less fun, more dominance and less zest, more shrewdness and less banter belong to these two; humour and gaiety have split off into the life of common men and women. Falstaff's mistaken dream of greatness is shattered and he hears himself reduced to a shadow of the King's imagination; for Henry V stands where his father had stood, for the life of reason and judgment against the life of fantasy.

> I have long dreamt of such a kind of man,
> So surfeit-swell'd, so old, and so profane;
> But being awak'd, I do despise my dream. (V. v. 50–3)

This was the formula by which the sovereign arose from a play – 'Think all is but a poet's dream', as Lyly had urged Elizabeth. But against the voice of reason and judgment may be set a feminine voice, which was to be heard again pronouncing Falstaff's epitaph:

> Well, fare thee well. I have known thee these twenty-nine years, come peascod-time; but an honester and truer-hearted man – well, fare thee well. (II. iv. 369–71)

Truth resides officially with Henry V, yet in spite of his double triumph (honour, that 'word', has been snatched from Hotspur as if it were a boxer's belt, and now the lie and opinion are banished), Kate Percy and Mistress Quickly remain unconverted; while the incorrigible Pistol produces a line which is both a theological definition of Truth or Constancy and a parody of the motto of Queen Elizabeth herself: 'Semper idem: for obsque hoc nihil est'.

Henry sweeps all the nation behind him, except two women and a few fools. Such exceptions, however, are not to be despised in the world of Shakespeare's England. The uncertainty of the public view of Truth has been demonstrated. 'Thou art a blessed fellow', says Truth's champion, Prince Hal, to Poins, 'to think as every man thinks; never a man's thought in the world keeps the roadway better than thine'. There is no need for an unconditional identification with Falstaff; indeed there is no possibility of it; for the virtue of Shakespeare is to present many incompatibles not reconciled, but harmonized.

Notes

1 The deposition scene was left out of the first printed version.
2 'Hal' a more vulgar abbreviation may be used only in Eastcheap: 'Young Harry' is the familiar form at court. Compare Falstaff's description of himself, 'Jack Falstaff with my familiars, John with my brothers and sisters, and Sir John with all Europe'.
3 No one would dream of calling John of Lancaster 'Jack'.

VII

Shakespeare's Hybrid:
All's Well that Ends Well

All's Well that Ends Well might have as its sub-title 'Two Plays in One'. In this chapter I shall be concerned with one of the plays only – the play that is revealed by the structure and the plot. Such a partial and one-sided approach is justified because, I believe, it reveals the governing idea[1] of the whole composition. This is perhaps a danger-ous assumption, for 'in attempting to isolate the idea that governs a play we run the risk of fixing it and deadening it, especially when the idea discerned is expressed as a philosophical proposition and stated in a sentence or two '[2]

The governing idea of this particular play is one which I believe belongs rather to Shakespeare's age than to all time. To display it therefore requires what may seem a humourless and over-detailed study of the background of ideas. The method by which the idea is presented is not quite Shakespeare's usual one, though not unlike that discerned by modern critics elsewhere in his work.[3] No one could dare to suggest that Shakespeare took a moral idea and dressed it up in human terms; yet the allegorical mode of thought and the conception that literature should promote good actions were still very much alive in his day. They were not secure.[4] Shakespeare himself, in that period of the mid-1590s when he more or less has the stage to himself – the period between the death of Marlowe and the arrival of Jonson – transformed the conception of dramatic art and produced those ripe and humane works which for ever made im-possible such plays as Robert Wilson's.

The modern reader of *All's Well* may feel that the play contains one superb character study, that of Bertram; and at least one speech of great poetic power, Helena's confession to the Countess. Seen through Helena's eyes Bertram is handsome, brave, 'the glass of fashion and the mould of form': seen through the eyes of the older characters he is a degenerate son, an undutiful subject, a silly boy. The two images blend in the action, as we see him sinking from irresponsibility to deceit, but making a name for himself in the wars. He ends in an abject position, yet Helena's devotion continues undiminished. Her medieval counterpart, patient Griselda, whose virtues are passive, is not called on for more than obedience,[5] and the audience need not stop to wonder what kind of a person the Marquis could be, whether such barbarity could be justified as an assay of virtue, and how the final revelation could leave his wife with any palate for his company. As a character, he exists only to demonstrate Griselda's patience. But Bertram is not 'blacked out' in this way. The connection of his character and Helena's feelings with the general theme can be explained, but they are not identified with it.

In *All's Well* the juxtaposition of the social problem of high birth versus native merit and the human problem of unrequited love recalls the story of the Sonnets; the speeches of Helena contain echoes from the sonnets,[6] but the story to which her great speeches are loosely tied does not suit their dramatic expression. It illustrates the nature of social distinctions, of which the personal situation serves only as example. It might be hazarded that this first tempted Shakespeare, who then found himself saying more, or saying other, than his purely structural purpose could justify. Helena's speech to the Countess is the poetic centre of the play, but the structural centre is the King's judgement on virtue and nobility. For once, the dramatist and the poet in Shakespeare were pulling different ways. *All's Well that Ends Well* expresses in its title a hope that is not fulfilled; all did not end well, and it is not a successful play.

My contention is that *All's Well* fails because Shakespeare was trying to write a moral play, a play which he proposed to treat with the gravity proper, for example, to 'a moral history'.[7] He was not writing allegorically, but his characters have a symbolic and extra-personal significance. To write such a play the writer must be detached and in complete control of his material; and Shakespeare was not happy when he was theorising. Here he is not driven to bitter or cynical or despairing comment on the filth that lies below the surface of life. Instead of the stews of Vienna, the activities of Pandarus and Thersites, we have the highly moral comments of the young Lords on Bertram. Yet compared with *Measure for Measure* – to which it is most closely linked by similarities of plot[8] – the play appears more confused in purpose, more drab and depressing, if less squalid. Both are concerned with what Bacon called Great Place; the one with the nature and use of power, the other with the nature and grounds of true nobility. The characters are occasionally stiffened into types: the King becomes *Vox Dei*, which means that he is merely a voice. Yet at other times, but chiefly in soliloquy, deep personal feeling breaks through. Angelo's temptations and Helena's love are not completely adjusted to the stories which contain them. These feelings burst out irrepressibly, and in a sense irrelevantly, though they are the best things in the plays.

To compare *Measure for Measure* with its source play, *Promos and Cassandra*, is to see the shaping process of imagination at work: to compare *All's Well* with Painter's translation of Boccaccio is at least revealing.[9] The alterations are perfectly consistent, tending to greater dependence, humility, and enslavement on Helena's part and greater weakness and falsehood on Bertram's. New characters are added to voice Helena's claims to virtue and dignity – this is the chief purpose of the Countess, Lafeu, and the additions to the King's part – while others are created to stigmatise Bertram. An outline of Painter will make this clear.

Giletta of Narbonne is brought up with Beltramo and several other children; though not noble she is rich, and refuses many suitors for love of him. After his departure she waits some time (years are implied) before following him, and she sees him before she seeks the King. The conditions of her bargain are that she cures the King in eight days or she offers to be burnt, the King spontaneously adding that he will give her a husband if she succeeds. She asks the right to choose and, somewhat to the royal chagrin, names Beltramo. The King almost apologises to the firmly protesting Count, but pleads that he has given his royal word. After the wedding Giletta goes to Rossiglione, puts the estate in order, tells the people the whole story and goes away openly with a kinsman and a good deal of treasure. She reaches Florence, ferrets out Beltramo's mistress, plans the substitution and eventually gives birth to twin sons. At her leisure she returns, and entering on a day of feast, presents her two sons; Beltramo, to honour his word, and to please his subjects and the ladies, his guests who make suit to him, receives her as his wife.

These shrewd, unsentimental, vigorous Italians, who come to terms after a brisk skirmish, resemble Benedick and Beatrice rather than their own Shakespearian descendants. Two principal characters, the Countess and Parolles, have been added by Shakespeare, and two lesser ones, Lafeu and the Fool. The climaxes are heightened, and in the last scene Bertram is in danger of the law.[10] Shakespeare's hero is a very young man, highly conscious of his birth. He is handsome, courageous in battle, winning in manners: he is also an inveterate liar.

The Elizabethan code of honour supposed a gentleman to be absolutely incapable of a lie. In law his word without an oath was in some places held to be sufficient.[11] To give the lie was the deadliest of all insults and could not be wiped out except in blood. Honour was irretrievably lost only by lies or cowardice. These were more disgraceful than any crimes of violence. Alone among Shakespeare's heroes Bertram is guilty of the lie. Claudio, in *Much Ado*, is clear, and Bassanio, though he thinks of a lie to get himself out of an awkward situation at the end of the play, does not utter it. By such conduct Bertram forfeits his claims to gentility: a gentleman, as Touchstone remembered, swore by his troth, as a knight by his honour.[12] For this he is shamed and rebuked openly, not only by his elders but by his contemporaries and even by his inferiors.[13] The feelings of a modern audience towards Claudio or Bassanio may be due to a change in social standards, but Bertram is roundly condemned.

The fault, however, is not entirely his, for like Richard II, Prince Hal, and all other great ones in search of an excuse, he can shelter behind ill company. Parolles, or Wordy, a character of Shakespeare's own invention, is perceived in the end by Bertram himself to be the Lie incarnate. From the beginning the Countess had known him as

> a verie tainted fellow, and full of wickednesse,
> My sonne corrupts a well-derived nature
> With his inducement
>
> (III ii 90–2)

whilst Helena describes him before he appears as 'a notorious Liar', 'a great way foole, solie a coward'. It is not till the final scene that Bertram too acknowledges him

> a most perfidious slave . . .
> Whose nature sickens: but to speake a truth.
>
> (V iii 207–9)

In the earlier part of the play he is completely gulled by Parolles, who gains his ends by flattery. To the Elizabethan, the flatterer was the chief danger of noble youth, and his ways were exposed in most of the manuals of conduct. In Stefano Guazzo's *Civile Conversation*, a book of manners designed for the lesser nobility, much of Book II is taken up with the subject. Shakespeare in his comedy makes little use of the figure of the flatterer, and this differentiates him from Chapman, Jonson and Middleton, who took the parasite of ancient comedy and furnished him with the latest tricks of the coney-catcher. Falstaff is in some sense a flatterer, but he is never more deceived than when he thinks to govern his sweet Hal.[14]

Flattery thrives on detraction, and Parolles' evil speaking, which finally exposes him, has been anticipated by his double-dealing with

Helena and Lafeu. His cowardice is of no power to infect Bertram,
but his lying is contagious, and in the last scene the Count shows how
deeply he is tainted. The unmasking of Bertram re-echoes the un
masking of Parolles.

Shakespeare is unlikely to have felt deeply about the minutiae of
social procedure, the punctilio of a modern and Frenchified fashion
like the duel, or the niceties of address. Saviolo's discourse on the lie
is put into the mouth of Touchstone, Segar's observations on Adam
armigero are given to the First Gravedigger, and Falstaff has the
longest if not the last word on Honour. But the question 'Wherein
lies true honour and nobility?' was older than the new and fantastic
codes of honour, or the new ideas of what constituted a gentleman. It
is the theme of the first English secular drama, *Fulgens and Lucres* (c
1490), where Medwall gave the lady's verdict for the worthy com
moner against the unworthy nobleman, thereby proving his inde
pendence of his original, Buonaccorso, who in *De Vere Nobilitate*
had left the matter open. In 1525, Rastell, *Of Gentylnes & Nobylyte*
treated the same subject, and it was an obvious theme for secular
moralities. The question of blood and descent had been touched on
by Shakespeare in *King John* in the triple contrast of Arthur, the legal
successor, John the King *de facto*, and Richard the Bastard, whose
royalty of nature makes him the natural leader. Civil nobility seen in
relation to courtly life was a different aspect of the same problem and
it is with this that Shakespeare is concerned in *All's Well*.

When at the turn of the fifteenth century, the ruling caste had
ceased also to be a fighting caste, there remained for the elder and
wiser the role of statesman or politician and for the younger sort that
of courtier. The feudal tenant-in-chief had derived his standing from
his military prowess and his local territorial responsibilities of
delegated rule. Although the military profession was no longer
paramount, the young noble was trained in war. The perfect courtier
was required to be witty, full of counsel and of jests, skilled in music
and poetry, a horseman, a patron of all noble science. Such arts of
living could be learnt only at the court. He should be ambitious of
honour – like Hotspur and Prince Hal – truthful and loyal, kindly
and modest. His life was devoted to glory, and his reward was good
fame. Such employments as the professions afforded – of which that
of physician was held least worthy, as too close to the barber and the
potecary – were the refuge of impoverished families and of younger
sons. As the king was the fount of honour, the young noble's place
was at court; but the vanity and corruption of court life were
especially dangerous for the young. In actuality, the scramble for
preferment was a dangerous game in which the player might lose his
all.[15] Warnings against the court had been set forth in literature for

more than a century. Spenser's *Colin Clout's Come Home Again* depicts both the glories and miseries of the court. A sick or ageing ruler left the courtiers exposed to all the natural dangers of the place without restraint. Such a situation is depicted at the beginning of *All's Well.* The metaphor of the sick king was always something more than a metaphor for Shakespeare. The Countess bids farewell to her 'unseason'd courtier' with open misgivings, and Helena, too, is openly afraid of the influence of the court on Bertram: Parolles' description is not inviting, and even the clown is not improved by it.[16] When the court is reached, all the virtuous characters turn out to be elderly. The King describes the perfect courtier in the person of Bertram's father, recalled to his mind by the young man's likeness (a resemblance already twice commented on):[17]

> Youth, thou bear'st thy Father's face,
> Franke Nature rather curious then in hast
> Hath well compos'd thee: Thy Father's morall parts
> Maist thou inherit too.
>
> (I ii 18–21)

The elder Rousillon is but lately dead when the play opens. In an extensive picture or mirror of his father, the King sets up to Bertram that model which had already been recommended to him by his mother. It constitutes one of the main statements of the play, embodying the idea of true nobility.

> He did look farre
> Into the service of the time, and was
> Discipled of the bravest . . . in his youth
> He had the wit, which I can well observe
> To day in our yong Lords: but they may iest
> Till their owne scorne returne to them unnoted
> Ere they can hide their levitie in honour:
> So like a Courtier, contempt nor bitternesse
> Were in his pride, or sharpnesse; if they were,
> His equall had awak'd them, and his honour
> Clocke to it selfe, knew the true minute when
> Exception bid him speake: and at this time
> His tongue obeyd his hand. Who were below him,
> He us'd as creatures of another place,
> And bow'd his eminent top to their low rankes,
> Making them proud of his humilitie,
> In their poor praise he humbled. . . .
>
> (I ii 26ff.)

The model which Bertram actually takes is the very antithesis of this. Parolles claims to be both courtier and soldier, but his court-liness is entirely speech, as his soldiership is entirely dress. Even the clown calls Parolles knave and fool to his face (II iv). He is ready to play the pander and to tempt Bertram ('a filthy Officer he is in those suggestions for the young Earle', III v 17–18), yet at the end he crawls to the protection of old Lafeu, who had been the first to meet with provocative insults the challenge of the 'counterfeit'.

Affability to inferiors was indeed not always recommended: Elyot held that courtesy consisted in giving every man his due, whilst Guazzo thought 'to be too popular and plausible, were to make largesse of the treasures of his courtesie, to abase himself, and to shew a sign of folly or flatterie'.[18] Yet on the other hand, Theseus's gracious kindness to the tradesmen, or Hamlet's sharp answer to Polonius's 'I will use them according to their desert':

> Gods bodykins, man better. Use everie man after his desert, and who should scape whipping: use them after your own Honor and Dignity. The lesse they deserve, the more merit is in your bountie

illustrate the same virtue which the King praised in the elder Rousil-lon.

The arts of speech were indeed in themselves the very stuff of which a courtier was made. Guazzo describes first of all the speech and bearing to be cultivated, and then the truthfulnesss, fair speak-ing, and modesty which should characterise the matter of discourse. Hence the ungraciousness of Bertram's petulance. 'A poore Phys-ician's daughter my wife?' did not perhaps sound quite so outrageous as it does now, for marriage out of one's degree was a debasing of the blood which blemished successive heirs. But Helena is of gentle, though not of noble blood, and all the other young nobles who have been offered to her have been ready to accept her.

The question that is raised by Bertram's pride and the King's act is one central to all discussion on the nature of nobility. 'One standard commonplace on nobility took shape: that lineage alone was not enough, but that the son of a noble family should increase and not degrade the glory of his ancestors.'[19]

Aristotle had said that Nobility consisted in virtue and ancient riches:[20] Lord Burghley, a potent authority in his day, lopped the phrase down: 'Nobility is nothing but ancient riches.' Whilst it was admitted that the King could confer nobility upon anyone, gentility was sometimes held to be conferred only by descent, hence the saying, 'The King cannot make a gentleman.' At the court of Elizabeth, herself the granddaughter of a London citizen and sur-rounded by new nobility, the more rigid views were not likely to prevail. Nevertheless 'nobility native' was inevitably preferable to 'nobility dative'.[21] Through inheritance it conferred a disposition to virtue, and even the degenerate were shielded in some manner by their descent, 'the fame and wealth of their ancestors serves to cover them as long as it can, as a thing once gilded, though it be copper within, till the gilt be worn away.'[22] Education and the example of his ancestors would also help the nobleman, though a bad education might corrupt him entirely.[23] The debate on old and new titles in Osorio's *Discourse of Civil and Christian Nobility* went in favour of blood, while Nenna's *Il Nennio* supported the lowly born. But all would agree with Mulcaster: 'The well-born and virtuous doth well deserve double honour among men ... where desert for virtue is coupled with descent in blood.'[24]

Desert for virtue is Helena's claim, and the two words echo significantly throughout the play. The causes for ennobling the simple were headed by 'virtue public', in other words, some great public service, and this it is which ennobles her. Learning and riches were other causes. Elyot declared that nobility is 'only the prayse and surname of virtue' and set forth the eleven moral virtues of Aristotle as the model for his Governor.[25] The essentially competitive nature of honour, while it was recognised, was not stressed.

In Helena and Bertram, the true and the false nobility are in contest. Helena seeks recognition: Bertram denies it. The King, with the Countess and Lafeu whom Shakespeare created to act as arbiters, are all doubly ennobled by birth and virtue and therefore judge dispassionately. By these three judges the young people are compared at intervals throughout the play, to the increasing disadvantage of Bertram. In the first scene, the Countess introduces Helena as inheriting virtue and yet improving on it. The technical terms of honour emphasise her point:

> I have those hopes of her good, that her education promises: her disposi-
> tions shee inherits, which makes faire gifts fairer ... she derives her
> honestie, and atcheeves her goodnesse (I i 47ff.).

Of Bertram she cherished hopes less assured, but wishes that his blood and virtue may contend for precedence, and his goodness share with his birthright.

By making his social climber a woman, Shakespeare took a good deal of the sting out of the situation. Helena's virtues were derived from her father and from Heaven, to whose intervention she ascribes all her power to cure the King. She protests she is richest in being simply a maid, and the King offers her to Bertram with the words

King of France about Cordelia ↳

> Vertue and shee
> Is her owne dower: Honour and wealth, from mee.

The promotion of a modest but dignified young woman is far from arousing jealousy.[26] Helena had been conscious of her lowliness and in her first soliloquy she almost despairs:

> Twere all one,
> That I should love a bright particuler starre,
> And think to wed it, he is so above me.
>
> (I i 97–9)

To the Countess, before making her confession, she says:

> I am from humble, he from honored name:
> No note upon my Parents, his all noble,
> My Master, my deere Lorde he is, and I
> His servant live, and will his vassall die.
>
> (I iii 164–7)

These words are not retracted by her confession for she protests that she does not follow him by any token of presumptuous suit: 'Nor would I have him till I doe deserve him' (I iii 199). At her first encounter with the King, Helena is almost driven off by her first rebuff. In stately couplets which mark out the solemnity of the moment she suddenly returns and offers herself as 'the weakest minister' of Heaven. She frankly claims 'inspired Merit' and warns the King that it is presumption to think Heaven cannot work through the humble. 'Of heaven, not me, make an experiment.' The King recognises the power of something greater than herself in Helena's voice and he submits. She is 'undoubted blest'.

Such claims shift the ground of Helena's nobility. To fail to recognise her as already ennobled in a superior way by the choice of Heaven is an aggravation of Bertram's offence in refusing the consummation of the marriage – itself a religious duty as Diana reminds him (IV ii 12–13). The Countess feels nothing but indignation with the 'rash and unbridled boy', for

> the misprising of a Maide too vertuous
> For the contempt of Empire.
>
> (III ii 27–8)

Even before the journey to court she had loved Helena as her own child (I iii 98, 143–4) and now she prefers her, disclaiming her proper son (III ii 68–9), who in rejecting such a wife has lost more onour than he can ever win with his sword. Helena's penitential pilgrimage raises her yet higher in the Countess's estimation, and finally, with the report of her death, she becomes 'the most vertuous gentlewoman, that ever Nature had praise for creating' (IV v 9–10).

In bestowing a wife on one of the royal wards, the King was certainly doing no more than Elizabeth and James had done. Much lesser persons regarded their wards as legitimate matrimonial prizes. The customary formula (which the King uses): 'Can you like of this man?' 'Can you like of this maid?' did not imply love but only the ability to live harmoniously together. Bertram, who is succinctly described by Lafeu as an 'asse', has, it is clear from the first scene, no dislike of Helena, but he knows her as his mother's servant and 'I cannot *love* her, nor will strive to doo't.' Only later does the brilliant idea occur to him that he was really in love with Lafeu's daughter.[27] His seduction of Diana 'contrives against his owne Nobilitie', and his responsibility for the death of Helena means that 'the great dignitie that his valour hath here acquir'd for him [i.e. in Florence], shal at home be encountered with a shame as ample' (IV iii 25–30, 79–82).

Bertram's 'folly', though excused as the fault of Parolles' ill-counsel (IV ii 1), and as 'Naturall rebellion, done i' th blaze of youth' (v iii 6), remains in the eyes of Lafeu a blot upon his honour. However much Bertram wronged his King, his mother, and his wife, he wronged himself much more (v iii 12–19). Lafeu champions Helena's memory rather in the way in which Paulina champions Hermione's, and the rapidity with which the King jumps to thoughts of murder when he sees the royal gem offered as 'an amorous token for fair *Maudlin*' is a proof of his feeling for Helena no less than of his well-merited distrust of Bertram. Like the rings of Bassanio and Portia, the jewels which are bandied about in the last scene are symbolic of a contract and an estate of life. The King's gem derived from him to Helena, and Bertram neither knows nor cares what it is. His own monumental ring symbolises all that he has thrown away.[28]

> an honour longing to our house,
> Bequeathed downe from manie Ancestors,
> Which were the greatest obloquie i' th world,
> In me to loose.
>
> (IV ii 42–5)

This jewel, with which he had taunted Helena, is found at the end in her keeping.

Nevertheless, though Helena is wise and Bertram foolish, though she is humble and he is proud, his final acknowledgement of her would constitute a strong ending. When Brachiano marries Vittoria, or when in *A Woman Killed with Kindness*, Sir Francis marries Susan, the condescension of the noble partner is matter for astonishment. Even in realistic comedy, such as *Eastward Ho!*, the marriage of court and city provides grounds for satire and for farce. Helena's success would lose all point if it were not a great exception. If this suggests that social theory enabled the judicious spectator both to eat his cake and have it, the answer is that the same dilemma lies at the centre of the play, and is expounded by the King in a full account of the nature of title and dignity – a speech which had tradition behind it, but which is sharply at variance with the nigglers who measured whether honour came with the first or third generation of a new title.

> Tis onely title thou disdainst in her, the which
> I can build up: strange is it that our bloods
> Of colour, waight and heat, pour'd all together,
> Would quite confound distinction: yet stands off
> In differences so mightie. If she bee
> All that is vertuous (save what thou dislikst),
> A poore Phisitian's daughter, thou dislikst
> Of vertue for the name: but doe not so:
> From lowest place, whence vertuous things proceed,
> The place is dignified by th' doers' deede.
> When great additions swells, and vertue none,
> It is a dropsied honour. Good alone,
> Is good without a name. Vilenesse is so:
> The propertie by what it is, should go,
> Not by the title. She is young, wise, faire,
> In these, to Nature shee 's immediate heire:
> And these breed honour: that is honour's scorne,
> Which challenges it selfe as honour's borne,
> And is not like the sire: Honours thrive
> When rather from our acts we them derive
> Then our fore-goers: the meere words, a slave
> Deboshed on everie tombe, on everie grave:
> A lying Trophee, and as ofte is dumbe,
> Where dust, and damn'd oblivion is the Tombe
> Of honour'd bones indeed. . . .
>
> (II iii 124ff.)

Helena already possesses the essential attributes and therefore the potentiality of honour, which the King by his recognition of her claims will bestow. 'The name and not the thing' is vanity.[29]

Medieval tradition recognised three classes of nobility:[30] Christian, natural and civil. Pre-eminence must be given to sanctity, but the saints included poor fishers, even slaves. Natural nobility or perfection of kind might be ascribed to animals, and a noble falcon justly so termed. The writers of books of honour often mentioned these two classes, but pointed out that they could not discuss them. One of the fullest treatments of the subject is by Dante in his *Convivio*. He denies civil nobility any real value.[31] Nobility, he says, cannot be defined by riches, which in themselves are vile,[32] or by time, because all men ultimately derive from a common stock, but only by its effects. The necessary outcome or effect of Nobility is Virtue: where Virtue exists, Nobility must therefore exist as its cause. Nobility descends upon an individual by the grace of God (*Convivio*, IV xv) and is 'the seed of blessedness dropped by God into a rightly placed soul.' Dante goes on to expound the eleven moral virtues (much like Elyot). The claim to nobility by descent is then refuted, natural and Christian nobility identified, and civil nobility wiped out. Dante's Third Ode, upon which this section of the *Convivio* provides a commentary, is addressed to Beatrice, who, like Helena, is an example of active virtue, received by a direct infusion of grace. The language of religion is used with particular frequency by Shakespeare in this play,[33] and the gravest words of all are spoken by the Clown (IV v 50–9) when he describes how 'the Prince of this world' entices nobility 'into his court'.

> I am for the house with the narrow gate, which I take to be too little for pompe to enter: some that humble themselves may, but the manie will be too chill and tender, and theyll bee for the flowrie way that leads to the broad gate, and the great fire.

Helena is 'a Jewell' (V iii 1) which Bertram throws away. His rejection of her must be seen not in isolation but as linked with his choice of Parolles.[34] The first dialogue of Helena and Parolles, the Liar and Vertue as she herself has labelled them, must be seen as the encounter of Bertram's good and evil angels, who, if this were a morality, would contend for his soul in open debate.[35] In the final scene Parolles turns the tables on Bertram, and though the King dismisses the informer with contempt, an elaborate and inexorable shaming of the now utterly silenced young man proceeds. This last scene, in which Shakespeare completely forsakes his original, has the closest affinities with *Measure for Measure*. It is a judgement scene with charge and countercharge piled up in bewildering contradiction till they are resolved as if by miracle in the sudden appearance of the central figure. In this scene the King appears as the fount of justice: he deprives Bertram of all honour (V iii 184–6), though the revenges with which he threatens the young man should not be taken in any personal sense. Such a finale, with a royal judgement, and a distribution of rewards and punishments, was a well-established comic convention,[36] though it is difficult to resist the thought that in offering Diana a husband, the King shows some inability to profit by experience. The riddles with which Diana led up to the *dénouement* recall those in which Portia swore she lay with Doctor Balthazar to obtain the ring, and they are not to modern taste.

 Bertram's conversion must be reckoned among Helena's miracles. What is well ended is her struggle for recognition, which he concedes her. Her devotion, tinged for the first time with bitterness, requires another mode of expression than the last dozen lines allow. She has been acknowledged by her lord: that her personal happiness is simply irrelevant, and the ending therefore neither hypocritical nor cynical, can be granted only if the play is seen as a study of the question of 'Wherein lies true honour and nobility?'

Notes

1 See Nevill Coghill, 'The Governing Idea, Essays in the Interpretation of Shakespeare – I', *Shakespeare Quarterly*, i (1948), pp. 9–16.

2 Ibid.

3 Two excellent modern editions appeared after this article was written, by G. K. Hunter (Arden, 1959) and Barbara Everett (New Penguin, 1970), see also Joseph Price, *The Unfortunate Comedy*, 1968.

4 Cf. Rosemary Freeman, *English Emblem Books* (London, 1948), pp. 19–22.

5 Helena shows herself similarly passive in her two scenes as wife (II iv; v). Unlike Parolles, she calls Bertram her 'master', both before and after marriage (I iii 166; III iv 9).

6 Helena's three great speeches (I i 91–110; I iv 199–225; III ii 102–32) have a number of parallels with the Sonnets, especially the second of the three. Cf. Sonnets xxvi, lvii, lviii, lxxxvii. The way in which Bertram is condemned recalls also the plain speaking which is so unusual a feature of the Sonnets (e.g. xxxv, lxvii, lxxxii, lxxxiv, xcv, xcvi).

7 A term defined by A. P. Rossiter in his edition of *Woodstock* (London, 1948): roughly, a chronicle history built on a moral theme.

8 e.g. the rejection of a devoted bride for insufficiency, and a compelled marriage ordered by the ruler: the substitution of one woman for another: the false self-accusation of the chaste woman, followed by prolonged lying from the culprit, culminating in his exposure through the arrival of an absent person: the slanderer who speaks ill of his lord and is unmasked in public.

9 William Painter, *The Palace of Pleasure* (1566), contains as the xxxviii novel the story of 'Giletta a phisition's daughter of Narbon', the original being Boccaccio, *Il Decamerone*, III ix. The subject of the relations of

All's Well to its sources is, I understand, being considered in detail by Professor H. G. Wright. See *Modern Language Review*, XLVI (1951), 431–5; and (1955) 45–8. Cf. Hunter, ed. cit., XXV–IX.

10 Bertram's own lies cause this, and the exposure of his treatment of Diana. Her use in this scene is entirely Shakespeare's own invention, and much increases the melodrama. Helena in Act II also increases the tension by offering to have her name traduced as a strumpet if she fails to cure the King, and by cutting down the period required from eight days to two.

11 R. Kelso, *The Doctrine of the English Gentleman* (Urbana, 1929), p. 78.

12 *As You Like It*, I ii. Cf. Mulcaster, *Positions* (reprinted London, 1898), p. 198.

13 e.g. IV ii 11–30 where Diana, who is perhaps his social equal, being descended from the ancient Capilet, rebukes him; IV iii 1–30, where the young Lords criticise him. Parolles' sonnet contains some nasty home truths: in the last scene the King and Lafeu are quite uncompromising. Bertram's word is not to be trusted (V iii 184–6).

14 Hamlet's discrimination between Polonius, his two schoolfellows, and Osric is a mark of the wise prince: Timon's failure to discriminate is his downfall.

15 See Lawrence Stone, 'The Anatomy of the Elizabethan Aristocracy', *Economic History Review*, XVIII (1948).

16 I i 71, 80–2; 182–93, 224: III ii 13–29. See Kelso, op. cit., pp. 50–2, for a comparison between the English and Italian courtly traditions, which suggests that English courtiers were more frequently employed in administration and that mere attendance at court was in England not considered an occupation in itself. Yet in spite of this, Sidney, like Bertram, stole away to the wars, though 'with a copy of Castiglione in his pocket'.

17 I i 1, 71–2.

18 S. Guazzo, trans. Pettie, *Civile Conversation* (reprinted London, 1925), i 158.

19 John E. Mason, *Gentlefolk in the Making* (Philadelphia, 1935), p. 8.

20 *Politics*, IV viii 9.

21 Kelso, op. cit., p. 22.

22 Sir Thomas Smith, *De Repub. Anglorum* (reprinted London, 1906), p. 38.

23 Kelso, op. cit., p. 24, quotes La Perrière, *Mirour of Policie* (translated 1598): 'If he be evilly instructed in his young years, he will as long as he liveth have such manners as are barbarous, strange, and full of villainy.' The education of a prince or noble was the subject of constant discussion.

24 Mulcaster, *Positions*, p. 199; quoted by Kelso, op. cit., p. 30.

25 *The Governor*, ed. Croft, ii 38; quoted by Mason, op. cit., p. 26.

26 Her many hesitations, her disclaimer of any aspiration to a royal match, show Helena's decorum. No Elizabethan could, like a modern writer, have called it 'canny'.

27 The King had long ago arranged the match, in the young people's childhood, and Bertram's affection may be assumed to be politic; but his

readiness to accept the plan undermines his claim to freedom of choice in his first marriage.

28 In Painter's story the ring is not an heirloom, but prized by Beltramo 'for a certain vertue that he knew it had'. Bertram's use of Diana's ring as a love-token should not be pressed as a point against him, though it is hardly suitable: but his lying repudiation and slander of Diana is ignoble.

29 So, when she has fulfilled Bertram's conditions, Helena turns to seek not her lord, but the King (IV iv), because public recognition of her right is essential.

30 Kelso, op. cit., p. 21, where it is mentioned that later writers tended to ignore these divisions, or to pay them lip-service only.

31 *Convivio*, Fourth Treatise.

32 *Nobile* is derived by Dante from *not vile* (IV xvi).

33 e.g. I i 109–10, 239–40; I ii 57–8, 65–7; I iii 20–i, 212–13, 253; II 139–44, 151–7, 163, 178–9; II iii 1–7, 28–9, 69; III iv 28–9; IV ii 21–9 66–8; IV iii 55–63.

34 The pride of Parolles and the humility of Helena have been contrasted in their use of the term 'master': they are shown at the beginning as more or less social equals.

35 Bertram's ultimate rejection of Parolles, though well-deserved, is expressed with a wilful petulance, not with shame: 'I could endure anything but a Cat, and now he's a Cat to me' (IV iii 242–3).

36 e.g. *Friar Bacon and Friar Bungay, The Shoemaker's Holiday, An Humorous Day's Mirth.*

VIII

What Shakespeare did to Chaucer's *Troilus and Criseyde*

Troilus and Cressida, unlike most of Shakespeare's plays, was designed to be read as literature and not only for the boards. The Preface to the Quarto calls it a comedy as distinct from a mere play, serving as 'commentary' to 'all the actions of our lives', and appealing to judgment as well as pleasure. This advertisement, though neither of Shakespeare's nor his company's devising, was written by one who knew his public and aimed at catching the select few, with the warning that Shakespeare's plays would soon be difficult to get hold of. The key word is 'wit', but such wit as does not exclude labour; for the writer adds that the play deserves to be properly set forth, with commentary and notes, like the classics. Could he return to survey the endeavours of Campbell, Hillebrand, Baldwin and others, he might write himself down no minor prophet.

Among the marks of conscious labour and effort are the formal debates in camp and citadel, the complex and strange vocabulary, and the great variety of sources. The tone and flavour of the play, disturbing and ambiguous, controls and directs the response; and the 'conclusion of no conclusions' is in keeping with it. A bitter comedy for the Inns of Court men may have been what Shakespeare set out to write; but no work of his can be pigeonholed, and *Troilus and Cressida* bears less resemblance to the formula of Comical Satyre than does *Hamlet* to Revenge Tragedy.[1]

In the division of interest between the two plots, most of the 'commentary' is put into the story of the siege; the dramatic excitement and the main channel of sympathy lies in the love story. My concern is chiefly with the story of Troilus and the way in which by comparison with the original work of Chaucer, Shakespeare's governing intention is revealed. I shall be less occupied with the extent of the borrowing than with the nature of the handling and the temper of approach.

II

Behind the story of the siege, there has been discerned the work of Homer, in French or in Chapman's translation of *Seven Books of the Iliads*, Lydgate, Caxton, and possibly a drama or two. Behind the story of Troilus there is Chaucer, Henryson and a general popular tradition.

The sack of Troy was to the sixteenth century the highest secular symbol of disaster, the 'great crash'; it was what 1914 was to writers of the twenties and thirties, and as such it had already been used by Shakespeare in his most ostentatiously literary work, *The Rape of Lucrece*, where the 'augmentation' of Lucrece's woes in the tapestry of Troy makes it the emblem of betrayal. Soon after *Troilus and Cressida* was finished, the image rose again to Shakespeare's mind in the passion of the mobled queen, and Hamlet's passionate soliloquy upon it. Pyrrhus, the true son of Shakespeare's own Achilles, minces the limbs of Priam in a blind violence which otherwise in the play of *Hamlet* remains hidden – for murder and lust, combined in the person of Claudius, are masked in more than Sinon's cunning.

Such accounts of the siege as Shakespeare might have read in English were from the literary point of view neither stimulating nor shapely. He had either to quarry from the rambling narratives of Caxton or Lydgate,[2] or stumble through Chapman's text of Homer, which the contortions of syntax no less than the pidgin-Latin vocabulary made very nearly unreadable (these first seven books became much clearer in Chapman's final version). The influence of Chapman on the language of *Troilus and Cressida* is at its greatest in the debating scenes, where something near a scholar's rhetoric was required to sustain the height of argument. Years before, in *Love's Labour's Lost*, Shakespeare had laughed at scholars' terms; here in a limited way he returned to them; but combined with the 'conceited wooing of Pandarus Prince of Licia', with the satyrical snarling of Thersites, and with the speech of the lovers themselves, which ranges from high terms to barest simplicity.

Those concerned with the sources of *Troilus and Cressida* have devoted most space to the story of the siege. R. K. Presson, whose treatment is the latest and most lengthy,[3] gives only twenty-five pages out of one hundred and fifty-seven to Chaucer's poem, with which however he 'inclines to think' Shakespeare was familiar. In depicting the siege, Shakespeare had relied upon at least two and possibly three versions; he selected, recombined, and rearranged the ingredients with the utmost freedom. For the love story he went to the greatest poet accessible to him in English; and his treatment of Chaucer is at once consistent and paradoxical. The high and heroic romance is in every way deflated. If the whole play reflects Shakespeare's reactions towards some deep betrayal, with roots vast, ramifying and obscure, it is not likely that only by chance he took Chaucer for this more intimate and dramatic half of the story: a poetic ideal was being ironically distorted and defaced. That the author of *Romeo and Juliet* had learned from the author of *Troilus and Criseyde* would seem to be one of those possibilities not to be measured by the number of detectable parallels. A poet learns his trade not from books of rhetoric but from other poets; and the Wyf of Bath and Harry Bailly still remain the only peers of Angelica and Falstaff.

In refashioning this story, Shakespeare was doing to Chaucer what Chaucer had already done to Boccaccio; but he was not the first to produce what the rhetoricians would call a 'correction' of Chaucer's work. In Thynne's edition of 1532, Robert Henryson's *Testament of Cresseid* was printed as a sequel to Chaucer's poem, and it was even copied by a sixteenth-century writer into a fifteenth-century manuscript.[4] If he read it, Shakespeare made no direct use of this poem; indeed it was Rollins' thesis that Shakespeare reversed later developments of the story in ignoring the pitiable end of the heroine.[5] But the imagery of disease, so violently presented in Henryson in his picture of Cresseid the leper, was dissolved into the general language, where, joining with the tradition of comical satyre, it appeared in the language and person of Thersites (a figure very much enlarged from hints in the original story of the siege). Henryson's stern and elliptic statement of the punishment wrought by Time and Change – Saturn and the Moon – upon Cresseid's beauty carries the concentration of a Scots ballad and the solemn retributory weight of Scots piety, as in the brief epitaph carved upon her tomb of 'merbell gray'

> Lo, fair ladyis, Cresseid, of Troyis toun,
> Sumtyme countit the flour of Womanheid,
> Under this stane lait Lipper lyis deid.

To encounter such a harsh, incongruous if noble ending joined to the delicate intricacy of Chaucer must have been jarring and bewildering to a sensitive reader ignorant of the history of its composition. Such a sequel would violate rhetorical decorum if read as part of the original, but it might supply a hint to be improved upon. Henryson, while inflicting the full horrors of the spital house upon Cresseid, does not question the beauty of the love that was once between her and Troilus, and her dying remorse and lament belong to an unperplexing if bitter world, where truth is honoured even in the breach of it. Shakespeare's exploration of betrayal goes further than either Henryson's or Chaucer's. There is no physical destruction; only, 'if beauty have a soule this is not shee'.

III

Compression and inversion direct Shakespeare's use of Chaucer. The original narrative is an inward one; experience, not events form the ground of it.

> The double sorwe of Troilus to tellen . . .

Each of Chaucer's five books is represented by one or two scenes in Shakespeare, the division between Chaucer's books corresponding roughly to the division between Shakespeare's acts. Book I, the love woes of Troilus, is represented by I. i; Book II, the wooing of Criseyde, by I. ii (with the scene of Helen, III.i, as appendage – Helen and Paris appear in Chaucer's second book); Book III, the consummation of love, is represented by III. ii; Book IV, the parting, by IV. ii and IV. iv; Book V, the betrayal, by V. ii. Chaucer's story is leisurely and, especially in the wooing, he protracted events; throughout, as Shakespeare tells it,

> Injurious time now with a robbers hast,
> Cram's his ritch theev'ry up hee knowes not how.   (IV. iv. 41–2)

Yet the clear inversion of every idealistic feeling save those of Troilus is so relentless that a 'mirror image' emerges. As Shakespeare shows them, Pandarus and Cressid distort Chaucer's two subtlest creations, for neither, in their Chaucerian form, is to be found in *Il Filostrato* or any of the earlier accounts; it was precisely to the most original parts of Chaucer that Shakespeare turned for his bitterest refashioning.

Chaucer, in Book I, shows Troilus as absurd and unreasonable; both his lovers are 'tetchy' – especially, in Book II, Creseyde. The raging of the hero and the hesitancy of the lady remain none the less wholly sympathetic, whilst in Shakespeare the tetchiness is transferred to Pandarus, whose cheap display of power in his petulance to Troilus conceals the salesman's trick of pretending indifference to stimulate the customer. He next opens his attack on Cressid with the same comparison with Hector that Chaucer's Pandare also employs (Book II, ll. 170–207; cf. I. ii. 50–95) but in Shakespeare by depreciation of the great hero, in Chaucer by admiring comparison. To whet Pandarus, Shakespeare's Cressid mockingly disdains Troilus, while Creseyde frankly acknowledges his prowess. For the delicate and subtle fencing with words between medieval knight and lady ('I shal felen what he meneth, ywis'), there is substituted a frank and brutal exchange, culminating in the open taunt 'You are a Bawde!' Cressid's soliloquy proclaims her simple creed, the art of the coquette raised to a rule of life, based on the assumption that what is to be looked for in man is simply 'lust in action'. Chaucer's Creseyde, on the contrary, will not admit to herself or to Pandare even the natural flattery which she feels at the prospect of a royal lover. She is a young widow, sensitive, loath to make any emotional commitment (Book II, ll. 750–6), but innocent enough to be deceived by Pandare's dramatic threat of a double suicide for himself and Troilus. Though on Pandarus' word, still a virgin ('How now, how now, how go maidenheads?') Shakespeare's Cressid is both wily and raw; unlike Chaucer's lady, she is unmoved by the sight of hacked arms and helm as the hero passes her on his return from battle; at the first interview she betrays her own arts completely to Troilus

Perchance my Lord I show more craft then love . . .   (III. ii. 49)

and, warm from her first encounter, generalizes glibly on her original theme;

> Prithee tarry, you men will never tarry,
> O foolish Cresseid, I might have still held of,
> And then you would have tarried.   (IV. ii. 15–17)

for Cressid, as Ulysses was shortly to observe, is a natural 'daughter of the game'.

Chaucer's lady, reading in her chamber, playing with her maidens, conducting her lawsuit under masculine tuition, is gracious and dignified; Pandare, though he does not disguise his ultimate hope that the lovers may be united, does not dare to press even for an interview. She is not ignorant of 'the right true end of love' but restrained by modesty and pride. Pandare sees ahead and is content to move slowly; she lives in the moment, as she is later bitterly to acknowledge (Book V, ll. 734–49) so that the delicately complex process of the wooing (which Chaucer admits to spinning out as long as possible, Book III, ll. 1195 ff.) allows her to dissolve her hesitancies only at the last possible moment, after three separate stages in the wooing have been depicted, and several years are supposed to have elapsed.

The wooing itself has acted as 'a spur to valiant and magnanimous deeds' and Chaucer's Troilus has become a more renowned fighter 'in hope to stonden in his lady grace' while Shakespeare's Troilus is enervated and drawn from the battle by his love. When the play opens, his protracted wooing is nearly over. The actual scene of Cressid's surrender (III. ii.) has several reminiscences of Chaucer. Troilus' rapture

I am giddy; expectation whirles me round . . .   (III. ii. 17)

though it leads him to fear 'sounding destruction' is not as acute as that of the medieval knight, who does actually fall in a swoon. At an earlier interview, Chaucer shows him feverish and overcome, for the physiology of wooing, as Chaucer understood it, though it leads to increased valour in war, involves deep disturbance and not unmanly tears (Book III, ll. 57–8, 78–84). All the gasping and palpitating is on the part of the knight, who like Shakespeare's Troilus, forgets his rehearsed speech; the lady remains inwardly calm enough to make even her final surrender with a laugh against herself, though by this time she too quakes like an aspen leaf (Book III, ll. 1210–1). The difference in tone between Shakespeare and Chaucer can be most easily gauged by a comparison of the song in praise of love which Antigone sings to Creseyde (Book II, ll. 827-75) with the bawdy verse that Pandare sings to Helen (III. i. 108–19). Shakespeare's destruction of the character of Pandarus is as thorough as that of Creseyde. In Shakespeare he gloats over what he does not see with obscene insistence, while in Chaucer he drily mocks, and comments to himself as he finally settles for a night before the fire. The greeting of Creseyde (or Cressid) next morning (Book III, ll. 1555–75 – cf. IV. ii. 24–34) contrasts very neatly the same jests as spoken in the 'high rhetoric' of courtesy and in the 'low rhetoric' of the stews.

While described on the title-page of the Quarto as 'Prince of Licia', Shakespeare's Pandarus calls Troilus simply his 'Lord' and would appear to be on much the same footing as is Parolles to Bertram or that later procurer, Webster's Flamineo, to Brachiano. Pandare in Chaucer is the Prince's comrade in arms, and his loyalty to both lovers is emphasized at the moment of initial success (Book III, ll. 239–343). Creseyde has just received Troilus 'to her service' and the ultimate outcome can hardly be doubted, though the lady's feelings must be observed. 'My dearest lord and brother', Pandar begins, 'I have become for your sake the kind of creature who brings men and women together. Take pity of her; I have betrayed her to you, but don't betray her to the world by boasting of her favours.' To which Troilus replies with fervent oaths, and indignant denial that Pandare's act of 'compaignie' should be classed as mercenary sale.

> Call it gentilesse,
> Compassioun and felawship and trist.   (Book III, ll. 402–3)

And he offers to get his own sister for Pandare as recompense – an offer which in Shakespeare is transferred to become part of Pandare's own assault upon his niece's feelings ('Had I a sister were a grace or a daughter a Goddesse, hee should take his choice'). Far from apologizing for his conduct, Shakespeare's Pandare identifies his role with that of the 'traders in the flesh'. At the end of the lovers' contract, in which they prophetically sketch their several fates and draw the moral, he bestows his name on 'all pitiful goers between to the world's end' and draws in the very spectators to the brothel.

> And cupid grant all tong-tide maidens here,
> Bed, chamber, Pandar to provide this geere.   (III. ii. 206–7)

The device is repeated in the epilogue, where Pandarus prays to those members of his livery present in the audience to condole with him:

> As many as be here of *Pandars* hall,
> Your eyes halfe out, weepe out at Pandars fall . . .
> Brethren and sisters of the hold-door trade . . .   (V. x. 46–50)

At the corresponding points in his story, Chaucer too directly addresses his hearers. After the bedchamber scene, he humbly appeals to all lovers to correct and improve his telling of the noble tale; and at the end, his formal address to his book, 'litel my tragedie', merges into another to the same 'yonge fresshe folkes, he or she' to forsake the love of man for the love of God; then comes the dedication to Gower and Strode, and finally the prayer to the Trinity which he took from Dante's *Paradiso*. The human tragedy, while subsumed into something greater, remains beautiful in itself.

> Thynketh al nys but a faire,
> This world, that passeth soone as floures faire.

Shakespeare chose to end with a reference to the celebrated brothels of the Bankside owned by the Bishop of Winchester. It completes his lacerative destruction of Chaucer's whole vision, which has already replaced the sensitive Creseyde, and the recklessly devoted, mockingly sympathetic Pandare, by a combine of amateur drab and professional agent.

The lengthy wooing and three years 'bliss' of Chaucer's lovers are condensed by Shakespeare into a single meeting and one night's enjoyment. Yet their secret is known to Paris and Aeneas; under pretence of arranging excuses for Troilus, Pandarus has dropt some broad hints. Troilus makes no attempt at concealment and assumes before Diomede the right to protect Cressid. She herself is the only one to take precautions, when she thrusts Troilus back into her chamber on the arrival of the Lords.

IV

With the exchange of Cressid for Antenor, Shakespeare draws his two plots together; the connection with Chaucer grows fainter. In Chaucer, Hector's noble instinct is to refuse the exchange – 'We usen here no woman for to selle'[6] – but he is overruled by the mob; while

Troilus, who is present at the council, does not speak for fear of compromising Creseyde. Later however both he and Pandare lament at length and propose to abduct Creseyde, who is herself the one to counsel moderation and to promise that she will steal or beg her way back to Troy. Shakespeare's Troilus stoically accepts the public decision in which he took no part: 'Is it so concluded?' and overrules Cressid, who is hysterically protesting; he promises to corrupt the Greeks' sentinels and make his way to her by night. Shakespeare's Troilus is altogether more disciplined and active; Cressid's lament recalls something of the original, though she does not go to the length of threatening suicide (Book IV, ll. 771–7, 813–9, 862–8; cf. IV. ii. 102–115).

Chaucer's Creseyde, handed over in silence by Troilus at the town's end, arrives at the Greek camp half-fainting and is received only by her father.

> She . . . stood forth muet, milde, and mansuete.   (Book V, ll. 194)

The slow dragging hours of her lover's vigil on the walls, the despair of Criseyde as she gazes at the towers of her home from the Grecian camp, the ruthless skill of Diomede prepare for the long-delayed end. The prisoner, caught in the war machine, is battered into subjection; she is in essentials the same as the Cressida of Walton's recent opera, and ends so broken that her final pitiful letter shows her incapable even of the consistent lie. Chaucer's lovers, after their parting, never meet again; Troilus, whose eagerness and trust had made him mistake every approaching figure for that of his love, whose obstinacy of belief had persisted against even the damning evidence of the letter, is finally convinced by the sight of his love-token upon Diomede's captured coat-armour. Pandarus, though his superior insight told him that Criseyde's return was not to be hoped, is as outraged by this proof of infidelity as Troilus himself. The 'doctrine' of the ending is set forth in the interpolated passage from Boethius which is put into the mouth of Troilus in Book IV (ll. 958–1078). It is Fate or Necessity which decrees the separation; but only after death can Troilus accept it. Shakespeare's Troilus gives to Cressid in the moment of parting the orthodox religious explanation; they are punished for idolatry;

> Cressid, I love thee in so strain'd a purity,
> That the blest Gods as angry with my fancy,
> More bright in zeale then the devotion which
> Cold lippes blow to their deities, take thee from me.   (IV. iv. 23–6)

Then, with utmost speed, comes the disaster. If the wooing was condensed, the betrayal is concentrated much further. While Chaucer dwells on the pangs of suspense, and of ebbing hope ('Hope is alwey lesse and lesse, Pandare!' cries Troilus), Shakespeare uses an extreme form of shock, of dramatic reversal and recognition. In the reception scene and the tent scene, by a blinding demonstration, first the spectators and later the hero are shown the quicksands of Cressid's faith.[7] The irony is pointed by Cressid's resumption of her old arts, in words that constantly echo earlier scenes.

> I prithee do not hold me to mine oath . . .   (V. ii. 26)
> Nay, but you part in anger . . .   (V. ii. 44)
> Come hither once again . . .   (V. ii. 49)

and, in reply to Diomede's 'Will you then?' perhaps the savagest line of the play;

> In faith I will lo, never trust me else.   (V. ii. 59)

After her maudlin tears over the pledge, in which she rises to verse at the thought of Troilus' 'memorial dainty kisses' to her glove, she veers again;

> Well, well, tis done, tis past; and yet it is not.
> I will not keep my word.   (V. ii. 97–8)

Ulysses, who reads her at a glance, watches half-incredulously the despair of Troilus: the gloating of Pandarus is replaced by that of Thersites; three different readings of the event are supplied by the three watchers.

In Chaucer the evasions, excuses and counter-accusations of Creseyde's final letter to Troilus display the collapse of desperate resistance; but what Shakespeare's Cressid here displays is spontaneous, strange, and yet horribly familiar. Shakespeare's Troilus, like Chaucer's, had had his fears (IV. iv. 79–85; cf. Book IV, ll. 1485–91), but the suddenness and completeness of this metamorphosis destroys more than the image of Cressid; it destroys his whole world. Chaos is come again. The principle of contradiction no longer applies; a thing may be itself and also something else.

> If there be rule in unitie it selfe
> This was not shee.   (V. ii. 139–40)

If beauty have a soul[8] – if the outward and inward ever correspond to each other – this is not she; the existence of truth, of the womanhood that was in 'our mothers', of sanctimony itself is questioned. Chaucer's hero accepts his fate as divinely ordained: Shakespeare's hero inhabits a world in which the natural sequence of events ('discourse of reason' as they are perceived) is utterly suspended. The varying and incompatible points of view represented by the three watchers are not further apart from the incompatible fighting within Troilus himself. From such a world the gods are altogether absent and, when at last they reappear in the last scene of all, they are hostile.

> Frowne on, you heavens, effect your rage with speed,
> Sit gods upon your thrones, and smile at Troy. (V. x. 6–7)

For to Shakespeare, the agony of Troilus over Cressid's falsehood is distanced and given final perspective, not as in Chaucer by the hero's death and the enlarged world of the epilogue, but by its place in the greater story. Hector falls by the unchivalrous butchery of the Myrmidons; but Troilus himself is in no chivalrous mood by then. In Hector's death, which leaves him the champion of a doomed city, Troilus finds the 'moment of truth';[9] and the Folio text borrows a climax of Chaucer.

> March away;
> Hector is dead; there is no more to say. (V. x. 21–2)

Namore to seye. No more indeed, but the final testament; which is not Cressid's but Pandar's, and spoken to the audience. This ending was perhaps among Shakespeare's second thoughts; yet it makes a very fitting contrast with the armed warrior of the Prologue. For the strength of this play lies in a vision not of the grandeur but the pettiness of evil; the squalor and meanness and triviality of betrayal, which here enjoy their hour.[10]

Notes

1 See O. J. Campbell, *Comicall Satyre and Shakespeare's 'Troilus and Cressida'* (San Marino, Huntington Library Publications, 1938). Peter Alexander, *Shakespeare's Life and Art* (London, J. Nisbet, 1939), mentions the Inns of Court.

2 The task of turning narrative romance into dramatic form is stressed as one of the chief dramatic problems of the Elizabethan playwright by Madeleine Doran, *Endeavors of Art* (Madison, University of Wisconsin Press, 1954), ch. 5.

3 Robert K. Presson, *Shakespeare's 'Troilus and Cressida' and the Legends of Troy* (Madison, University of Wisconsin Press, 1953).

4 LI, St John's College, Cambridge. M. R. James, *A Descriptive Catalogue of the Manuscripts in the Library of St John's College, Cambridge* (Cambridge, Cambridge University Press, 1913), p. 274. The 'explicit' at the end of the Chaucer would make clear that it *was* a sequel.

5 Hyder E. Rollins, 'The Troilus–Cressida story from Chaucer to Shakespeare', *PMLA*, XXXII (1917), 383–429.

6 Compare the refusal to chaffer for Helen in Shakespeare II. ii, and Paris' words to Diomede, IV. ii. 77–80.

7 In Henryson there is a sudden similar shock in the smiting of Cressid with leprosy; and later there is a poignant silent encounter of prince and lazar.

8 The various uses of the word *soul* in this scene are worth exploring.

9 The manner of Hector's death is taken from the accounts in Lydgate and Caxton of Troilus' own death.

10 Perhaps the final irony is provided by the writer of the preface to the Quarto who declares that Shakespeare's comedies (including this) 'seeme (for their height of pleasure) to be borne in that sea that brought forth Venus'.

IX

An interpretation of *Hamlet**

In this discussion of *Hamlet* I shall be concerned in the first place with the subjective view of this play, that is, I shall consider the play from Hamlet's own point of view, as the sympathetic reader or spectator might see it. But in the second place, I shall consider it from the objective point of view and look at the character of Hamlet from the outside and see it as a study of a particular kind of person as the detached observer might see it.

The view of *Hamlet* which I wish to begin with is that which could reveal the scepticism, the self-questioning of a man ill-adjusted to his world, built on the basis of a much simpler problem, the standard dilemma of the revenger. Keats spoke of the quality that went to form a man of achievement, especially in literature, and which Shakespeare possessed so enormously. I mean negative capability, that is, when a man is capable of being in uncertainties, mysteries, doubts. It seems to me that recently in criticism of *Hamlet* this capacity has been singled out as the peculiar strength of the play: the ability to tolerate a state of interior conflict, to reserve an area of mystery ('You would pluck out the heart of my mystery', Hamlet accuses Rosencrantz and Guildenstern); to reject the pleasure that comes of acting by rule and by rote.

This is not so in Shakespeare's other major tragedies. The darkness of *Macbeth* never occludes a clarity that keeps alive in Macbeth remorse and the knowledge of what he has done. 'Direness may become familiar' to his slaughterous thoughts. But he still calls them 'slaughterous'. There is a residue of clear judgment, as of sheer animal courage that remains with him to the end, and which leaves at

*This article was delivered as a lecture at the Faculty of Literature, Hiroshima University, on 30 April, 1964, to celebrate the fourth centenary of Shakespeare's birth.

the last something of a man, some lineaments of nobility.

Lear and Othello alike, being wrought on, are perplexed in the extreme; but in both these plays, there are standing on either side of the protagonist his good and evil angels, and though the depths of destruction leave him helpless at the end to do more than turn in the direction of the good, yet this he does. Having made the wrong choice, he then, after traversing a great arc of experience, reverses that choice. The dilemma for the spectator in this case is, rather, 'Why should such things be?' But the defeat (which is the triumph) leaves the spectator assured that this mystery is beyond sorrow and joy. In a region of 'calm of mind', all passion is spent. It is not so altogether with *Hamlet*.

Hopkins, the Victorian poet, wrote to his fellow poet Bridges:

> You do not mean by mystery what I mean. A mystery to you is an interesting uncertainty. The uncertainty resolved, the doubt settled, the interest vanishes. To me it is an incomprehensible certainty. But there are, you know, some suspensions so lovely in music, some moves so elegant in chess that the interest remains stronger after the problem is solved. How must it be, then, when the solution of the problem is the most pointed putting of the difficulty and the incompatibility itself the answer in which you are to rest?

Hamlet is a play of this kind.

Hamlet is an existentialist tragedy, a play at once of a great uncertainty, and yet one which affirms the responsibility of man. When I say that *Hamlet* is an existentialist tragedy, I mean of course in a sense in which Jean-Paul Sartre and Albert Camus define it. By way of illustrating how close the contemporary criticism of *Hamlet* may come to the modern idea of an existentialist play I shall quote two modern critics of *Hamlet* and then from Sartre and Camus.

Professor D. G. James in *The Dream of Learning* wrote:

> Shakespeare in *Hamlet* saw uncertainty, ignorance, failure, deceit. I do not say that he saw even in *Hamlet* only these things but that he saw at least these things we cannot deny. Hamlet certainly had no unquestioning faith. He had no philosophy, natural or other, and his problems were hardly to be solved by the use of scientific method or knowledge or experiments as Bacon's were. Shakespeare was using an old, crude and violent story; he was turning it to majestic usage, controlling and mending it as far as he could, to convey the tragedy of a man caught in ethical and metaphysical uncertainties.

And Harry Levin in *The Question of Hamlet* entitles his three sections 'interrogation', 'doubt' and 'irony'. *Hamlet* is one who questions, tests and probes, an intellectual whose first impulse is to jot down his thoughts. Hamlet's thought is primarily in the interrogative mood. The graveyard scene has seventy questions in

Muriel Bradbrook on Shakespeare

three hundred and twenty-two lines. 'Who's there?' opens the play. 'Long live the king!' is the watchword. But we are soon to ask 'Which king?'. Questions of 'What is the ghost?' haunts the play. Polonius, Rosencrantz and Guildenstern test Hamlet with questions. There are doubts of the ghost, of Ophelia's virtue, of Hamlet's intention towards her, of whether to kill the king at prayer, or whether to go on, or to seek suicide. Levin notes that Camus has written: 'Only one philosophical problem is really serious, that is, suicide. And to decide whether or not life is worth living is to answer the most fundamental problem of philosophy.'

Now, for an existentialist's statement of tragedy. Sartre in *Forgers of Myth* (1946) wrote:

> Man is not to be defined as a reasoning animal or as a social one, but as a free being, entirely indeterminate, who must choose his own being when confronted with certain necessities, such as being already committed in a world full of both threatening and favourable factors, among other men who have made their choices before him; who had decided in advance the meaning of those factors. He is faced with the necessity of having to work and die, of being hurled into a life already complete, which is his own enterprise, and in which he can never have a second chance, where he must play his cards and take risks no matter what the cost. A man is free within the circle of his own situations who chooses whether he wishes to or not for everyone else when he chooses for himself.

That is the subject matter of our play.

And this is Camus' description of Sisyphus in *The Myth of Sisyphus*:

> The gods condemned then Sisyphus to ceaselessly rolling a rock to the top of the mountain, when the stone would fall of its own weight. They have thought with some reason that there is no more dreadful punishment than futile and hopeless labour. You have already grasped that Sisyphus is the hero of the absurd. His scorn of the gods, his hatred of death and his passion for life won him that unspeakable penalty in which the whole being is exerted towards the accomplishing nothing. His is the price that must be paid for the passions of the earth. One merely sees the whole effort of a body straining to raise the huge stone, to roll it and push it up a slope a hundred times over. One sees the face screwed up, the cheek tight against the stone, the shoulder bracing the clay-covered mass, the foot wedging it, the fresh start with arms outstretched, the wholly human security of two earthclotted hands. At the very end of this long effort measured by skyless space and time without death, the purpose is achieved. Then Sisyphus watches the stone rush down in a few moments towards that lower world, when he would have to push it up again towards the summit. He goes back down to the plain. It is during that return, that pause, that Sisyphus interests me. A face that toils so close to the stone is already stone itself. That hour, like a breathing space which returns as sure as his suffering;

that is the hour of consciousness. At each of those moments when he leaves the heights and gradually returns towards the lairs of the gods, he is superior to his fate. He is stronger than his rock. The lucidity that was to constitute torture at the same time, crowns his victory. There is no fate that cannot be surmounted by scorn.

This is the ironic mood of Hamlet's soliloquies, especially of 'O that this too too sullied flesh would melt', and is the Sisyphus situation 'To be, or not to be'. Who would fardels bear?

The irony is strongest when divine vengeance overtakes the King at the end of *Hamlet*. The Prince makes the point with the harsh jest:

> Here, thou incestuous, murderous, damned Dane,
> Drink off this potion. Is thy union here?
> Follow my mother.   (V. ii. 317–9)

as well as to Laertes, who acknowledges more piously and devoutly: 'I am justly caught with mine own treachery'. Chance turns into a larger design. Randomness becomes retribution, as Professor Holloway observes. There is very little incertitude possible in a world governed by such mechanisms of dark precision. But Hamlet himself does not win by deep plots. He leaves those to his enemy, except insignificantly in putting on his antic disposition, and in the trap of the play scene; but otherwise his irresolutions serve him well, while the deep plots fail. The significant pattern that emerges is not of his devising. For he does not usurp the role of omnipotence, nor take upon himself the mystery of things as if he was God's spy.

Hamlet is both a scholar and a soldier. He has friends of both sorts, Marcellus and Horatio. Yet he is perhaps the first character in English who betrays the nervous irritability of the artistic temperament. He is vulnerable, a man who can be hurt in new ways, as when his grief is misunderstood. 'Why seems it so particular with thee?' asks the Queen, and he flinches from the word because it betrays such incomprehension of his feeling:

> Seems, madam! Nay, it is; I know not 'seems'.
> 'Tis not alone my inky cloak, good mother,
> Nor customary suits of solemn black,
> Nor windy suspiration of forc'd breath, . . .
> Nor the dejected haviour of the visage,
> Together with all forms, moods, shapes of grief,
> That can denote me truly. These, indeed, seem;
> For they are actions that a man might play.   (I. ii. 76–84)

At once, the old formal tableaux, the display of grief, is before us as in the earlier plays, but only to be rejected in the fluent, vehement sketch of Hamlet's critical revulsion from old, mere shapes of feeling. I thought that the performance of *Hamlet* last night brought out very clearly these changes of mood in Hamlet, and in particular the revulsion from pretence. When Ophelia returns his presents with the pious little platitude, that she must have learnt from Polonius:

> to the noble mind
> Rich gifts wax poor when givers prove unkind,   (III. i. 100–1)

Hamlet responds in instant exasperation against the banality: 'I never gave you aught' as much as in recoil against the memory that he cannot bear to have referred to. He recoils again from the shape of the actor's grief in playing the scene of Hecuba: 'What's Hecuba to him, or he to Hecuba?' He is not a stoic.

It is worth recollecting that the play, of itself, cannot be regarded as a finished composition which was composed by Shakespeare at one burst of easy fluency, to remain unmodified for the ten years after its composition, during which the author still remained an active member of the Chamberlain's Men. The play exists in various states and it seems probable that, like other popular forms of spoken literature, it received additions or deletions on different occasions. Speeches might be inserted, just as Hamlet asks the players to insert his speeches; or on certain occasion, omitted. The position of the soliloquy 'To be or not to be', is quite different in the Quarto and Folio texts. In the first Quarto we have an example of how badly the play could be treated by actors and how little understood. Shakespeare may have revised *Hamlet* just as Goethe spent his whole life revising *Faust*. The fascinating dynamics of *Hamlet*, the possibility of growth, the space for variant interpretations which allows such a wide legitimate scope to actors and producers may be dependent upon this original dynamic in its conception. There could be no final version of *Hamlet*. And, therefore, I think, the version given last night, which was essentially the tragic *Hamlet* with the comic scenes severely pruned and even some of the more witty aspects of Hamlet himself omitted, is a legitimate version. It is not a complete *Hamlet*, but it is a *Hamlet* which is quite legitimate and reasonable to present.

The nineteenth century saw Hamlet as an entirely pure and largely meditative character, and Claudius as entirely wicked. In the twentieth century there have been pictures of Hamlet as an egotistical Machiavelli, as a brutal and violent intruder on a peaceful citizenry. Salvador de Madariaga, L. C. Knights and Derek Traversi depicted him in this way. I have seen Robert Helpman's Hamlet played as a mere boy shattered by his first encounter with the cruelty of things, Sir John Gielgud's royal prince, scolding his mother for her failure to live up to the standard of behaviour suitable to her royal station. I have seen Hamlet in Napoleonic costume, Hamlet in late Victorian costume, and the last students' production I saw at Cambridge, the one before yours, was *Hamlet* played on a grassy bank beside a stream with a real willow tree, in a warm summer night in June; with the famous actors, Sir Lewis Casson and Dame Sybil Thorndike watching their young granddaughter playing Gertrude. So that many different Hamlets can mean different things. Yet there is a measure of continuity within these protean forms which I cannot better define than by the term with which I began, negative capability, that is, when a man is capable of being in uncertainties, mysteries, doubts without any irritable reaching after fact or reason.

What chiefly remains from the older drama in this Shakespearean version seems to me to be the figure of the Ghost. The Ghost offers Hamlet a traditional role, that of the revenger, but Hamlet is not to be confined within any simple presumption. Yes, Hamlet is a man who has seen a ghost and it is round the Ghost that the natural imagery of this play develops – and round that skull of Yorick which, in the graveyard scene, replaces it as the form of the dead. The Ghost of his father will speak only to Hamlet. The Queen thinks it, what Horatio called it at first, an illusion. Even to Hamlet it is but *like* the King that is dead. It is in fact the first character we meet, and deeply mysterious, bringing both airs from heaven and blasts from hell. The Ghost comes to tell the secrets of his prison-house, from which he has escaped to the chill glimpses of the wintry moon, beside the glittering waves of the sound where the great fortress palace stands with all its miles of cellarage, its underground fortifications. To Hamlet, the Ghost presents this image of imprisonment.

Hamlet, his own flesh and blood, learns how flesh betrayed the old King. The heavy stalk of the Ghost, the plated armour he wears, his telling monosyllabic greetings: 'List, list, O, list!', 'Mark me', 'Remember', accompany the issuing of an archaic but absolute command, 'Vengeance'. It is a compulsion, it is a *must*, laid on Hamlet by an archaic part of himself, a part which has been disturbed and reactivated by his mother's marriage following hard upon his father's death. These two shocking events, coming so close together, have roused up this commanding spectral figure with its ghostly truncheon and its final command, 'Swear, Swear, Swear' (which you left out, I noticed, last night). The compelling power of that part of ourselves, which we do not understand, can appear only in such images. Returning to daylight, Hamlet no longer feels sure what it is that has quenched for him the golden fire that adorns the firmament, covering it with vapours, and sterilized the earth to rocky barrenness. The prison of his own solid flesh, within which the prince (even at the beginning of the play) has felt depressed, is further darkened by this encounter. The whole world has become a prison for him. Yet he tells his companion: 'O God, I could be bounded in a nutshell and count myself a king of infinite space, were it not that I have bad dreams' (II. ii. 254–5). So he half acknowledges his own mood to be illusion, 'It goes so heavily with my disposition'. And it is because he knows he does not know, because at the centre of the play there are questions, doubts, disturbances, that Hamlet's part is everyman's. The unfocused, unacknowledged grief, 'the pang without a name, void, dark and drear', is common to all; and because there is a void at the centre of Hamlet the man, and the Ghost is at the centre of *Hamlet* the play, there is room enough for a whole multiplicity of Hamlets. He can be interpreted to suit all thoughts and conditions of man.

The motionless heaps that litter the stage at the end of *Hamlet* are but untenanted clay, which will be shovelled in rapidly to join Yorick, Ophelia and Polonius. Hamlet had thrice held discourse with the dead in his lifetime; once on the battlements, once in his mother's bedchamber and once, sardonically, and playfully, with the skull of Yorick; which he holds in his hand like a fool's bauble or a ventriloquist's doll, coaxing the chap-fallen jaw to utterance, putting a tongue in its mouth and sending it back to the bedchamber to speak to Gertrude the message she will not hear, that she must rejoin the Ghost one day. 'Go, get thee to my lady's chamber, tell her, let her paint an inch thick, to this favour must she come; make her laugh at that' (V. i. 187–9).

The relation of the characters with each other in this play extends not only to husbands and wives, parents and children, but to living and dead. And the relation of the living to the dead can be achieved only through that process which we call mourning. The ability to mourn is one which an eminent psychiatrist, Carl Rogers, of Chicago, has described as one of the leading characteristics of emotional maturity. And I shall conclude this account of *Hamlet*'s psychodynamics by considering it as study in mourning. I have done this in collaboration with a psychiatrist, a friend of my own, who works in London on clinical psychiatry.

According to my friend, Dr Heard, the process of mourning normally follows a fourfold development. In the first phase of shock or disaster, the mourner will not feel anything, but may be deeply numbed and almost paralysed. The second characteristic phase is anger or resentment, sometimes irrationally directed against the dead for having deserted the mourner. The third phase is one of restitution, the mourner tries to replace the dead or reincorporate them as if they were still alive. The last stage is the acceptance of loss and recovered stability.

In his first soliloquy Hamlet is still undergoing the first phase. 'O, that this too too solid flesh would melt!' This passes into the second. Grief for his father is converted into rage against his mother, the unworthy remaining half of what had been to him an inseparable image of authority and love. The Queen's failure to share his mourning is Hamlet's prime distress. The third stage of mourning (when in phantasy or imagination the dead is restored to life, preferably as a part of oneself), which the psychologist calls 'introjection', occurs between Hamlet's departure to England and his return. When he found the document that ordered his execution, he acted promptly and royally, writing an order in the royal style and sealing it with the royal signet of his father. He despatches his traitorous companions as coolly as Henry V despatches his traitorous followers at the opening of *Henry V*. And he announces his return by adopting the royal title; 'This is I, Hamlet, *the Dane*;' that is, the *King* of Denmark. Moreover, in the graveyard scene there emerges for the first time, and quite unrepressed, Hamlet's physical revulsion at the physical fact of death, as he faces it in his dialogue with the skull of Yorick. The corpse he mourns is still like his father, though there are fleeting recollections of Polonius, a politician, and Rosencrantz and Guildenstern, the flatterers that 'praise such a lord's horse when he meant to beg it'. Finally, the image of the great Alexander himself, a form of his father's military figure: 'Dost thou think Alexander look'd o' this fashion i'th'earth?' 'Even so', says Horatio. 'And smelt so? Pah!' (V. i. 192–4). The loathing that comes out here is transferred from Hamlet's original loathing, but it is much more natural and immediate. When he learns that the unsullied flesh of Ophelia is to be laid in the grave new-made, he breaks out in a passionate grief that transforms itself immediately to a passion of anger against Laertes, the two feelings appearing almost simultaneously (this, of course, because in his speech Laertes has very obviously reproached Hamlet as the cause of Ophelia's madness).

At the end Hamlet appears calm, resolute and prepared to meet death.

> If it be now, 'tis not to come – if it be not to come, it will be now, if it be not now, yet it will come – the readiness is all. Since no man owes of aught he leaves, what is't to leave betimes? Let be. (V. ii. 213–6)

And so he is content to rest in the absence of knowledge, content to accept the uncertainty of his too-likely end. And there are no thoughts of anything dark or uncertain after death, which to the dying Hamlet represents felicity ('Absent thee from felicity awhile'). By what pain and through what havoc this calm has been achieved and how much is left for the mutes and audience to this act to piece out with their thoughts! For here, as a later poet (almost in Hamlet's last phrase) has said, is where 'Words, after speech, reach into the silence'.

X

The balance and the sword in
Measure for Measure

Measure for Measure, performed at court before the king on St Stephen's night (26 December) 1604, marked the end of a climactic year for Shakespeare and his company. On 15 March, as the King's Men, they had marched in their royal livery from the Tower to Westminster, in coronation procession that took from eleven o'clock till five. Less than a month later on 9 April their theatre opened after a long closure for plague; during the whole of August with nine others, Shakespeare had been deputed to wait on the Spanish Ambassador, Don Juan Fernandez de Velasco, Constable of Castile; for peace with the old enemy, Spain, was sworn that month. They would savour thus a first taste of Spanish punctilio, and the religious household of a Spanish grandee, for none had been seen in England since the Armada years; the Constable brought a train of two hundred followers (see below, p. 168).

The company staged a courtly satire, starring a disguised duke which had been played by boys of the Chapel; entitled *The Malcontent*, it was the work of a young lawyer, John Marston. Three editions appeared in 1604.

Shakespeare's personal life had its difficulties; nine years later, a legal case in the Court of Requests showed that he lodged with a French family, near the royal court of justice at the Old Bailey. He was acting as go-between for the marriage of the daughter of this house, Marie Mountjoy, to a former apprentice; perhaps he knew that her mother was having an illicit love affair with a neighbouring tradesman. Possibly his younger brother Edmund lodged with him; for three years later in the neighbouring parish of St Giles, the burial of an illegitimate child fathered it on Edmund. In his country home at Stratford, his eldest daughter was undergoing some kind of religious crisis; for soon she was cited in the ecclesiastical court for staying away from Easter Communion.

So girls' dowries and girls' problems were on his mind, just as his company asked for a comedy; he threw together his memories of an old play, *Promos and Cassandra*, bits from his own earlier comedies, *All's Well that Ends Well* and *Much Ado About Nothing*, added a song of great beauty and pathos (he was also engaged on a tragedy in which a striking feature was to be 'the willow song'); then his imagination fired, and he found himself writing things that resembled passages from those very private poems, his Sonnets, which he never intended the world to hear.

* * *

The play itself was full of surprises. The man who proves not a judge but a blackmailer is given his infamous payment by his own betrothed in disguise; the executed criminal is not the young sinner Claudio, nor the old sinner Barnardine; the unknown Friar charged with conspiracy turns out to be the Duke; the judge then stands in the prisoner's place; the judge is being married, but sentenced also to death. The essence, as in a modern detective story, is surprise and speed. As the absent ruler returns to his city, praising his deputy, and promising new honours, Isabella raises her cry:

> Give me justice, justice, justice!   (V. i. 5)

The outward conduct of the Duke betrays the most elementary principle of justice, for he appoints Angelo, the accused man, judge in his own cause. Every law student who had crossed by Temple Stairs to the Globe Theatre would know that a judge or advocate is forbidden by oath to take any case in which he has the slightest personal interest; this is one of the principles of natural justice. And in disguise as the Friar, the Duke returns to accuse himself:

> The Duke's unjust
> Thus to retort your manifest appeal,
> And put your trial in the villain's mouth
> Which here you come to accuse.   (V. i. 293–301)

In Ben Jonson's *Sejanus*, which his company had staged, the same plea had rung out in the trial scene of Silius

> Is he my accuser,
> And must he be my judge?   (III. i. 199–200)

Shakespeare's London had seen Francis Bacon leading the prosecution against his former patron, the Earl of Essex, in 1601; it had also seen that very year, Essex's fellow prisoner, and Shakespeare's patron, Southanpton, released from the Tower where for two years he had lain under sentence of death. The deserved sentence was lifted, by the mercy of the new ruler, upon one whose dissolute youth had been a subject of lament in the sonnets. If some shadow of the Earl of Southampton's reprieve lies behind that of Claudio, this would of course have been a private matter for the playwright himself, for the 'justice' of *Measure for Measure* is not at all that of the law – of Astraea, the heavenly goddess with the balance and the sword, emblems of equity and of retribution. The Duke does not cease to judge his own cause; for when Lucio, the rake, is sentenced to marry Mistress Kate Keepdown, whose child he has fathered, rather than sentenced to death, he protests 'Marrying a punk, my lord, is pressing to death, whipping and hanging' – only to receive the retort from his former victim

> Slandering a prince deserves it.   (V.i.522)

This ducal forerunner of Gilbert's farcical Mikado is determined to make the punishment fit the crime in his own way, but he becomes ever more Gilbertian and even less like a judge in bestowing the last award – to Isabella. It is the solution of *Trial By Jury*, Gilbert's first farce

> Barristers, and you, attorneys,
> Set out on your homeward journeys;
> Gentle, simple-minded Usher,
> Get you, if you like to Russia;
> Put your briefs upon the shelf,
> I will marry her myself!

Something like this farcical note (though not for the marriage) is supplied by Lucio, especially in the last scene. This autocrat, in disguise, had promised Isabella

> Grace of the Duke, revenges to your heart,
> And general honour.   (IV.iii.132–3)

He is now speaking as the fount of justice, the fount of honour, and (though he is in a Catholic country) the head of the church. It is only if the roles are confused that farce results.

   A code of shame and honour, more efficacious and self-enforced than a code of crime and punishment, belongs particularly to sexual offences, and to slander. Claudio was paraded through the streets (this form of penance is found elsewhere in Shakespeare[1]) whereas the Duke had himself foreborne in person to press the laws he had left in abeyance lest this should bring slander upon him – as it does, though not in the way he had anticipated. He gave Angelo full scope

> So to enforce or qualify the laws
> As to your soul seems good . . .   (I.i.66–7)

which is to abrogate all statutory law in favour of equity. (It was in fact decreed under James that if law and equity were in conflict, equity should prevail.)

Angelo's open shaming is the object of the judgment scene. It is so complete that he does not wish to live; his pride, his very identity had been removed.

The repentant Juliet was prepared to 'take her shame with joy' (II.iii.30–36) and whilst the Friar told her her sin was the heavier, the Duke tells Claudio

> She that you wrong'd, look you restore.   (V. i. 123)

Confusion between ecclesiastical and civil law was nowhere stronger than in the matter of marriage and sexual offences. There has been much discussion about the validity of precontracts, such as Claudio and Angelo both admit, though the one was private and the other public; in such matters custom ruled, though the church had revised its canon law.

Whilst much of the law was ecclesiastical, the matter of dowries was of course within the civil law. Most noble marriages were regarded less as contracts between individuals than as the means of joining alliances, as part of a family power structure or an ambitious man's plan to rise. Thus, in 1601 John Donne had been thrown into prison for stealing a marriage with the niece of the Lord Keeper, his employer; and so had the priest who performed the ceremony.

The dowry of Juliet was the object of Claudio's concealment of the contract, whilst the forcible marriage of Angelo and Mariana was ordered with the object of giving her a dowry to wed a better husband – an idea taken over from the old play. In the earlier versions, of course, there was but the one feminine character, the sister (or in earliest forms the wife) of the condemned man, who really was killed.

By the magical double substitution of Mariana for Isabella and Ragozine for Claudio, Angelo's criminal intent is nullified; in her plea for mercy, Isabella eventually enters this fact, with the alternative pleas in the case of blackmail, a first offender; in the case of the judicial murder, that under the letter of the law, the penalty might be enforced.

The ruler's exercise of spiritual authority is as outrageous as his legal decisions. To assume a holy habit, and power of absolving sins which he did not possess, to hear confession (V. i. 524) and to betray secrets of the confessional given to himself (III. i. 165) and to others (IV. iii. 127) is so monstrous that a Spanish censor has simply cut the whole play out of the Folio in a copy at Valladolid.

Of course the Friar has been seen as a divine figure by some scholars – by others as a monster. Yet again he has been seen as a

surrogate for King James, but this view has been vigorously
rebutted.[2]

Whilst earlier humanist definitions of the Prince or Governor
required him to practise the four cardinal virtues of fortitude,
temperance, prudence and justice, the last was most essential.
Clemency was also a great virtue in a prince but Machiavelli thought
it better for a prince to be feared than loved, if he could not inspire
both feelings; he also thought that offenders should either receive a
free pardon or execution for crime against the state; and the Duke
seems disinclined for anything resembling a middle way. He 'dresses'
Angelo in his own love and lends him his terror; both attributes are
given at the end of *Henry VIII* to the future Queen Elizabeth. 'She
shall be lov'd and fear'd' for 'Peace, plenty, love, truth, terror' wait
upon her (V. v. 48). The short rhymed verses in which the ruler
defines his double office at the end of Act III, where the action veers
towards comedy, resemble those used for the god Jupiter in *Cymbeline*; both may represent some aural memory from Shakespeare's
youth of the octosyllabics used in the old craft mysteries for the
speeches of divinity.

> He who the sword of heaven would bear
> Should be as holy as severe;
> Pattern in himself to know,
> Grace to stand; and virtue, go . . .   (III. i. 254–7)

With such a standard the earthly ruler is almost inhibited from
action. Angelo takes a different and a more legalistic view: his office
is not holy.

> I not deny
> The jury, passing on the prisoner's life,
> May in the sworn twelve have a thief or two
> Guiltier than him they try   (II. i. 18–21)

but he adds 'what open lies to justice, justice seizes' adding

> When I, that censure him, do so offend,
> Let mine own judgment pattern out my death,
> And nothing come in partial.   (II. i. 29–31)

Later he declares to Isabella that strict enforcement of the law is
mercy –

> I show it most of all when I show justice;
> For then I pity those I do not know,
> Which a dismiss'd offence would after gall . . . (II. ii. 101–3)

In his disguise as a Friar, the Duke makes this point again at the end
of the play

> Laws for all faults,
> But faults so countenanc'd that the strong statutes
> Stand like the forfeits in a barber's shop.
> As much in mock as mark.   (V. 1. 317–20)

which Escalus immediately pounces on as 'slander to the state'.

But the state in this play appears to mean the Duke, or his deputy; he has no council, only friends and followers. In comedy the ruler is often in this position, and acts quite arbitrarily (as do the Dukes in *As You Like It* and *Twelfth Night* and the French King in *All's Well That Ends Well*). In some comedies, where a judgment often concludes the play, the judge is himself absurd, the most ludicrous being the Governor in Chapman's bitter comedy *The Widow's Tears*. In particular the most disgraceful sins of prodigal young men were apt to be overlooked – as Heywood's *If you Know not me you know Nobody*, Dekker's *The Honest Whore* or the anonymous play, *The London Prodigal*, performed by Shakespeare's company this very year, and on the title page attributed to him!

It is the *mercy* of the law according to the Duke that decrees the law should be enforced against Angelo as it had been against Claudio:

> The very mercy of the law cries out
> Most audible, even from his proper tongue
> 'An Angelo for Claudio, death for death'.
> Haste still pays haste and leisure answers leisure;
> Like doth quit like, and measure still for measure.   (V. i. 405–9)

The trite form in which it is stated reduces this proverbial wisdom to triviality. It also however recalls the verse from St Matthew's gospel which points to the difference between judgment as the Duke finally sees it and as Angelo sees it.

> Judge not, that ye be not judged. For with what judgment ye judge ye shall be judged; and what measure ye mete, it shall be measured to you again. And why beholdest thou the mote that is in thy brother's eye but considerest not the beam that is in thine own eye. (7. 1–3)

It is not the business of the individual to sit in judgment, except upon himself. The subjective aspect of judgment is put lightly by Orlando against the ready condemnations of Jacques: 'I will chide no breather in the world but myself, against whom I know most faults' (*As You Like It*, III. ii. 262–4). Isabella seems to envisage the judgment of souls, when they are weighed in the scales of heaven, as she warns Angelo:

> We cannot weigh our brother with ourself   (II. i. 126)[3]

and it is not herself she is putting into the scales when she later decides against the monstrous ransom – 'More than our brother is our chastity' (II. iv. 184). For, as another woman had pleaded 'My chastity's the jewel of our house' (*All's Well That Ends Well*, IV. ii. 46) and since Isabella is later prepared publicly to confess to an unchastity she did not incur, it is not her public reputation that deters her; nor, considering the situation of Claudio and Juliet, is it merely the life of her brother and herself that is involved, but a possible innocent:

> I had rather my brother die by the law than my son should be unlawfully born. (III. i. 187–8)

she tells the Friar. Angelo himself feared the revenge of Claudio for dishonour done to his house, while trusting that a woman's fear of shame (IV. iv. 21–3) would prevent any disclosure by Isabella.

Isabella's relations with Angelo and with Claudio provide the emotional conflagration of the play, its active heart. The most powerful tie is the stable one of brother and sister. In *The Family, Sex and Marriage in England, 1500–1700*, Lawrence Stone has observed that the fraternal relation of brother and sister was often the most disinterested and strongest of all family ties.[4] As the eldest son inherited an estate, the younger brothers were usually at odds with him, and he, very often with his parents, who used their children as bargaining counters in the struggle for power; but brothers and sisters were not rivals in the power structure and such famous examples as the Countess of Pembroke and Sir Philip Sidney, Penelope Rich and the Earl of Essex, the Princess Elizabeth and Henry, Prince of Wales had an important effect on public life. At his trial for rebellion, Essex pleaded that he had been under Penelope's influence, while she asserted she had been more like a slave than a sister. When the Prince of Wales lay dying, he was to call repeatedly for his sister who, when kept from him for fear of infection, tried to make her way in disguise. Shakespeare had developed this relation both in Viola and Sebastian and in Ophelia and Laertes.

When Isabella hears her brother at first willing to face death

> If I must die,
> I will encounter darkness as a bride
> And hug it in mine arms. (III. i. 84–6)

she recognizes a voice of their kinship, a voice from their father's grave; for she herself had used the very same metaphor in rebutting the suggestion of Angelo

> Were I under the terms of death,
> Th'impression of keen whips I'd wear as rubies,

> And strip myself to death as to a bed
> That longing have been sick for, ere I'd yield
> My body up to shame . . .   (II. iv. 100–4)

This is the familiar image of the martyrdom as a bridal, and Isabella's simile might be paralleled from Southwell or other devotionalists; but the sexual image has another context in the mind of Angelo.[5] The bleeding wretches laid upon hurdles, and drawn through the streets of London to their deaths, had been trained to imagine this as a glorious consummation. Claudio's mortuary preparation by the Friar with just such a religious exhortation – 'Be absolute for death' – only makes him more vulnerable when put to the test. Isabella, as has been seen, does not avoid the violent phrase, and she asks her brother

> Is't not a kind of incest, to take life
> From thine own sister's shame?   (III. i. 140–1)

Next, she is tempted to think him not her brother but a bastard. It is the same woman who on hearing of Angelo's final order for her brother's execution, which she believes to be carried out, cries 'O, I will to him and pluck out his eyes!' (IV. iii. 116). It is *this* woman who kneels as advocate for Angelo's defence.[6]

The retribution was to be exacted in a later play; another bastard was to hear in *King Lear* (given two years later, St Stephen's day 1606 at court)

> The gods are just, and of our pleasant vices
> Make instruments to plague us:
> That dark and vicious place where thee he got
> Cost him his eyes.   (V. iii. 170–3)

* * *

The purpose of all the reversals and surprises here is to turn the sight inward upon the self. When the Duke, who 'above all other strifes, contended especially to know himself' (III. ii. 219–20) decided as Friar that 'craft against vice I must apply' it is to meet falsehood with falsehood. Isabella is very reluctant to speak falsehood at the seat of justice:

> To speak so indirectly I am loath;
> I would say the truth;   (IV. vi. 1–2)

whilst the Duke's use of 'very mercy' is far from verity – for Claudio, as he well knows, is not dead. The word 'very' is thoroughly mocked in the comic attempt to find out what was done to Elbow's wife – where it occurs fifty-seven times; truth is trivialized, but the extreme difficulty and uncertainty that attends a quest for truth in this sense is at least fully attested.

Truth lives within, and it is the Duke's purpose to turn Angelo's eyes within. Angelo has to learn the full lesson set by Isabella

> Go to your bosom,
> Knock there and ask your heart what it doth know
> That's like my brother's fault.   (II. ii. 136–8)

These words achieve the opposite of their immediate purpose for they give Angelo the first prompting that something 'like my brother's fault' is indeed lodged within Angelo's heart. The well-trained young novice is applying the Lord's injunction 'Let him that is without sin cast the first stone' (John, 8. 7) as well as that prayer which is so often echoed by Shakespeare, as a personal utterance, in the last lines of Sonnet 120, in the last lines of the epilogue to *The Tempest*, 'Forgive us our sins as we forgive those that sin against us'. A mutuality of forgiveness means Desdemona forgiving her death, taking it upon herself, or Antony's generosity to the treacherous Enobarbus; such generosity is found again and again in the Sonnets

> Take all my loves, my love; yea, take them all   (Sonnet 40)
> For thy right, myself will bear all wrong   (Sonnet 88)

and finally in Prospero

> they being penitent,
> The sole drift of my purpose doth extend
> Not a frown further.   (V. i. 28–30)

The blunted sword, or sword of mercy, which in Spenser lay at the feet of Mercilla belongs to the world of external justice; the relationship in the Sonnets makes use only with playfulness of legal terms, and the aim of the Duke is rather regeneration or recreation.[7] The world reflects back upon each individual the image with which he confronts it; this psychological truism suggests that Angelo's neglect and contempt for a sexual object once attained is very easily converted to self-hatred when he is exposed. It is again a mood reflected in the sonnets (Sonnet 129).

The purpose of a play being to touch each individual member of the audience, the fantastic events of a comedy do not have the context of a public world. Yet here, Mistress Overdone, Elbow and Pompey are familiar figures from London comedy, while Lucio, who at the beginning of the play organizes what action there is, becomes as it were another deputy for the Duke; first giving his own character to the absent ruler, then fathering his own aspersions upon the Duke himself, in his role of Friar. The symbiosis between these two, almost as close as that between King Lear and his fool, permits Lucio an intolerable series of interruptions in the final scene, which are like subversive Freudian comments upon the justice being meted out.

Claudio's shopsoiled Mercutio, a figure out of John Donne's satires of London life, Lucio is dismissed to prison when the blind and obdurate Barnardine is given into the custody of a friar for spiritual education.

Justice being left with her balance, but not her sword, the Duke finally offers a share of his power to Isabella. This is not a wooing, but a species of coronation; perhaps as Angelo might be physically stripped of the insignia of a judge and of a noble (he is the Duke's cousin, apparently his next of kin), so perhaps Isabel should receive the coronet or the sceptre that honours Truth. In this final scene a surprising number of characters are mute; Angelo says nothing at his reprieve, Claudio and Juliet, Isabel and Barnardine, receive their awards as part of that whole interior exploration of the larger self, the little realm of man, which each spectator, in the depths of his own being, would register, when the mendicant Friar, the Beggar, becomes arbiter sovereign.

The alternative roles of Friar and Duke do not create a character in depth; they are rather like the alternative aspects of the monarch which are by now familiar from the cult of Queen Elizabeth.[8] Hence this play has become a subject of prolonged critical debate; which was perhaps Shakespeare's intention, for to win an audience to debate is to involve them, and here the young lawyers who formed the most intelligent part of his audience would find as much material for argument as the legally minded Scottish king.

The double action, inward and outward, in this play, would be seen by Shakespeare's contemporaries as working like the Ptolemaic spheres, enclosed within each other, moving in contrary directions. The outer world reflects back upon man that aspect with which he confronts it, so that measure for measure is the law of relations between man and man, but the retributive powers of the world are complemented by diabolic or angelic impulses from within the heart of each man, so that Isabella calls out lust unknown to himself in Angelo, the Duke by apparently satisfying his desire calls out an impulse to murder. Mariana, whose earthly hopes had been destroyed by her brother's death, calls out in Isabella an impulse of compassion, which expresses itself in hard and legalistic terms. Thus the two spheres join in her final plea.

Notes

1 In 2 *Henry VI*, II. iv. the Duchess of Gloucester does open penance in a white sheet in the London streets. This form of shaming was still observed, and in 1616 Shakespeare's son-in-law Thomas Quiney was so

condemned for getting an illegitimate child, by the Ecclesiastical Court at Stratford; a penance subsequently commuted.

2 See Richard Levin 'The King James version of *Measure for Measure*', *New Readings versus Old Plays* (Chicago, University of Chicago Press, 1979).

3 Cf. III.ii.258–9, V. i. 113–5 for other uses.

4 (London, Weidenfeld & Nicolson, 1977), p. 115.

5 Cf. Peter Milward, *Shakespeare's Religious Background* (London, Sidgwick & Jackson, 1973), pp. 58, 78; and Harriett Hawkins in *Shakespeare Survey*, 31 (1978), 105–13.

6 One of the titles of the Virgin Mary is the Advocate for Souls.

7 Cf. Isabella's plea, II. ii. 77–9.

8 See Frances A. Yates, *Astraea* (London, Routledge & Kegan Paul, 1973), Part II. The two halves of the disguised ruler in *The Malcontent* similarly do not cohere to make a naturalist character: they are rather alternative approaches to the world of courtly vice and depravity.

XI

Othello, Webster and the tragedy of violence*

Eloquent and spectacular, *Othello* is now the least discussed of Shakespeare's major tragedies, yet in his own day it was the most innovatory. It is more than half a century since the hero was condemned by T. S. Eliot; I don't believe that today anyone would imagine that in his last speech Othello is 'cheering himself up' – a remark that from the future author of *Sweeney Agonistes* and *The Family Reunion* tends to rebound against him. Leavis intensified the charge to 'brutal egoism'; Auden thought Iago more interesting than Othello. Certainly today he inevitably becomes the centre of dramatic interest. Othello as a role defeated Garrick; some think he defeated Olivier; and today on stage the helpful plainspeaker who turns out to be a killer by remote control calls out a response that mere wife murder cannot evoke in those who have supped full with the horrors of the large and small screens. He is brainwashing.

Yet Rymer, in the first attack on this play, hardly mentions Iago, and Leavis considers him but a plot device. The attempts at intervention from the audience have usually been directed to Othello, either to enlighten him ('You great black fool, can't you see?') or the Russian justification 'He wasn't to blame. A love like that could burn up a City'. Shakespeare has built both these responses into the final scene; the first is Emilia's, the second Cassio's.

Desdemona's piteous look as she lay at his mercy was noted for its great effect by an Oxford spectator as early as 1610; Samuel Pepys recorded gratification when a pretty lady sitting next to him 'cried out' as Desdemona was murdered. In his *Lettres Philosophiques* Voltaire cited the scene as the greatest of Shakespeare's barbarisms; in 1822 in Paris the curtain had to be rung down, and Talma was forced to supply a happy ending.

*The Folger Shakespeare Library's annual Shakespeare birthday lecture, 1981.

This scene has always been a favourite with painters, for its purely spectacular appeal is both to tenderness and violence and the picture therefore 'vibrates' naturally. 'The grieved Moor' was a contemporary tribute to Burbage's acting; 'Nay, lay thee down and roar' is Emilia's comment. Othello uses no weapon but his own hands to destroy Desdemona. Pity or sympathy is also essentially a tactile impulse, a movement to touch; pity or sympathy was what Desdemona evoked very strongly in the first audience. In contrasting the violence of wife murder with the atrocities of modern films I have blurred an important distinction. Violence implies the rupture of an existing relationship, with one partner seeking the absolute domination of the other. Perhaps to annihilation. Thus the violence involved in law enforcement represents the absolute domination of the general will upon the transgressor; such violence is authorized, again even to annihilation. War, a second form of legalized violence, represents for Othello the tranquil mind, it represents content.

An atrocity is a gratuitously criminal act between two without previous relationships; it is strictly a meaningless act. Iago may be committing violence on some opponents; but he appears incapable of relating to anyone reciprocally and therefore atrocious. To Othello's 'Why . . .?' no answer is given. Othello, in assuming the role of judge first on Desdemona, and then on himself, combines also the roles of prosecutor, executioner and finally victim. Yet paradoxically he pleads not guilty too: 'an honourable murderer, if you will'.

For violence in art, an equal combination of savagery and tenderness is therefore needed; without tenderness the situation is not tragic. The act of violence then becomes an act of self-violence also, since part of the self was denied. In Heywood's *Woman Killed with Kindness* which appeared in the same season as *Othello*, 1604, the pious husband severs relations with his guilty wife utterly, telling her she is the murderer of the relation between them:

> It was thy hand cut two hearts out of one.

Desdemona is the first to use the term – 'my downright violence and storm of fortunes' she tells the Senate, in marrying Othello has cut her off from the life she had known, to share that of 'an extravagant and wheeling stranger/Of here and everywhere' (I. i. 137–8). She wants to plunge into the sort of Marco Polo wanderings he had recounted; to share dangers; 'she wished that Heaven had made her such a man' as Othello. He has opened a new world to her, as she created one for him. When he thinks her false, Othello's occupation's gone, chaos is come again, heaven mocks itself; in his mind her death effects a huge eclipse in the cosmos.

As they land together in Cyprus, first stage of the wandering, he reaches an inner harbour of the spirit;

> If twere now to die,
> 'Twere now to be to be most happy; for I fear
> My soul hath her content so absolute
> That not another comfort like to this
> Succeeds in unknown fate.   (II. i. 187–91)

At the end of an agonizing interior journey, he finds himself in another harbour: and anchors upon the marriage bed.

> Here is my journey's end, here is my butt,
> And very seamark of my utmost sail . . .
> Where should Othello go?   (V. ii. 270–1, 274)

Recent studies have stressed Othello's insecurity, from B. McElroy, *Shakespeare's Mature Tragedies* (Princeton, 1973) to Jane Adamson (*Othello as Tragedy, a study in Judgment and Feeling* (Cambridge, 1980), who decides that in this play everyone misjudges everyone else because in defence of their own precarious identity they are so impelled; it is less painful for Othello to believe the worst than in his basic insecurity to tolerate a state of doubt. 'Away at once with love or jealousy!' Miss Adamson's own psychological and permissive approach makes her try 'to govern our loathing for Iago' (p. 202) and to place Bianca as only another woman. Her version is not related to performance, but well designed for those in analysis; blood is replaced by trauma; there are no spectators to cry out.

In attempting to present the kind of Othello that Heywood might have perceived, a Jacobean Othello, some paradoxes are encountered. The only tragedy by Shakespeare set in roughly contemporary times, it is also the only one in which he went straight to an exotic foreign tongue, the Italian of Cinthio. It deals with a limited domestic subject (tragedy being traditionally about the fate of kingdoms and the fall of princes), yet links this with the order of society and of the cosmos, in the manner that in his great marriage hymns Spenser had involved the eternal powers in two London marriages. Shakespeare had displayed this at the end of *As You Like It* when he brought in Hymen, 'God of every town'.[1] The sacramental theory of marriage, which St Paul terms *enosis* or unification – 'they shall become one flesh' – has joined the young Venetian noblewoman so completely to the mature black stranger that when asked on her deathbed 'O, who hath done this deed' she can reply quite truthfully 'No body, I myself'. She will not allow Othello to cut two hearts out of one. It is he who sees himself as separated and calls her a liar.

A few Blackamoors could be found in the City of London as in any great port,[2] but Shakespeare may have first met them as he was working on the play, when in August 1604 he was commanded with his fellow actors by his new master, King James, to attend on the Spanish Ambassador, the Constable of Castille. Two hundred followers, including perhaps some Moors and negroes, were in the train, the first Spanish embassy to be seen since 1588. He might even have learnt something of Spanish drama and the code of honour that sustained its violence.

In 'A Hispanist looks at *Othello*',[3] Edward Meryon Wilson pointed out that the Spanish code demanded death for any woman who by adultery contaminated the purity of noble blood. As a public duty a noble *must* so punish any of his female kin who offended, for the whole family were polluted by her unchastity. It is a stockbreeder's view of family life, an archaic and familial conception (with perhaps a dash of Muslim male dominance) incompatible with the British rule of law.

However, a Spanish lady who denied adultery must be given a careful hearing. Calderón's *El medico de su honra*, where an innocent woman was bled to death, convicts the husband of rashness but not of murder. Othello who claims that 'Naught did I in hate but all in honour' had been pitied by Ludovico as 'this rash and most unfortunate man' (V. ii. 298, 286).

He had never brought a rational accusation against Desdemona, for he breaks out not into accusations but laments and curses; she, while denying with oaths the charges she is so slow to conceive, does not press her demands for evidence till too late. She knows obscurely that he will probably kill her, yet she will not abandon that image of him that unconditionally she carries with her. She knows 'his unkindness may defeat my life' and although she protests against the injustice of her death ('O falsely falsely murdered') her last words are 'Commend me to my kind lord'. To this second trial (Cassio's having been the first) the Governor of Cyprus had brought the sword but not the scales of justice, and in two lines Emilia can destroy his case.

> O thou dull Moor! That handkerchief thou speak'st of
> I found by fortune and did give my husband.   (V. ii. 228–9)

Emilia's death bears witness that the 'universe of two' – the new freedom of hazardous choice, dangerous service and committed union made by Desdemona – won at least one convert. Emilia's death is of prime significance as validating this violent and catastrophic choice. An impulse of trust in the faithful service of her woman links this intimate tragedy once again to the larger world. By contrast the faithful servant in *A Woman Killed with Kindness*, Nicholas, who senses the collective wrong, the offence to the whole household, in the guilt of his mistress, refuses to do more than weep at the catastrophe, 'I'll weep, but by my faith not die'. Here the wronged husband having actually taken his wife and her lover abed, by Christian restraint drives the man away 'to the devil' and converts his wife to a state of contrition that constitutes a slow suicide.

The early Venetian scenes of *Othello*, which as has been observed, develop in the manner of a comedy,[4] present Othello facing someone very like the lord mayor in his capacity as chief magistrate. For Shakespeare Venice was not one of the interchangeable Italian cities like Verona, Padua, Milan or Mantua; the great international sea-port presented to him as to others a particular, enlarged image of London itself (as he had already shewn it in *The Merchant of Venice*). If in one perspective, London was Troynovant, in modern terms, like Venice, it was 'seated between the old world and the new'. Every year the republic of Venice was wedded to the sea by the Doge casting a gold ring into the Adriatic. Webster was later to recall this in the opening words of a Lord Mayor's Triumphal Entry: Thetis addresses Oceanus

> What strange sea music bids us welcome, hark!
> Sure this is Venice and the day St Mark,
> In which the Doge and Senate their course hold
> To wed our Empire with a ring of gold.
>
> *(Monuments of Honour*, 1–4)

The mayoral triumph was sometimes headed by a king of the Moors scattering fireworks or flourishing a great sword to keep back the crowd, a figure both of splendour and some terror. He was followed by the pageant or float that always led the procession – a beautiful girl, richly clad and decked with gems which she was permitted to keep against her wedding day. The Mercers' maid, 'device' of the Senior Company of the Livery, borne aloft by the bachelors of that company, doubtless represented a more exalted Virgin from an earlier age. Her image must have sunk deep in the popular mind.

Another pageant, the ship, sometimes scattered spices, or brought wine or (if the Lord Mayor were of the Fishmongers') live fish as gifts to the crowd. At the end of *The Merchant of Venice* the ships, described as 'the portly burghers of the Flood' have been replaced by Portia, entering once more in farthingale like a stately ship and scattering largess to Lorenzo and Antonio.

The equation of a beautiful bride with a great captured treasure ship is made when Iago says of Othello:

> Faith he tonight hath boarded a land carrack.
> If it prove lawful prize, he's made for ever.   (I. ii. 50–1)

and his interlocutor Cassio, greeting Desdemona at Cyprus, cried:

> O behold,
> The riches of the ship is come ashore.   (II. i. 82–3)

The image of a ship bringing riches up the Thames was traditional in many popular stories and dramas. Only that spring of 1604, their ships had come home in the grandest way for London, for Shakespeare and for King James.

On 14 March 1604 his three kingdoms of England, Scotland and Ireland were united in London for the triumphal entry of James from the Tower to the palace of Westminster to open his first Parliament. In his train, with a golden crown on the breast of their scarlet royal livery, marched the King's Players, including William Shakespeare. For him, a month short of forty, as for the king, two years younger, this daylong progress forged a new relationship with the City that crowned a lifetime's expectations. It followed in an enlarged form the annual mayoral procession of installation, in which the City expressed its sense of identity and its power; the City had stood firmly for James at his accession, when the Lord Mayor became temporarily the most powerful officer in the realm, all court offices being vacated at the monarch's death till reconfirmed. The King was the City's choice; they had averted the country's worst dread, civil war, so that to the sense of identity and power the City added a magnetic force of union. London epitomized the whole realm, as Dekker put it in recalling Shakespeare's great speech on England of *King Richard II* (II. i. 40ff) and transferring its sacramental grandeur to London:

> This little world of men, this precious stone
> That sets out Europe . . .
> The jewel of the land; England's right eye . . .

In the Lord Mayor's triumph, the metaphor that he was wedded to the City (Londinium, a woman crowned with towers) meant that like Peleus or Anchises he had married an immortal, thus ensuring his own immortal Fame. Imitating Queen Elizabeth, James was to use the image of marriage to his kingdoms ('I am the husband and the whole isle is my wife'); in his masque of *Hymenaei* Ben Jonson was to develop a magnificent variation on this image, enlarging it to cosmic proportions, where the king was the priest who wedded the kingdoms with the ring of the encompassing sea.

The Renaissance jewel offered a 'little world' in itself, often an exquisite and complex piece of goldsmith's fantasy, as in the work of Cellini; but gems also carried sovereign 'virtues' or powers – what we should call radiating influences – which warned of poison or averted its effects. Jewels were associated with black men because they came generally from India or Africa. One of the most famous is the

Armada Jewel given by Queen Elizabeth to Sir Francis Drake. On the outside of the pendant is the profile of a Negro of full African-type – behind him and half-eclipsed by him, an image of a white woman. Within, there is found a picture of the Queen herself and her emblem, the phoenix. Earlier Elizabeth had given to Thomas Walsingham's daughter on her marriage to Thomas Greasely the Greasely Jewel. This displayed an image of a full negro and two black cupids, opening to reveal double portraits of the bridal pair. From the imperial treasury at Vienna come fourteen cameos of black gods, the most striking being a black Diana, with a rich pearl suspended from her Ethiopean ear – as Romeo characterizes Juliet! (I. v. 47–8; cf. III. ii. 21–5)

The ultimate Biblical justification came from the *Songs of Songs* ('I am black but comely, O ye daughters of Jerusalem', 3. 6) where the black bride becomes identified with the whole human race united to Christ. Some years later, when the Chancellor of Cambridge, Francis Bacon, sent a diamond to the Public Orator, George Herbert, the poet replied by sending back 'a blackamoor' – some verses in black ink in George's best Latin, afterwards translated as 'A Black Nymph wooing a Fair Boy'. He replied with Iago's arguments.

> Black maid, complain not that I fly,
>   Where fate commands antipathy,
> Prodigious might that union prove
>   Where day and night together move,
> And the conjunction of our lips,
>   Not kisses mark, but an eclipse
>   (*Poems of Henry King*, ed. M. Crum, 1965, p. 151)

Here are the *disjecta membra* of images from *Othello*.

There were two paradoxical and opposite images of black men on the Elizabethan stage, as George Hunter and Eldred Jones in different ways worked out.[6] The treacherous evil Moor, the 'infidel' often coupled with some other infidel, such a Jew (as Ithamore with Barabas in *The Jew of Malta*) had been sketched by Shakespeare in Aaron of *Titus Andronicus*. The noble black warrior, from Peele's *Battle of Alcazar* (1589) descends through Marlowe's Calymath, Shakespeare's Prince of Morocco (in *The Merchant of Venice*) and Heywood's Mullisheg in *The Fair Maid of the West* to the union of the two in the disguised Machiavel, the Duke of Florence, in Webster's *The White Devil*.

The symbolic use of black and white imagery in *Othello* is too familiar to need any stressing now; Iago proves the black devil in the end; Desdemona appeared blackened in Othello's eyes, whilst Emilia stresses crudely the theological implications in rebutting Othello's accusation:

> The more angel she,
> And you the blacker devil!   (V. ii. 33–4)

an antithesis that Othello re-echoes in his own speeches of despair
(V. ii. 273–80). It is more significant now in tracing the submerged
images that make the play at once exotic and familiar, that bring
violence close to tenderness,[7] to observe the use of negroes with love
tokens and to see the variant here. A love token or indeed a token of
any kind is an activating gift of great potency for any dramatist in the
structure of his play. As symbol of the deepest exchange, of *enosis*,
the ring appears in many of Shakespeare's comedies.[8] Troilus' sleeve
and the love gifts which Ophelia returns are the chief tragic uses of
such tokens.

As he loses her, Brabantio recognizes Desdemona as his 'jewel' (I.
iii. 195) and so does Othello.

> Had she been true,
> If heaven would make me such another world
> Of one entire and perfect chrysolite,
> I'd not have sold her for it.   (V. ii. 146–9)

and in his death speech he characterizes himself as 'one whose hand

> Like the base Indian, threw a pearl away
> Richer than all his tribe.   (V. ii. 350–1)

The chrysolite, an infrangible stone that could never be flawed or
broken, represents the new world that neither he nor she could find
except in each other; it represents also the unflawed virginity that she
brought him. She was the pearl of great price but she could not
protect Othello from Iago's poison, the deadly 'medicine' he set to
work in Othello's veins.

Instead of a jewel, the actual dramatic object is the handkerchief
upon which so much of the action turns, which caused so much mirth
to Thomas Rymer and other classicists ('Let this be an example to all
housewives, that they look better to their linen'). However, in his
attendance on the Spanish Ambassador Shakespeare may have seen
the Spanish ladies with their ceremonious handkerchiefs. Any Spanish painting is likely to show a fine handkerchief prominently
displayed (as at the wedding of the Infante Isabella to Francesco de
Medici). In a Mediterranean climate a handkerchief, like a fan, was a
necessary piece of equipage, and could be as obvious as royal regalia.

In Shakespeare's very first tragedy, the napkin spotted with the
blood of the murdered boy Rutland is given to his father Richard of
York tauntingly by Queen Margaret and calls out the celebrated
tirade 'O tiger's heart wrapped in a woman's hide!' (*3 Henry VI*, I. iv.
110–49). (Here the religious analogue is of course the Veronica

napkin.) Othello's handkerchief, spotted with strawberries, is noted only when it is dropped (or possibly cast away by Othello himself) and picked up by Emilia, initiating the start of the tragic movement in the second half of the play

> She so loves the token
> (For he conjured her she should ever keep it)
> That she reserves it evermore about her
> To kiss and talk to.   (III. iii. 297–300)

Later only is it revealed that the magic in the web 'dyed in mummy which the skilful Conserved of maidens' hearts' (III. iv. 73–4) is to work magic not on the bride but the bridegroom. Othello's witchcraft if any is originally directed against himself. In a pathetic attempt to counter the lost magic, Desdemona asks Emilia to lay on their bed the wedding sheets (a delicately wrought work that every young girl prepared for her own bridal) spotted not with blood from maiden hearts but with the hymenal blood that had witnessed to her virginity, to the integrity of 'the perfect chrysolite'. Desdemona asks to be buried in one of these sheets. If the handkerchief represents all that Bertram's ring does in *All's Well That Ends Well*, Desdemona exchanged what Helena also offered. These tokens are more fragile and more intimate than jewels.

Iago had opened the action with a most offensive description of Othello ('an old black ram', 'thicklips') with the implications of fornication but none of marriage rites, only 'the beast with two backs'. It was commonly believed that Africans were more fierily volatile and emotional than the Mediterranean races, because they were born nearer the sun. Yet in these opening scenes Othello shows a calm patience, an ability to absorb shock and insult rendering it insignificant, that is truly African. 'Big Otto' uses without inflation the natural voice of command, as Desdemona addresses the Senate in a rhetoric as dignified and judicial as Portia's. In a quiet aside, Othello indicates to a subordinate his royal descent.

But when passing through the tempest, they reach Cyprus (or the London expedition, shall we say, reaches Ireland?)[9] what follows happens outwardly but also within Othello's mind, in 'the small circle of pain within the skull'. Each character casts a double shadow, and the shadows change erratically. The one real object remains the handkerchief; so that in the scene of shadow play where Othello is deceived by seeing it in Cassio's hand and tossed to Bianca, he then enters a living dream, a state of madness where all actions are profoundly unreal.[10] The audience must move at once in empathy with, and in judgment upon, what is happening. Desdemona is never as explicit as Hermione in *The Winter's Tale*:

> My life stands in the level of your dreams,
> Which I'll lay down.   (III. ii. 78–9)

but in the willow song she implies that he is mad – and therefore she is mad too. Adopting the language of Iago, Othello imagines Desdemona copulating with his entire command down to the blackened 'pioneers', the sappers. In the last scene he too for the last time 'tastes her sweet body' whilst invoking external codes to legitimize his violence as husband, commander of the troops, governor of the isle.

> O balmy breath, that almost doth persuade
> Justice to break her sword!   (V. ii. 16–7)

These perhaps the most purely sensuous lines of love in the play, initiate an epitome of that firm structure in which Othello develops from the African calm of Act I to the African frenzy of Act V. The disjunctive technique of a series of scenes in which tableaux punctuate long speeches, and quick exchanges suggest continuity is sustained by the two time-clocks that make the pace seem both gradual and violent. Iago, who like Othello lives by creating an imaginary world for himself, transmuting actions, treats his own wife as messenger, decoy or catspaw; although she holds all the clues, including the name of Cassio, which Othello gave her in the brothel scene, Emilia never suspects Iago. The hapless Roderigo, never seen anywhere but in Iago's company, serves to mirror his success with Othello, Cassio and lastly with Desdemona herself; the first blood he draws is upon Roderigo, until finally by killing his wife, Iago puts himself on an equality with Othello in the eyes of the law, where authorized violence decrees that his death be prolonged by tortures.

Although it was not printed till 1622 and therefore could have been known only in the theatre, *Othello* is a central influence on the two tragedies of John Webster, *The White Devil* (1611) and *The Duchess of Malfi* (1613). *The Duchess of Malfi*, his masterpiece, given by Shakespeare's own company, evoked the same pity for the Duchess that had been called out by Desdemona;[11] her momentary revival after strangulation, and the conversion which the sight of her dead face miraculously works in her murderers, intensify the local effect of the scene, yet the structure of Webster's tragedy, though related, is different, and far more disjunctive. Webster's Italy is not a blend of the exotic and the intimate, of London and her wedding to King James and Shakespeare, with the country of dreams. The Italy of Jacobean tragedy was a literary convention, a country of the mind that Webster shared with Marston and Tourneur. It is a dreamworld where the struggle for power is played out by characters whose force is evinced not in any political dimension – each moves in a bubble world of his own, of brightness or darkness, mist or brilliance. It might be said they are all mad, and like the vision of the madmen in Act IV of *The Duchess of Malfi*, this vision works collectively.[12]

The Duchess cannot reconcile her regal and her feminine selves; she moves first within her own dream of security, then in the prison of her insane brother's fancy. Her faithful woman says at the first proposal of the second marriage to her steward:

> Whether the spirit of greatness or of woman
> Reign most in her, I know not; but it shows
> A fearful madness: I owe her much of pity.   (I. i. 576–8)

Social distinctions operate here as powerfully as racial ones, with the added violence to natural sequence that the widow is here the active partner, wooing more directly than Desdemona. Antonio, her 'dis-qualified' choice, plays a feminine, passive role; it is she who plans the union, directs the flight and then unwarily exposes all to one who betrays her. We never meet her by her personal name Giovanna; she is Duchess of Malfi still. Except possibly in the echo scene after her death where Antonio recognizes the voice of 'my wife'. This home-less voice had been heard once before, offstage, crying out in the night in the pains of childbirth. The echo tells Antonio he will never see her more. Webster added the pathos of infants, a proof of tenderness that counterbalances the extreme horror of his mad Spanish royalty, the princes of the House of Aragon, or his cold Medici in violence directed onto women who here first give their names as title roles to tragedy.

The violence in Webster is continuous, and his language is no more diluted by the commonplace than his princes are restrained by precepts of morality. 'Tush for justice!' is the comment of the Duke of Florence on learning that his revenge is authorized by his sister's having been murdered. The power game is played out in a setting which like that of the drug addict is compulsorily attractive or repulsive. Bosola, the professional spy who betrays the Duchess wears many disguises, betrays and then doublecrosses his betrayer, dooming himself in the act. He is inevitably a masquer, an actor of roles, who never till the end finds true 'integrity of life'.

The Spanish code of honour is assumed but not accepted. The Duchess's brother finally asks Bosola:

> By what authority didst thou execute
> This bloody sentence?
> *Bosola:*   By yours.
> *Ferdinand:*   Mine? was I her judge?

> Did any ceremonial form of law
> Doom her to non being? did a complete jury
> Deliver her conviction up i' th' court?
> Where shalt thou find this judgment registered
> Unless in hell?   (IV. ii. 298–304)

Webster, a student of the Middle Temple, wrote no play without a trial scene, but the sword of heaven replaces the imperfect legal cruelties of men. Of the negative vision in Bosola and in Flamineo, George Hunter said: 'These patterns (of negation) are important if the author can convey some sense of the value they exclude.'[13]

The deepest insights come near to madness; in an insane world, madmen can see some things more clearly. Webster's scenes move by flickerings, jumps and reversals; his characters also develop in this way. There may be brief moments of absolute security as when Brachiano first meets his White Devil, and they exchange jewels as love tokens.

> Give credit, I could wish time would stand still,
> And never end this interview, this hour.   (I. ii. 192–3)

As her Moorish maid spreads a rich carpet and cushions for the encounter, the words are stately or emblematic but the actions intimate, Flamineo, her treacherous brother, providing the innuendo:

> 'His jewel for her jewel'; well put in, Duke . . .
> That's better; 'she must wear his jewel lower' . . .
>   (I. ii. 215, 218)

Heroic in pride and energy Vittoria (described as 'the famous Venetian courtesan' though she is not Venetian) surmounts her subsequent trial for adultery; whilst Brachiano's Duchess, who like Desdemona has taken his guilt upon herself, has been divorced with a kiss and murdered for reward. Built from opposing beauty and evil, the sharply disjunctive scenes of Vittoria's life end in

> O, my greatest sin lay in my blood,
> Now my blood pays for't.   (V. vi. 240–1)

These broken forms carry the possibility of character development which, as modern psychologists observe, proceeds by vibrations, leaps and jumps. Webster's 'poetry of the gaps' allowed his actors to breathe inside their parts, insert their own contribution and make their own interpretation. He worked very closely with the men of Queen Anne's troupe, and with the King's Men. Any actor will recognize the expertise of this 'poetry of the gaps'.

The Duchess of Malfi is subjected to tests of mockery and torture, through the grisly parody of an exchange of love tokens, when she receives the dead man's hand with a wedding ring upon it which she had given; Ferdinand's first gift to her had been a dagger of their father, his last the gift that 'brings last benefit, last sorrow' of the coffin and cords.

Ritualized cruelty (a kind exploited in such Spanish dramas as *Justice without Revenge*) culminates in grotesque parody as the Duchess's waiting maid is killed beside her mistress.

Other features of Webster's earlier life are reflected in the darkness of these tragic visions,[14] which have been revived with such powerful effect upon the modern stage. The sometimes gratuitous atrocity in Webster (as Flamineo's murder of his brother) can provoke the crazed tenderness of their mother's dirge.

> Call for the robin redbreast and the wren . . .

and in the darkness of her 'last presence chamber' the Duchess finds freedom. Iago's words on Othello

> Not poppy, nor mandragora,
> Nor all the drowsy syrops of this world
> Shall ever medicine thee to that sweet sleep
> Which thou owedst yesterday.   (III. iii. 334–7)

become transformed by her to

> Come, violent death,
> Serve for mandragora to make me sleep.   (IV. ii. 241–2)

The affirmation of Shakespeare and of Webster is that such beings have witnessed to their faith, so that the final act still carries tenderness. The hope may be eschatological only, yet in both of Webster's tragedies the last murders spring from devotion to two good women, whose young sons survive the general holocaust.

Notes

1 See D. J. Gordon, *The Renaissance Imagination*, ed. Stephen Orgel (Berkeley and Los Angeles, University of California Press, 1973), p. 115.

2 See Eldred Jones, *Othello's Countrymen* (Oxford, Oxford University Press, 1965), p. 12, for an order to a Lubeck merchant in 1601 ordering the return of 'Negars and Blackamoors' who had come 'since the troubles between her Highness and the King of Spain'.

3 In *English and Spanish Literature of the Sixteenth and Seventeenth Centuries* (Cambridge, Cambridge University Press, 1980).

4 See e.g. Barbara H. C. de Mendonça, in *Shakespeare Survey*, 21 (1968) 31–8. Susan Snyder has also made this point.

5 The riches of the great carrack, brought to Plymouth in 1592 had included a great diamond, bartered in a London theatre. Heywood in his *Fair Maid of the West* had displayed the riches of Barbary; the story of Dick Whittington has survived to this day.

6 George Hunter 'Othello and Colour Prejudice', in *Dramatic Identities and Cultural Tradition* (Liverpool, Liverpool University Press, 1978), (originally presented 1967); Eldred Jones, *op. cit.* note 2. Cf. Marvin Spivack, *The Anatomy of Evil* (Oxford, Oxford University Press, 1958) for black Iago, and also Leah Scragg, *Shakespeare Survey*, 21 (1968), 52–65.

7 Since the craft plays, the black king of Ethiopia, Balthazar, had been linked with rich gifts at the epiphany; in Heywood's *Golden Age*, Pluto, the black king of Tartarus, is made King of Tartary, associated with rich camel trains, evidently on the Venetian trade route from the East! The most famous image is the Daughters of Niger in Jonson's *Masque of Blackness* (1604/5) played by the Queen and her ladies at Court. Compare the older use of spotting the face with ink to denote sin in Morality plays e.g. *Three Ladies of London*.

8 Love tokens range from the rings of *Romeo and Juliet, Merchant of Venice, All's Well* and *Twelfth Night* to the absurd dog of *Two Gentlemen of Verona*, the shower of pearls, gloves, diamond studded pictures of *Love's Labours Lost*, the rain of gifts in *Timon* to the ring and bracelet of *Cymbeline*. Florizel buys no fairing for Perdita, but the 'fardel' supplies identity proof and includes a jewel. There are no gifts in *Comedy of Errors, Taming of the Shrew, Midsummer Night's Dream*, or *Merry Wives of Windsor* since all are farcical in some degree.

9 Cf. the hopeful expectation of a triumphal entry of a victorious Essex returning from the Irish wars (*Henry V*, V, Chorus) and its tragic sequel.

10 He emerges most clearly in the brief exchange with Cassio, 'Dear General, I did never give you cause' [to kill me] 'I do believe it, and I ask your pardon' (V. ii. 301–2).

11 See Middleton's commendatory verses for the play: 'Thy epitaph, only the title be Write *Duchess*; that will fetch a tear for thee.'

12 A subtle treatment of madness in *Othello* is Arthur Kirsch, 'The Polarization of Erotic Love in *Othello*', *Shakespeare and the Experience of Love* (Cambridge, Cambridge University Press, 1981).

13 George K. Hunter 'English Folly and Italian Vice', *op. cit.* p. 125.

14 See M. C. Bradbrook, *John Webster, Citizen and Dramatist* (London, Weidenfeld & Nicolson, 1980) for the story of the Princess of Eboli and Antonio Perez. For Overbury's murder see Beatrice White, *Cast of Ravens* (London, John Murray, 1965). Webster could have met the young Duke of Brachiano, who closes *The White Devil* on a strong note, for in 1601 he visited London after escorting his cousin Marie de Medici to France to wed the French king.

XII

The Origins of *Macbeth*

A very broad definition of 'sources' must be my excuse for considering so familiar a topic as the origins of *Macbeth*. In this, the most concentrated of the tragedies, a particularly wide diversity of material was fused into unity. 'In the quick forge and working-house of thought', Shakespeare wrought at white heat. The material to be considered falls into three classes. First, the Scottish and English Chronicles supplied the facts, and one important scene; secondly, various works on witchcraft and demonology, including those of King James, gave some material for the witches' scenes (but here the interest lies rather in Shakespeare's innovations than in his borrowings); thirdly, earlier works by Shakespeare himself present in a simpler form some of the ingredients of this play, and an examination of what might be called the internal sources elucidates its inward structure. The repetitions, echoes and restatements which are to be detected in Shakespeare offer more than mere opportunity for pedantic correlation; they are alternative statements, varied embodiments of those deep-seated and permanent impulses which underlie all his work and make it, in spite of its variety, a vast and comprehensive whole – a single structure, though of Gothic design.

In reading through Holinshed's voluminous Scottish Chronicles, Shakespeare would come, about a third of the way through, upon the story of Duncan, the eighty-fourth king according to that account, and the narrative with which we are all familiar. The Chronicle gives a brief and bald summary of reign after reign, describing the same round of violence, murder, rebellion and general turbulence. It is as monotonous as the series of apocryphal portraits of these early kings to be seen in Holyrood Palace; and the power of its monotony is considerable. The picture of a strange, bleak, haunted world emerges, where savage beings fulfil the passionate cycle of their dreadful lives as if under enchanted compulsion.[1] But why, in reading through these legendary stories, did Shakespeare stop where he did?

The story of Duncan and Macbeth glorified the ancestors of King James, both the ancient house of Macalpine, and in Banquo, an imaginary figure invented by Hector Boece during the fifteenth century, the later Stewart line. It also introduced the weird sisters, whose prophecies might be adapted to foretell the happy future rule of King James himself, and who were at the same time akin to the North Berwick witches whose practices against him had provided one of the most celebrated witch-trials of the age. Moreover, Malcolm Canmore, husband of the English princess Margaret and initiator of many new customs, stood at the beginning of one new age in Scottish history, as James, heir to the united crowns of Scotland and England, stood at the beginning of another. A royal command performance was clearly in view from the very inception of the play.

In the Chronicle, the history of Macbeth is briefly told, but Shakespeare shaped it both by expansion and compression. He crammed into a single act of war the rebellion of Macdonwald, two Danish invasions and the revolt of Cawdor – which happened only *after* the prophecy in Holinshed. The whole account of how Duncan was murdered he took from elsewhere, the murder of King Duff; though Macbeth's stratagem to send into the Danish camp supplies of drugged food and surprise them 'so amazed that they were unable to make any defence' might have suggested the drugging of the grooms. In the Chronicle, Macbeth slew Duncan in open revolt, and no indications of remorse are given either before or after the event. The long reign of Macbeth Shakespeare shortens into a few weeks; the wizard who prophesied to Macbeth about Birnam Wood merges with the weird sisters; Macbeth's death takes place before Dunsinane, and not at the end of an inglorious flight. In sum, the debt to the Chronicle is of the slightest; so bald a narrative gave Shakespeare the merest skeleton of a plot. There is, however, one scene, that between Malcolm and Macduff in England, which is reported in very great detail. Indeed, it is out of all focus in the Chronicle and occupies almost as much space as the whole of the rest of the reign. This scene represents Shakespeare's greatest debt to Holinshed; clearly it took his eye, and here perhaps is the germ of how he first conceived the play.

Malcolm's self-accusations are much more convincing to the present age than they were to the nineteenth century, when this scene was generally disliked. It was usual to cut it for stage performance. Yet an exile trying to evade the trap of his totalitarian enemy might plausibly test the reactions of his promised supporters. In a world still full of displaced persons and *agents provocateurs*, this scene can be harrowing. In Holinshed, the whole incident is weakened by the fact that both Malcolm and Macduff know of the murder of Macduff's family before the dialogue begins, so that it is hardly conceivable that Macduff could at this time be Macbeth's agent. Shakespeare, on the other hand, makes his leaving of the defenceless 'wife and child' a reasonable cause of suspicion to the young prince. Macduff does not answer Malcolm's query on this point. It is the silence of a man embittered and mature, deeply mortified by such incomprehension of the depths of sacrifice for which his loyalty prepared him.

Here again the modern reader may add his personal endorsement. In 1942 I had the honour to meet in London one of the highest officers of the French Navy, who had escaped from France after the German occupation to fight from this country. He too left his wife and child exposed to the retaliation of the enemy. In those days no one asked him why.

In Holinshed, Malcolm accuses himself of licentiousness, avarice and promise-breaking, and it is only the last which drives Macduff to renounce him. Promise-keeping is so essential to the ruler that although as all treatises on government declared – and particularly King James's[2] – it is the bounden duty of the subject to conceal the ill deeds of rulers and not even to let his *thoughts* harbour any treasonable reproof of them, yet this particular crime is indefensible. Holinshed makes the rather subtle point that while Malcolm is diffident about his other crimes, he seems to expect Macduff to conceal the last. Shakespeare omits the irony, but he was engaged in adding to the list of crimes, mentioning especially contentiousness, which, as Dover Wilson points out,[3] would be particularly obnoxious to the pacifist James. Malcolm's final speech constitutes almost a definition by contraries of the perfect ruler.

Such ingenious dissimulation would appear to the royal auditor a proof of his wisdom, more striking that it was precocious – and the more likely to foreshadow that of his illustrious descendant. Might not James also remember those ten painful months following the Ruthven Raid in 1582, when as a boy of eighteen he had to practise dissimulation with the gang who kidnapped him and forced him to govern in accordance with their faction? 'Better bairns greet nor bearded men,' exclaimed Lord Ruthven, when James at his first capture burst into tears. The King never forgot, and years later he contrived Lord Ruthven's death should pay for it. Such memories might well have recurred and given to the scene of Malcolm's exile a deep personal significance.

The ruler was always allowed to practise extraordinary stratagems in view of his extra responsibilities, as the Duke of Vienna did in *Measure for Measure*. Malcolm was showing himself fit to rule – cleverer than his father, who knew no art to find the mind's construction in the face, and did not probe below a fair appearance.

In his book on Shakespeare,[4] Hardin Craig has classed *Macbeth* among the political tragedies, and there is no doubt that it was more than a personal tragedy which happened to be about princes. The natures of an ill-governed and a well-governed kingdom are contrasted throughout the latter half of the play. Here Shakespeare moved away from the Chronicle, and relied partly on other works, including those of King James, and partly on those views which had formed in his own mind during the writing of his English histories.

The relation between the King and the body politic is a sympathetic one. When the King is sick or disordered, the land is disordered too. First we are given the picture of a happy kingdom, in which Duncan and his thanes support and respect each other. Duncan plants honours, and labours to make them full of growing. His subjects return to him all the bounties with which he nourishes them, in duty and service. In her welcome Lady Macbeth falsely strikes this note of devotion, which Duncan repays with an old man's gallant politeness.

After his coronation, Macbeth tries vainly at his feast to recreate the atmosphere of close-knit amity. But 'honour, love, obedience, troops of friends' he must not look to have. His thanes look forward to the time when they may 'do faithful homage, and receive free honours', but the Scotland they inhabit is disordered, sick, a distracted body swollen with evil humours. This picture of the distracted kingdom is familiar from the plays of *Richard II*, *Henry IV* and *Richard III*, where it is described at more length. Even Macbeth sees that his land is diseased (v iii). He himself is haunted with the sleeplessness that tormented the usurper Bolingbroke, and to read the opening of the third act of *Henry IV Part II* is like listening to an overture to *Macbeth*:

> O sleep, O gentle sleep,
> Nature's soft nurse, how have I frighted thee,
> That thou no more wilt weigh my eye-lids down,
> And steep my senses in forgetfulness? . . .
> Then you perceive the body of our kingdom,
> How foul it is; what rank diseases grow,
> And with what danger, near the heart of it?
>
> (III i 6–9, 38–40)

Malcolm is 'the medicine of the sickly weal', the 'sovereign flower' who comes with the blessing and aid of the saintly Edward. The reference in IV i to the Confessor's sacred powers of healing was an especial compliment to James who prided himself on the inherited gift of 'the healing benediction'; but it was also necessary as a counterweight to the picture of Macbeth's unholy rule; as such, Shakespeare took it from the English Chronicle and inserted it in his main political scene.

Further, into Macduff's reproaches of the supposedly vicious Malcolm, Shakespeare inserts an account of the forebears from whom he has degenerated; his father Duncan was 'a most sainted king', and his mother one who 'Oftener upon her knees, than on her feet, died every day she lived.' This is Shakespeare's Duncan, not Holinshed's; while of Malcolm's mother nothing is known. Shakespeare has borrowed the saintliness from the description of Malcolm's wife, the English princess, St Margaret, who transmitted the blood of the Saxon line to the Scottish royal house, and whose little chapel still stands within the walls of Edinburgh Castle. It was she and Malcolm himself who rivalled each other in pious practices and holy living. But by putting this picture a generation earlier, Shakespeare has brought into the play yet another contrast with Macbeth and his fiend-like Queen, whose land is described in terms of the plague:

> where nothing
> But who knows nothing, is once seen to smile:
> Where sighs, and groans, and shrieks that rend the air
> Are made, not mark'd: where violent sorrow seems
> A modern ecstasy: the dead man's knell,
> Is there scarce ask'd for who, and good men's lives
> Expire before the flowers in their caps,
> Dying, or ere they sicken.
>
> (IV iii 166–73)

As rightful heir Malcolm alone has the power to depose an anointed king, usurper though he be; but the conquest is almost unopposed. 'The time is free.' An immense feeling of relief surges up as Macduff appears on the battlements with these words. Malcolm, encompassed with his kingdom's pearl,[5] proceeds to inaugurate a new era by bestowing new honours. He thus fulfils his father's words that 'signs of nobleness, like stars shall shine on all deservers.' He also introduces the principle of feudal monarchy, with hereditary succession, and tenancy of the crown, which in fact Malcolm Canmore did institute in Scotland, following the unsuccessful attempts of his great-grandfather and grandfather, Kenneth II and Malcolm II.[6]

This particular theme, however, Shakespeare does not emphasise, and for good reason. The ancient succession of Scotland had been by tanistry, that is, the monarchy was elective within a small group of kinsmen, the descendants of Macalpine. In consequence, the King was almost as a matter of course assassinated by his successor, who chose the moment most favourable to himself to 'mak siccar' an inheritance that could never be regarded as assured. In spite of earlier attempts to make it hereditary, elective monarchy still persisted; by tanist law Macbeth had as good a claim as Duncan, and his wife a rather better one. By nominating Malcolm as his heir, the historic Duncan committed a provocative act which Macbeth might not unreasonably resent, and in Holinshed his real notions of murder are formed only at this point. Shakespeare did not wish Macbeth to have any such excuse for his deed. It must be unprovoked to give the full measure of pity and terror. Therefore by suppressing the conflict between tanistry and the hereditary principle, he was bound to slur over the full nature of Malcolm Canmore's innovations.[7]

On the contrary, the principle of hereditary succession is firmly emphasised by the prominence given to Banquo and his descendants, and in the cauldron scene Shakespeare has gratified the family pride of his royal patron by a pageant of his ancestors. Henry Paul has pointed out[8] that the Stewart line presented the striking picture of nine successive sovereigns in *lineal* descent the one from the other. This direct lineal descent of the crown was a matter of pride to James, who referred to it in his speeches to Parliament and in his writings. Shakespeare's interest in genealogy had been amply shown in his English histories. Edward's seven sons, seven branches growing from one root, are recalled to mind by the family tree which has Banquo as its root – he so describes himself.

Banquo was a purely imaginary character, inserted into the Chronicle by Hector Boece to provide a proper ancestry for the Stewarts. Fleance's escape to Wales and his marriage with a Welsh princess 'explained' why the Stewarts did in fact come from the Welsh borders. But after 1603 the original expansion of the weird sisters' prophecy, whereby Banquo was hailed as father to a line of kings, was expanded still further, so that they also prophesied that his descendants should unite the kingdoms of England and Scotland. In the pageant of the three sybils given at St John's College, Oxford, in 1605, James and his family were greeted in this fashion, and moreover an endless progeny was promised him.[9] The show of the eight kings was an apotheosis of the Stewart line, and must have been staged with great grandeur. To a Jacobean audience it symbolised all the stability and order which they hoped from a settled succession. A family which had produced nine kings in lineal descent offered a fair hope of escape from those dynastic difficulties which Elizabeth's reign had made familiar. The eight phantoms are all 'too like the spirit of Banquo'. They are physical replicas of him, but in the last Henry Paul would see the person of Mary Queen of Scots, the eighth Stewart to wear the crown. At all events this scene would have a very powerful topical significance.

These two scenes, then, the cauldron scene and the scene in England, are the *political* highlights of the play. They are the scenes in which Shakespeare relied most heavily on his immediate sources – those he would start from. And they are the two scenes which would most particularly appeal to King James. They are also the least tragic in tone. One is spectacular, and the other, although, as I have said, it is much more poignant to the present age than to the previous one, is still in rather a different manner from the rest of the play. What have the theoretically well-justified dissimulations of this canny young man, this perfect looking-glass for princes, to do with the agonised visions of Inverness and Dunsinane? How do they fit one who has a father murdered as well as revenges to execute on the tyrant who popped in between the election and his hopes? Malcolm is own brother to that other canny young man, Harry Monmouth, who is likewise justified by all the textbooks on government, including *Basilikon Doron*; but we are not moved. He is impersonal. The man is lost in the ruler. He may be *Vox Dei*; it means that he is merely *vox*.

Because of the close relation to source material, the impersonal subject and the specific appeal to royal interest, it seems to me that these two scenes are probably the earliest to be written. I do not believe that Shakespeare, or any original writer, starts inevitably with Act I and ends with Act V. Nor do I think that, once submerged in his tragedy and well away from his sources, he would suddenly curb himself in mid-career and begin to treat these cooler matters. At the same time these scenes are too well articulated with the main plot to be additions, though small additions may have been made to them. The cauldron scene and the English scene are both in a quite laudatory, or at least a quite neutral sense, superficial. They belong to the top layer of the play.

The character of Lady Macbeth owes nothing to the Chronicle; it has been suggested that Shakespeare might have seen the MS. of William Stewart's *Buik of the Chroniclis of Scotland*, a metrical and expanded translation of Boece finished in 1535 which contains a few very crude hints on the behaviour of Donwald's wife during the murder of King Duff.[10] The resemblances seem to me negligible and unconvincing.

But a passage from the *Description of Scotland* which is prefixed to Holinshed's Chronicle and which to my knowledge has not hitherto been noted seems to be relevant. It is from chapter XIII:

> each woman would take intolerable pains to bring up and nourish her own children. They thought them furthermore not to be kindly fostered, except they were so well nourished after their births with the milk of their breasts as they were before they were born with the blood of their own bellies: nay, they feared lest they should degenerate and grow out of kind, except they gave them suck themselves, and eschewed strange milk, therefore in labour and painfulness they were equal [i.e. with the fighting men]. . . . In these days also the women of our country were of no less courage than the men, for all stout maids and wives (if they were not with child) marched as well into the field as did the men, and so soon as the army did set forward, they slew the first living creature that they found, in whose blood they not only bathed their swords, but also tasted thereof with their mouths, with no less religion and assurance conceived, than if they had already been sure of some notable and fortunate victory.[11]

The intimate relation between tenderness and barbarity, suckling and bloodshed in this passage seems to me to give the fundamental character of Lady Macbeth as it is embodied in the most frightful of her speeches, that in which she invokes the spirits of murder to suck her breasts, and that in which she finally goads Macbeth:

> I have given suck, and know
> How tender 'tis to love the babe that milks me,
> I would, while it was smiling in my face,
> Have pluck'd my nipple from his boneless gums,
> And dash'd the brains out, had I so sworn
> As you have done to this.
>
> (I vii 54–9)

Lady Macbeth is siren as well as fury. The tenderness of Macbeth for her is reciprocated; they are indeed one flesh. There are a number of parallels between her part and that of Webster's *White Divel*[12] which suggest that her seduction of Macbeth should not be too far removed from Vittoria's seduction of Brachiano in the manner of its playing. When Macbeth comes out of the death chamber she says two words: 'My husband?' The usual form of address is 'My thane' or 'My lord', but in this supreme moment she uses the more intimate, and for an Elizabethan the more unusual form.

The double crime of treason and murder is also deadly sin. In 1604 William Willymat, the translator of *Basilikon Doron* under the title of *A Prince's Looking-Glass*, followed it with an original work, *A Loyal Subject's Looking-Glass*, in which he described the prime causes of rebellion as pride, ambition and envy. All three animate

Macbeth. 'Pride can in no wise brook to be at command, and to submit himself willingly . . . to the obedience of magistrates, rulers and governors . . . be they never so well worthy of their place.' Macbeth cannot brook 'the boy Malcolm', who has only been saved from captivity by the sergeant, should be nominated heir. Almost his last words are 'I will not yield / To kiss the ground before young Malcolm's feet.' The stripling – he should be of an age with his cousin, young Siward – provokes his pride; the weird sisters have stirred up ambition, always thought of as evil; and his very hunger for golden opinions makes him envy imperial dignity and the graces of kingship which he discerns in Duncan, and which he so vainly tries to reproduce. By the end of the play, Macbeth is accused of the other deadly sins also (IV iii 55–7) – in fact he is equated with the devil:

> Not in the legions
> Of horrid hell, can come a devil more damn'd
> In evils, to top Macbeth.

He is 'this fiend of Scotland', a 'hell-kite' and a 'hell-hound'.

In its treatment of the supernatural, the play shows the same subtle blending of a variety of material which is seen in the political theme; and it was again especially calculated to interest James, hero of *Newes from Scotland* and author of *Daemonologie*.

There was no real scepticism about witches. *Macbeth* comes at the end of a decade when the convictions for witchcraft in the Middlesex circuit reached their highest point. New statutes had been passed in 1604 reinforcing those of 1580, which made the consulting and feeding of spirits, the use of dead bodies as charms, and even unsuccessful efforts to harm by enchantment into indictable offences.[13]

It is rather surprising that before *Macbeth*, witches had appeared on the stage only in such harmless forms as Mother Bombie or the Wise Woman of Hogsdon. *Faustus* had been the only great tragedy to be based on the supernatural. The magician is a magnificent and powerful figure, a man of intellect. He enters into a formal pact with the devil and consciously chooses damnation; in return for the sale of his soul he obtains supernatural powers (*Daemonologie*, Book I, chapter VI). Henceforth, though still free to repent, the devil coaxes and bullies him out of such wishes. The equal poise of Heaven and Hell that characterised the moralities is not maintained; the scales are weighed for Hell, dramatically speaking. The emissaries of Hell are more active, numerous and powerful than the emissaries of Heaven. The sinner, however, is led to will and choose his own damnation. He is never *possessed*.

Macbeth was the first play to introduce to the stage in a serious manner the rites and practices of contemporary witchcraft. The witch differed sharply from the magician, as King James observed (*Daemonologie*, Book I, chapter III). William West of the Inner Temple thus distinguishes them in his *Symbolaeographie* (1594):

> *Soothsaying Wizards.* Of this kind . . . be all those . . . which divine and foretell things to come and raise up evil spirits by certain superstitious and conceived forms of words. And unto such questions as be demanded of them do answer by voice, or else set before their eyes in glass, crystal stones, or rings, the pictures or images of things sought for.
>
> [Witches] . . . shake the air with lightnings and thunder, to cause hail and tempests, to remove green corn or trees to an other place, to be carried of her familiar which hath taken upon him the deceitful shape of a goat, swine, or calf etc. into some mountain. . . . And sometimes to fly upon a staff or fork, or some other instrument. . . .[14]

Whilst Dee or Forman consorted with kings and princes, the witch was generally a poor, solitary, ignorant old woman. King James points out that magicians were learned and sought public glory; witches were unlearned and sought revenge. They blighted man and crops, were ugly and bearded, and went accompanied by a familiar. The more lurid practices of the continental sabbat are not recorded of English witches; though in *Daemonologie* and in the record of the North Berwick case, elaborate rituals are described, blasphemous as well as mischievous.

Shakespeare's play, though the first to deal with this topic seriously, was quickly followed by others. *Sophonisba* (1606) and *The Divil's Charter* (1607) were succeeded by a number of Chapman's plays introducing spirits, and in 1615 by Middleton's *Witch*, a song from which was incorporated in *Macbeth*. Jonson's *Masque of Queens*, with its celebrated anti-masque of hags, was produced in 1609. As in *A Midsummer Night's Dream*, and later in *The Tempest*, Shakespeare created a new kind of supernatural drama and one which was very widely and generally imitated.

In all these plays, however, witches are used for spectacular and intermittent effects, and the marvellous elbows out the sinister. Marston and Jonson drew largely on classical sources. Hecate, in *The Witch*, is used to supply love charms and is surrounded by familiars but her influence is not decisive. Barnabe Barnes in *The Divil's Charter* is mainly indebted to *Faustus*, but the crimes of Alexander Borgia and Lucretia occasionally parallel those of Macbeth and Lady Macbeth, and the conjuring scene especially seems modelled on the cauldron scene, whilst Alexander is cheated by a riddle at the end, in much the same way as Macbeth.

In *Macbeth* Shakespeare combines many different traditions, so that the weird sisters, or Three Destinies of Holinshed become assimilated with the North Berwick coven in their malevolent rites, yet they also acquire something of the magician's power to raise and command spirits and to foretell the future. Shakespeare's witches, like those of North Berwick, appear capable of flying 'through the fog and filthy air'. They are able to sail in a sieve, to assume animal forms, and control the weather. All this Agnes Sampson and her coven claimed to do in their attempts to destroy the ship carrying King James from Denmark.[15] But Shakespeare's hags also have marks of the English witch – their beards, their animal familiars and their acts of petty revenge against the sailor and his wife. These were the things charged against many a poor old woman at the sessions. Their gift of prophecy expressed in riddles – the riddling form of words is not found in Holinshed – links them with such characters as Mother Bombie, or Erestus, the 'white bear of England's wood' in *The Old Wives' Tale*. Incidentally, Rosalind, in the last Act of *As You Like It*, makes her promises to the lovers in the riddling form proper to the Magician which she professes herself to be:

> I will marry you, if ever I marry woman, and I'll be married tomorrow: I will satisfy you, if ever I satisfied man, and you shall be married tomorrow. I will content you, if what pleases you contents you, and you shall be married tomorrow. (V ii 122–6)

The prophecies of the witches about Birnam Wood and the man not born of woman are sprigs of folklore which also recall the earlier comedies; for instance, Erestus's prophecy that Eumenides is to be released from enchantment by a dead man.[16]

On the other hand, they have powers superior to those of common witches. Bishop John Leslie called them devils disguised as women (*De Origine, Moribus et Rebus Gestis Scotorum*, Rome 1578). They can vanish instantly like bubbles, which suggests a demonic power assuming and discarding human shape. They have no trace of any fear of or subjection to higher demonic forces; though the spirits raised in the cauldron scene are called 'our masters', yet the witches conjure them up and speak to them with authority, such authority as belongs to the magician like Faustus, the friar in *Bussy d'Ambois* and Owen Glendower. Macbeth, who sells his eternal jewel to the common enemy of man, is himself in Faustus's position, but he makes no formal compact, nor is he given any supernatural powers. He is tempted by rousing of his own worse instincts and led to natural crimes; but, on the other hand, he never renounces God and his baptism, as both witches and magicians were compelled to do.

After the murder of Duncan there is no possibility of his going back. He has crossed the invisible boundary which cuts him off from his kind. His hand is against every man. He is no longer a member of the human community, and finally he sinks to the level of a hunted rogue animal.

Yet although Macbeth's career recalls a descent into Hell, it is not presented openly as a descent into Hell. In the end he finds himself deceived in the witches, as the witch or magician was so often deceived by the Devil.[17] 'Be these juggling fiends no more believ'd,' he cries. In murdering Duncan, he committed mortal sin – the sin against the Holy Ghost as James called it in *Daemonologie* (Book I, chapter II) – that is, he consciously and deliberately did that which he knew to be evil, and which he detested even as he did it. The act brings the punishment which he foresaw, he loses this clear sight, wades in blood so far that he is blinded and becomes in the end insensible even to the death of his wife.[18] But the overt theological issue is never bluntly put. Hence H. B. Charlton can deny any religious significance to *Macbeth*, while W. C. Curry, Helen Gardner and Hardin Craig, not to mention Roy Walker,[19] see the play as 'essentially medieval and Christian'. The Prince of Darkness is present only through the acts of his emissaries, but they, while in many ways recalling the realistic witch, are 'creatures of another sort'. I would not be prepared to say whether they are human or not; they are more recognisable as human in Act I than in the later scenes, where they replace Holinshed's 'wizard', and have something of the Devil's power of deceit.

Lady Macbeth's relation with the dark powers is more mysterious. Women were thought far more susceptible to demons than men, and were far more frequently accused of evil practices. King James put the proportion as high as twenty women to one man (*Daemonologie*, Book II, chapter V). In her invocation to the spirits 'that tend on mortal thoughts' Lady Macbeth offers them her breasts to be sucked and invites them to take possession of her body; this was as much as any witch could do by way of self-dedication. Professor Curry considers the sleep-walking scene to be evidence of possession, and if she did lay 'self and violent hands' upon herself, Lady Macbeth committed the final act of despair.

Neither Macbeth nor his wife has any defences. Though his conscience at first speaks clearly, he has no Good Angel as Faustus has. Banquo may pray to the merciful powers to restrain his cursed thoughts, Malcolm and Macduff appeal to Heaven, old Siward commit his dead son to the soldiery of God, but Macbeth lives in an amoral world of old wives' tales and riddles – except for that one vision of the pleading angels with their trumpet tongues, and

Heaven's cherubim horsed upon the sightless couriers of the air, which recalls Faustus's vision of Christ's blood streaming in the firmament.

The portents which accompany the death of Duncan, and fore-shadow that of Banquo, are such as on the stage always appeared with the death of princes. The strange screams in the air and the horses that ate each other are developed from hints in Holinshed, but they are distinguished from other portents by the tone and colour of the language in which they are described. The thick darkness which hangs over the sky, the raven, owl and cricket's note are much less distinct than the fiery warriors who fought above the clouds in *Julius Caesar*. It is the thick night, the fog and filthy air, the smoke of Hell which create the peculiar horror of this play, and the omens are chosen to accord. How quickly it rolls down on the sunlit battlements where the martlet flits, as a Scotch mist will roll from a mountain! Just as the witches are more horrible because we do not know what they are – it would be a relief to meet Mephistopheles – so the whole treatment of the supernatural in *Macbeth* is characterised by a potent and delicately controlled imprecision. Hell is murky. The creatures of *Macbeth*, like the ghost in *Hamlet*, are not susceptible of any one theoretical explan-ation, religious or natural.

Yet in the end justice, whether God's or Nature's, prevails. There is no direct intervention, but in the final vengeance the ingredients of the poisoned chalice are commended to the sinner's own lips. (This happens literally in *The Divil's Charter*, where Borgia is poisoned with his own wine: it also happens, of course, in *Hamlet*.) Macbeth, who had begun as Bellona's bridegroom, ends in the same role as Macdonwald, his head hacked off and put on a pole. (Did Macdon-wald's head appear in the early scenes? According to Holinshed it was cut off.) The early description of Macbeth in battle which is given by the sergeant seems to me indubitably Shakespeare's. By the violence of it we are made unforgettably aware that bloodshed of itself is familiar to Macbeth – that his trade is hand-to-hand fighting. The physical side of Duncan's murder can cause him no qualms at all. Lady Macbeth, on the other hand, is not quite Holinshed's Valkyrie; perhaps she had not smelt blood before, and though she goes through the scene unflinchingly, she is haunted by the physical atrocity of it. To Macbeth, we may believe that the dastardly act of stabbing a sleeping old man was as instinctively repugnant as stabbing a kneeling man in the back was to Hamlet: 'Look on't again, I dare not,' he cries – he, who had unseamed men from the nave to the chaps.

It is here that we approach the deepest levels of the play and that we must leave external sources and seek within Shakespeare's own earlier work the foreshadowing of the terror and the pity which we feel. In the speeches of Macbeth, especially his five great speeches,[20] lies the heart of the mystery. They embody the experience which fundamentally gives rise to the play; and there are no sub-plots, no digressions to modify it.

Macbeth acts, according to Bradley, under a horrible compulsion; Dover Wilson imagines him following the air-drawn dagger in 'a horrible smiling trance'. The murder fascinates him as damnation fascinates Faustus. It is the inevitable, the irrevocable deed, after which he too dies in some sense:

> Had I but died an hour before this chance,
> I had liv'd a blessed time: for from this instant,
> There's nothing serious in mortality:
> All is but toys: renown and grace is dead,
> The wine of life is drawn. . . .
>
> (II iii 40–53)[21]

A period of intense and almost delirious anticipation is followed by complete collapse. There is one earlier picture of an 'expense of spirit in a waste of shame', one earlier picture of conscious guilt calling in night and the creatures of night for aid, one act of physical violence followed by as swift a repentance, one equally dishonourable breach of hospitality and trust. It is the one to which Macbeth himself refers:

> Now o'er the one half-world
> Nature seems dead, and wicked dreams abuse
> The curtain'd sleep: witchcraft celebrates
> Pale Hecate's offerings: and wither'd murder,
> Alarum'd by his sentinel, the wolf,
> Whose howl's his watch, thus with his stealthy pace,
> With Tarquin's ravishing strides, towards his design
> Moves like a ghost.
>
> (II i 49–56)[22]

What is to be learnt by turning back to the sententious *Rape o Lucrece*, with its emblematic description of the heroine, its lengthy complaints and testament, its studied ornament and its formal indictment of Night, Time and Opportunity? Here, I think, are the emotional components (as distinct from the narrative components of *Macbeth* lying separate, isolated, and more crudely and simply expressed. Tarquin's feelings before the deed, and Lucrece's feelings after it, are identical with the central core of feeling in *Macbeth*.

Night, Opportunity and a deceitful appearance are accessories to the deed. In her lament, Lucrece indicts these three. An atmosphere of tragic gloom and murk is diffused in the description of Tarquin's rising and stalking through the darkened house towards his victim. Like Macbeth, he tries to pray in the very act of entering her chamber and is startled to find that he cannot do it. There is a remote likeness to the physical horror of Duncan's corpse in the sight of Lucrece's body at the end, so ghastly inert in its great pool of blood

> Who like a late sack'd island vastly stood
> Bare and unpeopled, in this fearful flood.
> (1740–1)

But it is, above all, in the opening soliloquies of Tarquin that the likeness is apparent. Tarquin foresees the emptiness of his satisfaction, which Macbeth does not fully understand till after the deed; but the comment with which Tarquin's inward debate is introduced might serve as prologue to the later story.

> Those that much covet are with gain so fond,
> That what they have not, that which they possess
> They scatter and unloose it from their bond,
> And so by hoping more they have but less,
> Or gaining more, the profit of excess
>   Is but to surfeit, and such griefs sustain,
>   That they prove bankrupt in this poor-rich gain.
>
> The aim of all is but to nurse the life,
> With honour, wealth, and ease in waning age;
> And in this aim there is such thwarting strife,
> That one for all, or all for one we gage:
> As life for honour, in fell battles rage,
>   Honour for wealth, and oft that wealth doth cost
>   The death of all, and altogether lost.
>
> So that in venturing ill, we leave to be
> The things we are, for that which we expect,
> And this ambitious foul infirmity,
> In having much torments us with defect
> Of that we have: so then we do neglect
>   The thing we have, and all for want of wit,
>   Make something nothing, by augmenting it.
> (134–54)

In his protracted debate with himself, Tarquin points out the shame to his family, his blood and his posterity, the transient nature of the gain (and here Macbeth echoes him):

> Who buys a minute's mirth to wail a week?
> *Or sells eternity to get a toy?*
>
> (213–14)

He dreads the vengeance of Collatine even while he recognises th
ties of kinship and hospitality which bind them:

> But as he is my kinsman, my dear friend,
> The shame and fault finds no excuse nor end.
>
> (237–8)

Finally he rejects the counsel of reason in words which anticipa
Lady Macbeth's 'tis the eye of child-hood, That fears a painted devil

> Who fears a sentence or an old man's saw,
> Shall by a painted cloth be kept in awe.
>
> (244–5)

The crime which Tarquin commits, even more clearly, though n
more truly, than Macbeth's, destroys the natural ties between hi
and the rest of the community. It is a sort of suicide. Both Macbe
and he commit a violence upon themselves from which they cann
recover. Examples have been known in the modern world where ac
of sufficient violence will destroy the personality of the perpetrato
and even periods of acute nervous strain and danger, such as those
which combatants were subjected, will issue in nervous prostratio
and a feeling of complete emptiness of being. It is this identi
between violence and self-violence (though in *The Rape of Lucrec*
the effects of the crime are given in the soliloquies of the victir
which a comparison of the two works reinforces as the central ide
the germ of the play. Macbeth's real victim is himself. Both *The Ra;
of Lucrece* and Macbeth reflect with very different degrees of skill
deep-seated and permanent experience; and the difference serv
only to emphasise the unity of Shakespeare's art, the modifying ar
shaping power which his work as a whole seems to exert upon ea
of its parts. I think it is not fancy to say that *Macbeth* is the greater f
being demonstrably by the hand that wrote *Othello*, or even the har
that wrote *Lucrece*; since the likeness which is discernible with
such variety is proof that the play was written from the very depths
his mind and heart, and together with the multiplicity of sourc
which have furnished the subject of this paper, it gives a measure
the power, the intellectual and spiritual strength and pressure r
quired, to weld them into one.

Notes

1 The atmospheric strength of the Chronicle is noted by Dover Wilson in the New Cambridge edition of *Macbeth* (Cambridge, 1947), p. xii. He quotes the earlier edition of Sir Herbert Grierson and J. C. Smith at this point in support of the Celtic atmosphere of the story. In a paper read at Cambridge in November 1950, Mrs N. K. Chadwick suggested that the earliest chronicle, Wyntoun's, incorporates material from lost Celtic sagas on Macbeth, particularly in the parts relating to the supernatural. She bases this on changes in the style, indicating a Celtic original. There is an independent Norse saga of Macbeth.

2 *Basilikon Doron*, and *The true lawe of free monarchies* (Edinburgh, 1597, 1598).

3 Wilson, op. cit. pp. xxxi-xxxii.

4 Hardin Craig, *An Interpretation of Shakespeare* (New York, 1948).

5 Henry Paul points out in his article, 'The Imperial Theme in *Macbeth*' (*Adams Memorial Studies*, ed. J. G. McManaway et al., Washington, 1948, pp. 253–68), that the *pearls* set in the base of an imperial diadem represented the several dependent fiefs (*loc. cit.* p. 264). What follows in my text is indebted to this valuable article.

6 St Margaret, Malcolm's wife, and a strong influence in the shaping of his policy, obtained from the Pope the privilege that Scottish kings should be anointed (i.e. hallowed) at their coronation.

7 It is melancholy to note that Donalbain returned from Ireland to the Isles and (after Malcolm's death) slew his nephew, David, but was in turn succeeded by another of Malcolm's sons. With this one interval, the line of Malcolm Canmore retained the throne.

8 Paul, 'The Imperial Theme', p. 258.

9 It has been much disputed whether Shakespeare knew this pageant or not. Paul thinks he did.

10 See Dover Wilson, *Macbeth*, p. xvii, for a summary of the material.

11 *The Description of Scotland*, chapter XIII (translated from the Latin of Hector Boethius by William Harison, and prefixed to Holinshed's *Historie of Scotland*, 1577). As in the other quotations the spelling has been modernised.

12 Vittoria's 'Terrify babes, my Lord, with painted devils' and the words of Flamineo about her, 'If woman do breed man, She ought to teach him manhood', recall respectively ''tis the eye of child-hood / That fears a painted devil' and 'Bring forth men-children only.' The figure of the great lady, great in wickedness, was popular on the Jacobean stage. Lucrezia Borgia in *The Devil's Charter* also recalls Lady Macbeth in her laments and swoon over the husband she has slain, her invocation of the furies and her careful concealment of the murder by staging a mock suicide.

13 C. H. L. Ewen, *Witch Hunting and Witch Trials* (London, 1929), pp. 19-21, 31. I am indebted for this reference and for much general information on the subject of demonology to Mrs Florence Trefethan.

14 Ibid., p. 23.

15 See *Newes from Scotland*, 1591 (reprinted with King James's *Daemon ologie* in the Bodley Head Quartos, London, 1924).

16 *The Old Wives' Tale* (*The Dramatic Works of George Peele*, ed. C. T Prouty, vol. 3, 1970, p. 402).

17 In the words of King James (*Daemonologie*, Book I, chapter v) – which seem to be recalled by Banquo in I iii – the Devil tries 'to make himself so to be trusted in these little things, that he may have the better commodity thereafter, to deceive in the end with a trick once for all; I mean the everlasting perdition of their soul and body.' Cf. the deception o Alexander Borgia, unmasked at the end of *The Divil's Charter*.

18 This insensibility is contrasted with the Christian stoicism of Macduf and old Siward, who endure their bereavements courageously, no barbarously.

19 H. B. Charlton, *Shakespearian Tragedy* (Cambridge, 1948); W. C Curry, *Shakespeare's Philosophical Patterns* (Baton Rouge, 1937) Helen Gardner, 'Milton and the Tragedy of Damnation', in *Englisf Studies*, 1948, ed. F. P. Wilson (London, 1948); Hardin Craig, 'Motiva tion in Shakespeare's Choice of Materials', *Shakespeare Survey* 4 (1951 pp. 31–2; Roy Walker, *The Time is Free* (London, 1949).

20 *Macbeth*, I vii 1–28; II i 31–64; III ii, 13–26, 46–53; V iii 40–53; V v 17–28.

21 Cf. the line below, from *Lucrece*: 'Who . . . sells eternity to get a toy? and the lassitude of Cleopatra at Antony's death:

> The odds is gone,
> And there is nothing left remarkable
> Beneath the visiting moon.
>
> (IV xv 66–8)

22 It may be noted that this atmosphere is recalled again in Iachimo' speech over the sleeping Imogen: night, 'our *Tarquin*' with his stealthy tread, the crickets' cry (*Cymbeline*, II ii 11–14).

A Retrospective Review

In one of his *Nonsense Novels*, Stephen Leacock describes how 'Lord Ronald leapt upon his horse and rode off madly in all directions'. Shakespearean studies today might be seeming to do the same; but my own aim, here, is to stay with the interpretation of the text, watching two time-clocks – the time of their composition – co-ordinated with the present.

Any line of general studies is liable now to develop its own image of Shakespeare: the psychoanalysts' Shakespeare, the dogmatically Christian Shakespeare, and the Marxists' Shakespeare are all familiar; recently, the feminists' Shakespeare has been extrapolated from his plays. In 1981, at the Third World Shakespeare Conference, a seminar on translation disclosed a Shakespeare multiform as the Homers of the ancient and modern world, whose language, it was claimed, in some respects could be better understood by those who did not inherit it as their mother tongue.

If English scholars have become accustomed both to the claims of International Shakespeare and the Shakespeare of the Footlights, one of the functions of historic criticism in a permissive field has been to control the vagaries of personal response. The risk of seeing Shakespeare merely as an enlarged version of the self is intensified because he himself aimed at an individual response from each participant in a social event, the play in performance (above, p. 57). The end of performance being, as Hamlet put it 'to show the very age and body of the time his form and pressure', Shakespeare is modified even as he is transmitted; yet his poetry retains continuity, thereby moulding society whilst binding it together.

Through his magic evocative sympathy, even a great scholar like Malone, who was a lawyer, suggested that Shakespeare in his youth must have worked in a lawyer's office; whilst dons have preferred the early tradition that he served as a schoolmaster in the country, Duff Cooper, a man of military interests, recruited him into the Earl of Leicester's expeditionary force as Sergeant Shakespeare. And in 1983, the Chancellor of the Exchequer, quoting 'Take but degree away, untune that string/ And hark, what discord follows' proclaimed him a Tory.

The most illuminating discovery of the nineteenth century was that of the plays' order of composition, enabling them to be seen, in spite of their variety, as a vast and comprehensive whole (above, p. 143). The most illuminating discovery of the twentieth century has been the recovery of their context in performance, so that the text is enlarged by what used to be termed the subtext – the non-verbal languages of gesture, blocking, symbolic acts of presentation. Many plays unacted since the seventeenth century are revived, not as antiquarian exercises but as live theatre; great stage productions have sometimes led the way to critical understanding. Granville Barker discovered the acting potential of *Love's Labours Lost*: *Troilus and Cressida*, staged after World War I in modern dress, presented a vision of contemporary disillusion, comparable with that in T. S. Eliot's *The Waste Land* – a poem that itself had been rooted in Jacobean drama. As an under-graduate, I learnt how to read the Elizabethans from Eliot.

In the fifty years and more which have elapsed since my *Elizabethan Stage Conditions* (1932), I have observed three phases in the continuous re-interpretation and remaking of Shakespeare. The first, from the late twenties to World War II, was that of poets and scholars; in the second, from 1945 up to the end of the sixties, historians of the fine arts and social historians provided new backgrounds and contexts, whilst drawing together with men of the theatre. This is the period to which most of these essays belong. The seventies and eighties, a period of do-it-yourself Shakespeare, saw the foundation of world organizations for study, many new editions, and, in the two-text theory of *King Lear*, advanced by the Oxford editors, the encroachment of drama as performance upon the last stronghold of pure scholarship; the field of textual criticism. The first annual bibliographies of Shakespearean studies, produced after 1921 by growing professionalism in University studies, especially literary study, have culminated in the communications explosion of the age of computers and xeroxing. The *International Shakespeare Bibliography*, now appearing computer-aided as a special number of *Shakespeare Quarterly*, includes annually upward of 3,000 items, in many languages.

As an undergraduate at Cambridge in the late 1920s, I found drama related to social history in the volumes of E. K. Chambers,

The Medieval Stage and *The Elizabethan Stage*. The founding fathers of our English school had been historians by training; but T. S. Eliot shaped our personal responses. He sponsored G. Wilson Knight, *The Wheel of Fire* (1930), introducing a thematic approach to the Tragedies and the Last Plays; Wolfgang Clemen eventually based this on a more strictly historic reading. The fashion for anthropology seized also on the Last Plays as embodying myths of rebirth, seasonal rituals. Although production was not yet affected, this opened perspectives beyond tragedy in the old sense.

After World War II, history of art became applied, especially in the form of iconography, to Renaissance drama. Such work as that of Frances A. Yates and D. J. Gordon now fed spectacular elements into the theatre, influencing current production. From 1946 critics and men of the theatre came together in bi-annual conference at Stratford-upon-Avon, many members of the Royal Shakespeare Company themselves being recruited from the universities. The line of Shakespearean scholars who bridged the gap included Granville Barker, Dover Wilson, Allardyce Nicoll. They were reinforced from America, where the drama departments of great universities constituted centres of production. In the early fifties, the first English department of drama opened at Bristol, where Glynne Wickham began his study of the interaction of early drama with other forms of court spectacle and popular art. The splendid vitality of medieval craft cycles was revealed in performance, from York to Perran Round in Cornwall. As early as 1937, Eliot had taken the late medieval *Everyman* as model for *Murder in the Cathedral*, in order – he said – to escape from Shakespeare's overwhelming influence.

Conversely, it became fashionable to read Shakespeare in terms of early-Tudor morality plays – conservatively in *The Taming of the Shrew*, as I have shewn here, more radically in *Troilus and Cressida*. The main stress fell upon the English histories, in Dover Wilson's *The Fortunes of Falstaff* (1943), followed by Tillyard's *Shakespeare's History Plays* (1944), where as the supreme 'Mirror for Magistrates' their construction was seen to form two 'tetralogies'. This was parallel to the grouping of the Last Plays as a Series culminating in *The Tempest*. The new look of the forties hardened into dogma, until astringently corrected by A. P. Rossiter (died 1957) in *Angel with Horns* (1961). However, he surpassed Wilson Knight when he declared that Macbeth, his wife and Banquo 'are parts of a pattern or designs; are images or symbols . . . those symbols we call *dramatis personae*. It is in us that Macbeth, his Lady and Banquo happen' (p. 217, 219).

Meanwhile Tyrone Guthrie, who believed that 'Theatre is ritual' had established in 1953 his theatre at Stratford, Ontario, preparing the way for the strong lead given from Canada in theatrical studies, both in the bi-annual conferences at the University of Waterloo, Ontario, and in the production of *Records of Early English Drama* from the University of Toronto. My paper on *King Henry IV* was delivered at Stratford, Ontario.

The paper on *Macbeth* – an invited piece for the English Stratford, printed first in *Shakespeare Survey* – belongs to the early fifties. Those on *All's Well* and *Troilus and Cressida* reflect a growing emphasis on the Problem Plays, a third distinctively Shakespearean genre, which joined the Last Plays and the English Histories. In the late 1950s, the vogue for Brecht favoured their 'black comedy', the darkening of the English histories and such tragi-comedy as *The Merchant of Venice*; it curdled even the happy comedies with bitterness. On the other hand, the satiric Ben Jonson, if revived at all, was apt to be represented by his most genial entertainments, *The Alchemist* and *Bartholomew Fair*, for the bitterness had to reflect a contemporary deconstruction.

In 1964, when Shakespeare's fourth centenary evoked hundreds of books, festivities of all kind, I was invited to the Far East, where Japan, Hong Kong and Korea all celebrated. At the University of Hiroshima, where I delivered the lecture on *Hamlet*, students gave a performance in English, which they had been rehearsing for a year. Hamlet, relying on Olivier's film, wore a blond wig above his Oriental countenance. Tragedy I found universally understood; comedy transplanted chiefly as farce. For example, conventions of the love-game in *Twelfth Night* meant nothing in Djakarta; but Sir Andrew Aguecheek had the audience rolling in the aisles of the old Dutch theatre.

International Shakespeare provided a secular mythology, comparable to that of sacred history. The effect in Eastern Europe of the performance of *Hamlet* and *Titus Andronicus* is well-known. After the collapse of the Prague Spring of 1968, a friend who had survived the German concentration camps wrote to me 'I have retreated to Shakespeare's impregnable fortress'. In the tragic clowns of Václav Havel, his pupil, which derive from Shakespeare and Beckett, the protest – not political, but existential – has been dramatised. In 1968, in his attack on 'The Deadly Theatre' in *The Empty Space*, Peter Brook with one reservation (a strong one) praised Brecht's adaptation of *Coriolanus*. A Russian said to me: 'Why not a Russian Shakespeare? You have an English Chekhov!'

To bring together the English History plays, which were given at Stratford in sequence, John Barton began adding some lines to *King Henry VI*. When the sense of a cultural centre or norm has been lost, as it largely has in the seventies and eighties, then the pliability, the

Protean qualities of Shakespeare themselves offer a tempting target. In 1967, Tom Stoppard exploited them in *Rosencrantz and Guildenstern are dead*. The Royal Shakespeare Company in their *Hamlet* of 1981, in turn absorbed the effect of Stoppard. Professional directors searched for the bizarre – the Kabuki *Timon*, the British-India setting for *Much Ado*. In one production the voice of the Ghost in *Hamlet* was piped through the air-conditioning system; in another, Hamlet ventriloquised. Such shock 'insults' the Shakespeare of the Establishments. What power it has, depends on the ability of Shakespeare to survive and absorb all this; but it often depends also on a previous viewing of different versions, and may prove very disconcerting to the innocent foreign visitor.

The case against 'Directors' Theatre' was put by John Russell Brown in *Free Shakespeare* (1974), just when television had brought a new form. Some effects of the plays are heightened on the small screen, but the invisible interference between audience and actor imposed by technicians may belie the appearance of intimacy. It is no coincidence that the eighties see the first attempts to rebuild Shakespeare's original play-house both in London and in Detroit. Like playing early music on original instruments, this experiment will enlighten audience and actors in a way which can be utilized in the live theatre and on the screen (the television version of *King Henry VI* points to this). We cannot turn ourselves into Elizabethans, but we can physically experience their opportunities and constraints.

The two latest essays in this collection, those on *Measure for Measure* and *Othello*, were designed for Tokyo and Washington respectively. They reconstruct the immediate circumstances of the first performances. For if Shakespeare is now as international, and as much a performer's possession, as music, the origins grow even more significant as the stock from which new variations may be propagated. The bounty of the poetry does not fail:

> an autumn 'twas,
> That grew the more by reaping. His delights
> Were dolphin like; they showed his back above
> The element they liv'd in.
> (*Antony and Cleopatra* 5.2.86–9)

Bibliographical Note
Periods other than those covered here are represented in books I have written on Shakespeare: *Elizabethan Stage Conditions, a study of their Relations to Shakespeare's Plays* (1932, new impression 1968); *Shakespeare and Elizabethan Poetry* (1951, 1979) covers the six-

teenth century and the connexions with non-dramatic poetry; *Shakespeare the Craftsman* (1969, 1979) the middle years up to *Hamlet*; *The Living Moment* (1976) the Jacobean Shakespeare. *Shakespeare the Poet in his World* (1978) is a general contextual study. In addition to general works, *Themes and Conventions of Elizabethan Tragedy* (1935, 1980), *The Growth and Structure of Elizabethan Comedy* (1955, 1973) and *The Rise of the Common Player* (1962, 1979), I have written on George Chapman (1977) and John Webster (1980).

A bibliography of my published work to that date appears in *English Drama: Forms and Development*, ed. Marie Axton and Raymond Williams, 1976.